DISPLACED
BY WAR

DISPLACED BY WAR

GERTRUDE POWICKE AND QUAKER RELIEF IN FRANCE AND POLAND 1915–1919

SUSAN PARES

Francis Boutle Publishers

First published in 2015 by
Francis Boutle Publishers
272 Alexandra Park Road
London N22 7BG
Tel/Fax: (020) 8889 7744
Email: info@francisboutle.co.uk
www.francisboutle.co.uk

Displaced by War © Susan Pares and the heirs of Gertrude Mary Powicke 2015

All rights reserved.
No part of this book may be reproduced, stored
in a retrieval system, or transmitted, in any form
or by any means, electronic, mechanical
photocopying or otherwise without the prior permission of the publishers.

ISBN 978 1 903427 92 7

Contents

- 3 List of illustrations
- 5 List of maps
- 7 Acknowledgements
- 8 Picture acknowledgements
- 9 Preface
- 13 Chapter 1. Life before the First World War
- 40 Chapter 2. The Society of Friends and war relief
- 64 Chapter 3. Work in Bar-le-Duc
- 92 Chapter 4. Bar-le-Duc at war
- 123 Chapter 5. Change and movement
- 151 Chapter 6. Life in the équipe
- 173 Chapter 7. Poland
- 200 Chapter 8. The final weeks
- 209 Afterword
- 210 Additional material
- 210 Sermaize
- 216 Verdun
- 222 Gertrude and Wilmer in Paris, 1918
- 225 Luxembourg and Germany, May 1919
- 228 Visit to Eastern Galicia, November-December, 1919
- 233 Biographical notes
- 241 Notes
- 252 References
- 257 Index

This book is dedicated to Mary Jones and to the memory of
Gertrude Powicke and of Catherine Wray

List of illustrations

Page
- 13 1. Hatherlow United Reform church
- 14 2. Powicke House, Hatherlow
- 17 3. Milton Mount College, letter heading, 1911
- 19 4. Letter addressed to Gertrude in her brother Maurice's hand, 1907
- 21 5. Gertrude with Form III Middle, Manchester High School for Girls, 1914
- 24 6. Office holders, Romiley branch of North of England Society for Women's Suffrage, 1908-1910
- 27 7. Flyer for open air meeting in Bredbury, 6 June 1913, organised by the Romiley branch of the NUWSS
- 30 8. Harry Pickles and a fellow-trainee, Frensham Camp, Farnham, Surrey, November 1914
- 34 9. Christmas card from George Glover, 4th Division, to Gertrude, Christmas 1917
- 37 10. Driving licence issued to Gertrude Powicke, 28 October 1914
- 54 11. Plaque in the foyer of the Hôtel Britannique commemorating the Society of Friends' use of the hotel as its headquarters, 1914-1920
- 56 12. One of the FWVRC's pre-fabricated houses on display at the Exposition de la cité reconstituée, Paris, 1916
- 60 13. FWVRC distribution of bedding at Couvonges, Meuse, 1916
- 65 14. View of Bar-le-Duc at the time of the First World War
- 66 15. Corner bend from boulevard de la Rochelle into the rue St Mihiel
- 68 16. Rue de l'Horloge in the upper town, Bar-le-Duc
- 71 17. Bar-le-Duc, 30 June 1915: Gertrude Townend, Eliza Dalglish, Gertrude
- 81 18. Bicycling permit issued to Gertrude

84   19. Gertrude's dog Peter in what was probably the Hupmobile
93   20. Café-restaurant des Ruines, Vassincourt
94   21. Soldiers and townspeople in the rue Oudinot, Bar-le-Duc
95   22. Refugees passing through Bar-le-Duc, 1914-15
97   23. Entrance to the covered market, August 2012
100 24. Military lorries parked on the place Reggio, Bar-le-Duc
101 25. Soldiers' huts in the woods
103 26. Interchange between lorries and trains: the station at Bar-le-Duc
108 27. The café in the soldiers' club, Bar-le-Duc
112 28. Dining room at the Maison des parents, Bar-le-Duc
113 29. Sitting room at the Maison des parents, Bar-le-Duc
118 30. Effects of the bombing raid of 30 September 1917, Bar-le-Duc
119 31. Damage to the Crédit Lyonnais bank, Bar-le-Duc, following the bombing raid of 2 October 1917
121 32. Concrete bomb shelter constructed in place Exelmans, Bar-le-Duc
127 33. Refugees in the Oise leaving their village
142 34. 7 place de la Fontaine, Bar-le-Duc, August 2012
144 35. The 'shop' at Bar-le-Duc, March 1919: Edith Sheffield, Gertrude, Mary Sterling
147 36. Varennes co-operative store, Meuse
150 37. Médaille de la reconnaissance française, awarded to Gertrude
152 38. View of 99 boulevard de la Rochelle, Bar-le-Duc, August 2012
155 39. Photograph of Gertrude Powicke in her FWVRC uniform
165 40. Breakfast invitation, 21 April 1919
174 41. Group transit visa issued by the Swiss Legation, London, on 17 July 1919
185 42. Clothing disinfecting, Baranowiczi (now Belarus)
186 43. Ethel Dunbar in disinfecting kit
187 44. The 'disinfecting engine', Zawiercie delousing post
195 45. Opera programme for *The Tales of Hoffmann*, 12 November 1919, Warsaw
199 46. Menu for dinner offered on 24 November 1919 by the French military medical unit, Borszczów, Poland
204 47. Gertrude's grave, Warsaw, June 2013
206 48. Bathing tent at Nadworna
211 49. Sermaize in early 1915
213 50. Cité des Amis, Sermaize

214 51. One of the two remaining houses, Cité des Amis
219 52. The *voies sacrées* leading to Verdun: road and rail
220 53. La Suzanne, a survivor of the Meusien rail network, August 2012
221 54. Menu for a lunch given in Verdun, 17 February 1918

Maps
   47 1. Western front, 1914-18, showing German advances and retreats
   52 2. Area north and east of FWVRC's main area of activity, showing the front line, May 1917
  179 3. Poland, 1920

Acknowledgements

In London I have had the enormous benefit of access to a number of libraries and the rich collections they contain and would like to thank the staff at the British Library, Dr Williams's Library, the London School of Economics and Political Science, and the Women's Library in its Old Castle Street incarnation, for their help at various points. At the Library of the Religious Society of Friends in Britain, I am especially grateful to Melissa Atkinson, Visual Resources Development Officer, John Blake, head of Library and Archives, Josef Keith, archivist, Jane Kirby and their colleagues for continued interest and support. At the Imperial War Museum, Jane Rosen has assisted with releasing Gertrude's 'official' photograph. In Manchester, the staff of the John Rylands Museum have likewise been of help.

Among the pleasures of researching my great-aunt's life have been the sympathetic response and willingness to assist among so many people in various parts of the world. In Britain, my thanks go to Chris Ball, who generously shared with me her grandparents' experiences in the FWVRC; Margaret Clark, archivist of the Miltonian Guild, who helped with research into Gertrude's connections with her old school; Bob Clarke, secretary of Hatherlow United Reform church, who arranged for my husband and me to visit the church; Professor Peter Gatrell, University of Manchester, for his interest; Paul Hartley of Stockport Metropolitan Borough Council; Dr Anne-Marie Hughes, of Manchester Metropolitan University, for discussion and encouragement; Dr Christine Joy, archivist at the Manchester High School for Girls, for making available photographs and much information on my family's connection with the school; and my sister Jenny Pares for additional research. Thanks are also due to Kate Tattersall, who drew the maps for Chapters Two and Seven.

In France, a number of people have given their assistance, for which I am happy to record my thanks: first and foremost Jean-Michel Althuser, photographer in Bar-le-Duc and animator of the historic local rail network, le Meusien, and his colleague Daniel Labarthe, who has alerted me to useful documents; also in Bar, Monique Hussenot and Vincent Lacorde of the Archives départementales de la Meuse, who furnished us with useful material, and Marguerite Préau of the Musée barrois. At Sermaize-les-Bains, the then mayor (in 2012), Raymond Dzieja, and his two deputies, Alain Pauphilet and Pierre-Marie Delaborde, answered questions about the FWVRC presence in their town and took us on a tour of Sermaize. Ingrid Kolb-Hindarmanto, now back in Germany, answered my questions on infant nutrition. In Poland, Daria Borkowska of the Central Archive of Modern Records and Maria Sierocka of the Central Archive of Historical Records dealt with my queries; our friends Alison and Ian Fox have kept an eye on Gertrude's grave, aided by Dorota Pietrzyk; and Jan Pospiszył has supervised its renovation. Further afield, Patricia Chapin O'Donnell of Friends Historical Library of Swarthmore College in the United States has given assistance; and Brian Spears, Librarian of the Hupmobile Club, has kindly applied his expertise to identifying the model of Gertrude's car. In New Zealand, Alan Tunnicliffe, who edits the Powick family newsletter, has given me the benefit of his detailed knowledge of the clan.

Picture acknowledgements
Althuser collection: 14, 15, 16, 21, 22, 24, 25, 26, 27, 28, 30, 31, 32, 52; Archives départementales de la Meuse: 29 (AD055_FI_056FI1_0062); Author's collection: 3, 4, 6, 7, 8, 9, 17, 18, 19, 40, 41, 45, 46, 54; Alison and Ian Fox: 47; Jim Hoare: 2, 10, 11, 23, 34, 37, 38, 51, 53; Imperial War Museum: 35 (image number Q8073, part of the First World War Official Collection, Olive Edis, IWM photographer of the women's services in France, 1919), 39 (photograph of Gertrude Mary Powicke, IWM accession number SUPP.20/49 (Women's Work Collection). IWM signifies 'Held at the Department of Collections Access, the Imperial War Museum.'); Manchester High School for Girls: 5; ©Religious Society of Friends in Britain, 2014: 12, 13, 20, 33, 36, 42, 43, 44, 48, 49, 50; Stockport Metropolitan Borough Council: 1

Preface

This is a story with no happy ending. My great-aunt Gertrude Powicke died in Warsaw of typhus on 20 December 1919, the day after her thirty-second birthday. Before that, her life had been filled with work, activity and travel, and it is with those things that this book is concerned. Letter-writing and diary-keeping came readily to her, and the greater part of her correspondence and diaries has survived, along with photographs, documents and souvenirs. From this material an image, a personality emerges and a sense of a life that was already maturing.

She came from a Nonconformist background and was part of a large family for whom education was the way forward. Gertrude was among the early women graduates of Manchester University. She taught at the Manchester High School for Girls, one of the new schools offering higher education to girls. She was an active worker in the non-militant suffrage movement. When war broke out in August 1914, her energetic spirit drove her to seek work where she could feel she was really 'doing her bit'. She was accepted by the Society of Friends for their relief efforts in first France, then Poland, working always among the civilian victims of war. Throughout the four and a half years, June 1915 to December 1919, she spent with the Friends, she continued to record events, people and experiences and her reactions to them, for her family's benefit, but also as an act of analysis and self-examination.

As I have progressed with this memoir, I have come to realise that it incorporates two other accounts: the activities of the Friends' War Victims Relief Committee (FWVRC) in northeast France and Poland, and the wartime experiences of Bar-le-Duc, the town where Gertrude spent four years, though of course, neither of these accounts should be regarded as in any way official. Both, however, have their place for an understanding of the nature of Gertrude's work and of the spirit in which it was carried out. I have been disappointed to find that some of the new research on the impact of the First World War on civilians in France makes only very partial reference to the presence of the FWVRC. Quakers do not talk much about their contribution to public life, and the Friends' missions to France and Poland were small in comparison to those of other relief organisations such as the various national Red Cross groups, but they acted vigorously and effectively where they were present, were administered along carefully thought-out lines and to some extent may be regarded as embryonic forms of the larger international relief movements that developed during the twentieth century. On Bar-le-Duc, even without any extended study on my part of how small French towns coped with the demands of the war, I suspect that Bar's response – eventually sustained and imaginative – could be taken as typical

Six diaries cover Gertrude's work with the FWVRC, varying in size from pocket to notebook format. They are mainly written in ink, but towards the end in pencil. Ninety items of correspondence, seventy-one from France and nineteen from Poland, are to hand, some of them illustrated with stick drawings. Other family correspondence, sometimes written to her, sometimes about her, and the letters of condolence sent to her family after her death fill out the picture. Her own earlier letters and diaries from the years before she left for France have been used to outline her character, interests, studies and work up to that time. Drafts of articles, in at least one instance published, reveal her ability to instil her experiences into vivid, informative and often entertaining pieces of text – and her capacity for composing in French.

The opportunity to work on these sources has only come about through the generous co-operation of my family and Powicke cousins, who, as Gertrude's co-heirs, agreed to my plan of working up the material that was accumulating into a book and have let me quote and use this material. As can happen, letters and diaries had become dispersed around the family. Over a number of years various relatives have entrusted me with such elements of the archive as had come into their keeping. My particular gratitude goes to Mary Jones, Gertrude's last surviving niece, who initiated the process when she let me have such of Gertrude's letters and diaries as were in her possession and two earlier memoirs prepared by Gertrude's sister Agnes. Since then, other cousins have sent me further letters, diaries, documents and memorabilia. It is a pleasure to record this good family spirit.

I have drawn on Agnes' memoir, which exists in a long, unpublished typescript dated 28 October 1957 and in a shorter, undated manuscript in her hand. The text is invaluable for its continuity and amplitude, even if it confusing in places and follows a generally chronological pattern. Agnes was fulfilling an earlier wish by her brother Will, who in 1927 was already thinking of putting together material relating to Gertrude, with the aim of giving readers "a real picture of her". He does not appear to have got very far at the time and was hoping to finish his life of his sister after his retirement in May 1950, but his sudden death three months later cut that project short. Within the wider family, Alan Tunnicliffe of Christchurch, New Zealand, has made an exhaustive study of the Powick clan, and I have used some of his information.

Gertrude's diaries and letters offer a kind of counterpoint to the record that the organisation which sent her to France and then Poland, the Religious Society of Friends in Britain, was compiling. Quakers are generally meticulous noters, and Friends' Library in London contains much unpublished archive material relating to the FWVRC, reports that were circulated internally and publicly and, in the Society's weekly bulletin, *The Friend*, a continuous narrative of the FWVRC's work that presented the information received in London in a smoother, broader flow which emphasised the scope of the work and the purpose and vision behind it. A formal account is thus available that often confirms and enlarges the informal observations contained in Gertrude's diaries and letters, but sometimes passes over in silence some of the activities that she and her colleagues were engaged in. All this material has been placed at my disposal and I have been permitted to quote from the archives, from FWVRC reports and from *The Friend* and to draw on the resources of the Library's photographic collection. I have received continuous support and interest from Friends' Library, in particular from Josef Keith, who read a first draft of the text and offered essential corrections to my interpretations of Quaker belief and practice. Any remaining misapprehensions and errors are entirely my responsibility.

In Bar-le-Duc, the town where Gertrude lived and worked for four years, Jean-Michel Althuser, photographer and enthusiast for Bar's First World War history, has accumulated a fine photographic resource. He has most generously allowed me to reproduce some of the items from his vast collection of contemporary postcards and has pointed me to important written sources. In the neighbouring town of Sermaize-les-Bains, the then mayor and his staff made my husband and me welcome. In Poland, friends both British and Polish have helped me to construct the wider story surrounding Gertrude's grave. The sense of a collaborative project stretching across borders has been very strong at times.

Other material, both published and unpublished, has been quoted in this book. I have endeavoured to contact the holders of rights, but where I have been unsuccessful, no breach of copyright has been intended. I will willingly include acknowledgement of missing copyright in any future reprint or edition, if requested.

More detailed acknowledgements are made elsewhere in this book, but I must state here the encouragement and interest of my publisher, Clive Boutle. Above all I must record the sustained support of my husband, Jim Hoare, and my daughter, Joanna Hoare, for whom Gertrude has been a presence almost as long as she has been for me. From acting as travel companion, chauffeur and photographer to reading material in French archives and tracking down books and references, Jim has shown himself to be the researcher par excellence. He has all my thanks.

Lastly, I must acknowledge Gertrude herself. It has not always been easy to work on the material she left, knowing how the story ended; but by moving at the pace of her vivid accounts and staying with her lively spirit I have been able to accompany her all the way.

Susan Pares
July 2015

Chapter One

Life before the First World War

Gertrude Mary Powicke was born on 19 December 1887 in the Parsonage at Hatherlow, near Stockport in Cheshire. She was the fifth child and third daughter of Frederick James Powicke and Martha Collyer. The family occupied their home by virtue of her father's position as Congregationalist minister of Hatherlow. That part of Cheshire had supported a Congregationalist community since the seventeenth century, and the church, a fine building dating to 1845, was its third place of worship.[1]

As the family expanded, it moved into the neighbouring redbrick house, which bears the date 1887 and is now known as Powicke House. Gertrude had two elder brothers, Maurice and William, known as Will, and two elder sisters, Elizabeth, or Betty and Agnes. Nancy, born in 1891, was the youngest.

1 Hatherlow United Reform Church

2 *Powicke House, Hatherlow*

The family lay firmly in the Nonconformist tradition of English life. Frederick Powicke (1854-1935) was a scholar, working for and receiving a doctorate of philosophy from the University of Rostock in Germany in 1893, and was an authority on Richard Baxter, a theologian and Puritan minister of the seventeenth century, of whom he wrote a life, published in 1924. He was also a staunch exponent and defender of Congregationalism and sent some of his children to the local British School, run by the British and Foreign School Society, which offered non-denominational Christian instruction, rather than to the National School, which was supported by the established church. Maurice's wife Susan, writing to her husband on 3 December 1916, told him he spoke of his father "as though he were a comet", and indeed, Frederick was a man of spirit. Some of this fiery temperament flowed through Maurice and Gertrude too. Of Martha Powicke (1845-1935), known also as Patty, a less clearly defined picture emerges. She was said to have been "a woman of rare charm and sweetness" and was much loved by her children.[2]

Finances were a constant anxiety to both parents. The family was not poor, but it was a question of establishing priorities, among which education ranked very high. Fortunately, the children were all able, and scholarships, a necessity, could be won. The eldest, Maurice (1879-1963), became a distinguished mediaeval historian. Studies at

Owens College (later Manchester University) and Oxford University were followed by periods of research at Oxford and lecturing at Liverpool and Manchester universities. In 1909, at the age of thirty, he was offered the chair of history at Queen's University of Belfast. After wartime service from mid-1915 to March 1919 in the intelligence sections of government departments dealing with the blockade of enemy territories, he returned to Manchester University as professor of history, from 1919 to 1928. In that year he was named Regius professor of history at Oxford University. His scholarly and academic achievements brought great joy to his father.

Gertrude's second brother, Will (1880-1950), followed his father into the Congregationalist ministry. After lengthy studies, first at Glasgow University, then at Oxford, he was ordained in January 1911 to the Congregationalist church at Ross-on-Wye. Four years later he married Gwladys Evans, a friend of Agnes from Manchester University and Gertrude's fellow-teacher at the Manchester High School for Girls (MHSG). When war broke out, as an ordained minister he was exempt from military service, but family letters of 1915 and 1916 suggest that he was exercised about how best to make a contribution to war work. Eventually, in 1918, he was offered a post as a (Nonconformist) army chaplain in Egypt and left England in the spring or summer of that year. Gertrude noted briskly in her diary for 1 April 1918 that she was glad to hear he was going – "as he will then have done his 'bit' and I'm sure he is too ... it will be more satisfying as things are." On his return to England in 1920, he took up the first of three successive posts as a Congregationalist minister in and around the Manchester area.

Gertrude and her three sisters were very attached to each other. Some of this closeness may have dated to school days, when, over a period of fifteen years, the three older sisters were boarders at the same school. Agnes and Gertrude then studied in turn at Manchester University. Gertrude's early life to some extent ran in parallel to that of Agnes (1884-1965), from school through to university and, for a while, work. Agnes's choice of study at Manchester from 1903 to 1906 was English, and she went on to teach it throughout her career. In 1909, she was awarded an MA degree in English, again from Manchester, and in 1910 she gained her teaching diploma. A brief change of direction in spring 1919 involved work for the Educational Section of the Young Men's Christian Association (YMCA) in France and Germany, and she and Gertrude met for a few days (see section on Luxembourg and Germany). By the close of 1919 she was back in teaching.

Nancy (1891-1972) attended the Manchester High School for Girls. Her career was divided between social work and nursing, particularly with children, and teaching. In 1913, she embarked on a year's Social Service diploma course at Woodbrooke, the Quaker study and training centre at Selly Oak in Birmingham,[3] and acquired a further qualification in health visiting in 1915. In 1917 she was appointed assistant to the superintendent of the Manchester Child Welfare Centres, who was a family friend. A few years later she was superintending the School for Mothers at Cheetham Hill Centre. She returned to the MHSG in 1924 as a teacher of scripture, spelling and dictation, but also as registrar and medical clerk. In 1927 she was awarded the Certificate in Biblical Knowledge from Manchester University. She remained at the MHSG until 1930, then became matron at the Jewish Fresh Air Home and School, near Warrington.

Betty (1882-1967) did not pursue her education beyond fourteen. Over time she assumed a role as the domestic lynchpin in the household, overseeing its good regulation. Betty's view on things is not recorded, but from comments by other members of the family, the impression emerges of a competent and resourceful person who, for whatever reason, accepted the position of family manager. It was certainly a role much appreciated and valued by her family.

Gertrude's passport gives the customary brief factual description of her appearance: 5 feet (1.5 metres) in height; an oval face with a "small straight" nose, medium mouth, pointed chin and fair complexion; grey-blue eyes; and light-brown hair. She was indeed small, taking a size 3 in shoes. Her fellow-workers in the Friends Emergency and War Victims' Relief Committee remarked on her tiny frame, and her nickname 'Robin', acquired during university days, suggests the bright eyes and alert approach that seem to have characterised her. The whole family were of short stature. Alan Tunnicliffe's research[4] notes that her father, "[i]n common with other Powicks ... is believed to have been rather short, about 5'4''" (that is, 5 feet 4 inches or 1.62 metres). Photographs of Martha Powicke in old age show a tiny woman dressed in black with a white shawl and white hair knotted in a bun on top of her head.

In her memoir (page 1), Agnes Powicke notes that a few months after Gertrude's birth, their brother Will caught croup, a contagious respiratory infection. In consequence of this, Gertrude had to be fed on Nestlé's milk. (It may be that their mother was looking after Will and unable to feed the baby herself, or may have feared being a carrier of infection.) This diet appears to have contributed to bow legs in Gertrude as they became "too weak to carry her weight". Nestlé's milk is rich in calories, and its high sugar content may have led to Gertrude becoming overweight; Agnes admits that it made her sister "a bonny baby".[5] At the age of two and a half, she had an operation to correct the bowing and returned from the nursing home with her legs in splints.

Gertrude started school at the age of five, at the local British School favoured by her father. From there she moved on in 1897 to board at Berkeley House, the preparatory school for Milton Mount College in Gravesend in Kent. The College was intended primarily for the daughters of Congregationalist ministers and had already received first Betty (from 1892 to 1896), then Agnes (from 1895 to 1902) as pupils. The fees were £15 per annum.[6] Gertrude moved up to the College proper in 1899 and remained until 1907. The College's range of instruction was fairly wide, covering maths, science, music and gymnastics as well as Latin, modern languages, history, geography,

3 *Milton Mount College, letter heading, 1911*

English and scripture. Girls were prepared for the Cambridge Local Examinations. Their religious education was addressed seriously, with an emphasis, Agnes reports in her memoir (page 4), on Christian service. By 1907, her third year in the Sixth form, Gertrude was concentrating on history, English literature, French, German and maths, but also took in gymnastics and piano tuition. She had always been keen on sport, particularly hockey and swimming. In 1906, she took the Cambridge Higher Local examinations (the equivalent of today's A-levels), acquiring a distinction in French history[7] and winning a scholarship that allowed her to complete this final year at school as a pupil teacher entrusted with small supervisory duties.

Gertrude left Milton Mount College in July 1907. With her interest turning towards modern languages and, it would seem, to university entrance, she spent six months, from October 1907 to April 1908, in Germany, almost entirely at a German finishing school for girls in

Schwerin, east of Hamburg. Her stay there was a mixed success. She had hoped to have plenty of opportunity for study, but found that other activities made this difficult. A visiting teacher did lecture in German literature, however, and she and another English girl managed to read German, French and English literature together. Another disappointment was the lack of German conversation in favour of practice in French. The school, which had about fifteen students in all, took Norwegian, Swedish, Danish, French and English girls, but no Germans. Some of the girls were as young as sixteen or seventeen, some older than Gertrude. Many of them smoked. Gertrude was horribly homesick in the early weeks, but given her resilient character, ended up by making friends, seeing the value of new experiences and getting some enjoyment out of the situation.

What did not cease to worry her, however, was the financial cost of her stay, and this despite the fact that she attended the school on an au pair basis, teaching English to small groups of her fellow students or to individuals, and so seems to have been excused some of the fees. Her parents met many of the travel and living expenses, at least initially, and this exercised her. She insisted that she was trying to keep within her financial limits, but what she (and probably her parents) had not bargained for were the constant charges for laundry, postage stamps, even baths, in addition to the standard school charges. Presents had to be given all round at birthdays and Christmas and on leaving. Outings to theatres and concerts had to be paid for, so a free ticket to a concert was a bonus. Many of the other students had considerably more to spend than she did. Gertrude had to resort to borrowing from the other English girl and to asking her mother for funds. Her brothers also sent her small amounts, and she received clothes from home. This pattern of gifts, borrowing, taking advances and repaying was to recur throughout her life. In December 1907, however, she received news that she had been awarded a scholarship, possibly from her old school. Agnes reports it was for £15.

Attempts at finding a German family where she might be able to get some practice all failed, and Gertrude left Schwerin in early April 1908. She managed to spend nearly a week in Hamburg with a German family who had been asked to look after her while in the city. In those days, according to Agnes (memoir, page 10), Gertrude "learned to speak more German ... than during all the six months at Schwerin".

On her return to Hatherlow, Gertrude immediately applied herself to hard study – nine hours' work a day – in preparation for further Higher Local examinations and a county scholarship for university.

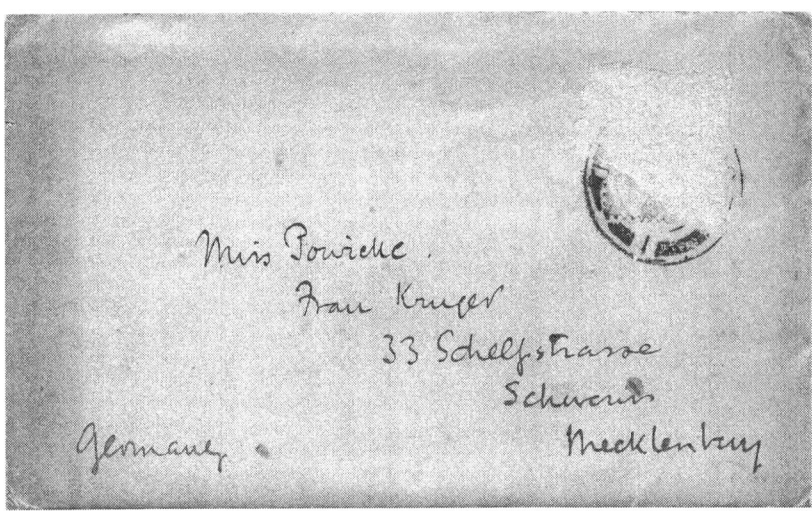

4 *Letter addressed to Gertrude in her brother Maurice's hand, 1907*

Agnes indicates that this was at Maurice's wish, and there is no doubt that he supported Gertrude in her studies, but we may also suppose that Gertrude herself wanted to pursue this course. She also wanted to sit for a Newnham scholarship. Her French and German did not need so much work, but she also had to present English, history, geography and maths as well as General English, which came with a long reading list. A year's work had to be crammed into nine weeks. She took the exams at Manchester University between 23 June and 14 July 1908, passed successfully and in August obtained a university scholarship offered by Cheshire County Council. The money was not sufficient for Newnham, but secured her a place at Manchester University. She was the third in her immediate family to attend the university.

Gertrude registered in the school of modern languages and literature for an honours degree in French and German, starting in October 1908. She combined these subjects with intermediate courses in history and Latin. In a letter of 31 January 1909 to Connie Lansdell, a friend from school days, she admitted to not yet caring much for languages, but could not go over to the history school since she was held back by her poor knowledge of Latin. She indulged her interest in history through joining the Historical Society, going on their trips and making friends among those taking the history school. She joined the university Athletic Club and the university Christian Union and became an active supporter of women's suffrage. During her three years' course she lived at home, her studies supported by her county scholarship. Maurice, by then established as a university lecturer and subsequently professor, was contributing to both her and their sister Nancy's educational costs, financing book purchases and academic fees. On 2 October 1910, for instance, he sent his mother a cheque for £10, explaining in his covering letter that out of this sum Gertrude was to have £3, or £2 if that was enough, for her books etc. for the coming academic year. He adds: "I arranged to give her a lump sum so as to save sudden appeals!" which suggests that Gertrude's calls for help may have been somewhat frequent.

In September 1910, in preparation for her final year, she secured funding from Cheshire County Council to spend a month on French language study at St Servan, on the outskirts of St Malo, in Brittany. Regular study, with coaching from a French woman, a former teacher of English, in translation and composition, was relieved by sea bathing and visits to historical sites. She worked hard during this third year, too hard, according to Agnes, "for a short time before the Finals she got influenza and was scarcely convalescent when the three weeks ordeal began" (memoir, page 19). She obtained a second class degree, to her disappointment, as she had hoped for a first. Will, Betty and Nancy accompanied her to the graduation ceremony in early July 1911. Their sister-in-law, Susan Powicke (writing to Maurice on 9 July from Hatherlow), described the three sisters in their finery. She had already given Gertrude 3/- to buy a pair of gloves for the occasion, as she had no suitable pair, and "I wanted her to look her best".

Gertrude now had to think of earning a living. The only avenue she appears to have explored was that leading to teaching. Her sister Agnes had already started on such a career. For a young woman of her background and education, teaching was deemed an appropriate means of supporting herself. One of the particular openings that may have been available was as an assistant or répétitrice within the French school system, but in the event, at around the time of her graduation Gertrude was offered a post as French mistress at the Manchester High School for Girls. The only flaw, according to Susan Powicke, writing to Maurice on 11 July 1911, was that Gertrude herself was "not quite sure if she will have always to be a teacher in a school or if she will have a chance of becoming a lecturer later on…" Whatever her reservations, it was at the High School that she took up work in 1911.

There is no doubt that a post at MHSG was a good opening. The school, founded in 1874, took its place in the expansion of school and university education for girls that marked the second half of the nineteenth century in Britain. It expanded rapidly in terms of numbers of pupils, accommodation and the range of the curriculum, and in 1876

5 Gertrude with Form III Middle, Manchester High School for Girls, 1914

opened a preparatory department for girls aged six to eleven. A maximum number of pupils, 600, was reached in 1914, but was later expanded. By the time Gertrude joined the staff in the autumn of 1911, the school was installed in premises in Dover Street under Miss Sara Burstall, a Cambridge mathematician and highly qualified teacher, who was headmistress from 1898 to 1924. The teaching staff were able to contribute to a pensions fund. The Powicke family already had a connection with the school through Nancy, who had been a pupil from 1904 to 1910.[8] More influentially, a family friend, Professor T. F. Tout, was chair of the board of governors.

Her experiences as a new teacher, and one new to teaching, were doubtless those of anyone starting up in her profession: the transition from study to employment, the task of mastering the techniques of teaching and exam setting and marking, the challenge of judging her pupils' capabilities and characters and of maintaining discipline, and the need to assess relations with staff old and new and adapt to the social life of the school. The actual content of teaching does not seem to have thrown her. The classes allocated to her were all *gamma* forms and thus rather dull. In a letter to Connie Lansdell of 29 October 1911, she admitted that she found that the girls' poor grasp of English grammar made it difficult for them to get to grips with French, particularly verbs (the complaint sounds all too familiar!). To her sister Agnes she wrote in a letter of 1 October 1911 that her teaching was confined to the present tenses of *avoir* and *être* and the Selected Poems of Victor

Hugo. More difficult was finding the right balance in her dealings with the girls outside of the classroom – a friendly approach was encouraged, but could not slide into laxness – and with some of the older teachers, who were inclined to snub the new staff. Writing to Agnes on 7 April 1912, to whom, as an experienced teacher, she confided many of these problems, she said that she had decided she should "walk warily and *be* humble too".

The first weeks at the MHSG were unsettled by the failure of her and her friend Dolly Lunn to find satisfactory lodgings. Dolly, who came from Halifax, had been a fellow-student at Manchester University and also took up a teaching post, in geography, at the High School in September 1911. The two friends decided to take rooms in Rusholme, in inner Manchester, but made a disastrous choice in their landlady, as Gertrude told one of her sisters in a letter of 4 November 1911. Mrs Petrie, a widow who made much of her "genteel" circumstances, wished to absorb the two young women into her family circle and resisted their attempts at independence. After two weeks, the strain was too much, and she asked them to leave, not before lamenting the failings of modern young women towards "poor lone widows" and accusing them of having broken up the family circle and lowered the tone of the house. By that time, it was impossible to find good rooms, and Gertrude decided to return to live at home and commute daily to work.

Exercise, which for Gertrude seems always to have been a necessity, was provided by hockey, which she played twice a week. She continued her suffrage activities, her involvement in the Christian Union and her support for the university German Society and Historical Society. Friends were abundant, many from university days. She attended school socials and dances, went to the theatre and in the summer vacation of 1912, took a four-week bicycling holiday with a woman friend in Normandy. With a regular income, many things were possible.

At some time early in the summer term of 1914, Gertrude asked for a year's leave of absence. Her reasons for this are not clear. Whatever the motive, the manner of accomplishing it was that she should apply for a post as a teacher of English in a French school. Her headmistress was prepared to release her for a year and gave her what can for once be described as a "glowing testimonial":

> Miss Powicke is a gentlewoman, with a charming personality, a good English accent and some social experience. She is an efficient and careful teacher, giving lessons in English here as well as in French, and manages a class of rather difficult girls effectively. She is well read

and thoughtful, and has very high ideals. Her influence would be excellent.

Nothing, of course, came of these plans. On 4 August 1914, Britain declared war on Germany. Gertrude was to get her year and more in France, but in wholly different circumstances.

Suffrage activities
Manchester was in the forefront in the long struggle for women's enfranchisement in Britain. Of the first three women's suffrage societies to be formed, all in 1867, one was in Manchester (the Manchester National Suffrage Society), the other two being in London and Edinburgh. The move followed John Stuart Mill's unsuccessful petition to parliament in 1866 in favour of women's suffrage. The first public suffrage meeting in the country was held in Manchester in 1868, in the Free Trade Hall. The city's power and wealth as a manufacturing and trading base and its strong political traditions all worked to foster the city's emergence as a centre for suffrage arguments and action. It was the home city of Emmeline Pankhurst (1858-1928), whose work there as a Poor Law Guardian in the mid-1890s exposed her to the appalling conditions of life which many women and children had to endure. Initially Emmeline Pankhurst and her daughters were members of the Manchester National Suffrage Society until, discontented with what they saw as the ineffectual tactics of the Society, they broke away to form the Women's Social and Political Union (WSPU) in 1903.[9] The Manchester Society itself changed its name to become the North of England Women's Suffrage Society and, along with other similar societies that had emerged in various parts of the country to campaign locally for women's suffrage, came under the aegis of the National Union of Women's Suffrage Societies (NUWSS) formed in 1897 by Millicent Garrett Fawcett.[10] From the early 1890s, Millicent Fawcett (1847-1929) led the constitutional wing of the British women's movement and in 1907 became president of the NUWSS. The NUWSS participated in marches and demonstrations, but never abandoned its commitment to constitutional means of persuasion, petitioning and campaigning. The gap between it and the WPSU sharpened until in 1912, the breach between the two organisations became permanent.[11]

From 1908, Gertrude became an increasingly active supporter of the constitutional suffrage movement. During the summer of 1907, the subject of women's rights had already come up in family discussion. In her memoir (page 7), Agnes reports that while the sisters were

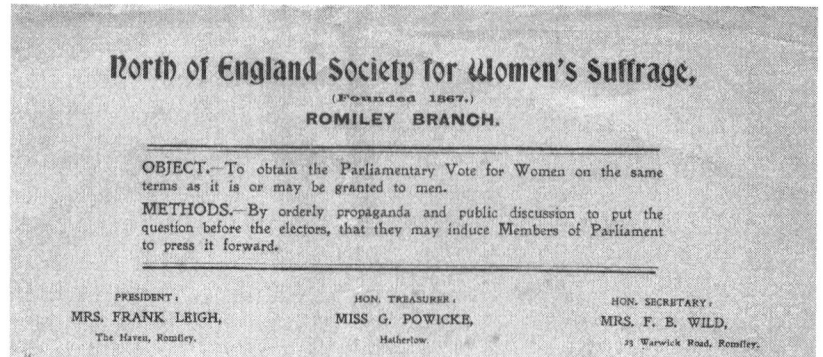

6 Office holders, Romiley branch of North of England Society for Women's Suffrage, 1908–1910

in favour, their father was initially much against the idea. After her return from Germany, Gertrude was drawn into the movement by a family friend, Mrs Leigh, who lived in Romiley, close to the Powickes. In November 1908, she joined with Mrs Leigh and other women to form the Romiley branch of the North of England Women's Suffrage Society. The NUWSS, which by 1913 had more than 50,000 members, operated in an organic fashion, drawing its strength from many small branches clustered into regional federations, which in turn were represented at the national level. In the Women's Suffrage Diary and Handbook for 1914, of which Gertrude had a copy, Romiley is listed under the Manchester and District Federation, which implies some re-organisation of the NUWSS structure. The Federation's president from 1906 was Miss Margaret Ashton, a formidable campaigner for women's and children's rights in the Manchester area, organiser of the 'Great Demonstration', a procession and open-air meeting on women's suffrage that took place over 23 and 24 October 1908 in Manchester, and the city's first woman councillor, elected in 1908.[12] She was also a member of the NUWSS executive from 1907 to 1915, and from 1912 to 1920 a governor of the Manchester High School for Girls. Through the two channels of campaigning and teaching, Margaret Ashton clearly knew Gertrude and indeed, sent her a present of boots for Christmas 1915, when she was already in France.

The Romiley branch of the NUWSS was headed by Mrs Leigh as president, Mrs Wild as secretary and Gertrude as treasurer. In January 1909, the group organised a public suffrage meeting, with two speakers, which attracted several new members. She reported to her friend Connie Lansdell in a letter of 31 January 1909 that the branch had nearly forty members, from the four who had launched the group the preceding November. Their MP had just retired, and Gertrude foresaw "an exciting time". She solicited Connie's views and in this and two succeeding letters to her friend, all written in the first half of 1909, set out the moderate suffragists' arguments on the legal, social and economic advantages of giving women the vote. The voice of perhaps Mrs Leigh, certainly of other campaigners, can be picked out here, but the enthusiasm is Gertrude's as she says she "would do anything to get a voice in government".

Gertrude and her sisters achieved their father's conversion to the cause. Persuaded by his daughters and by John Stuart Mill's essay of 1869 on the *Subjection of Women*, in early March 1909 the Reverend Frederick Powicke chaired the first in a series of meetings the Romiley branch held for its members and made a public confession of his change of heart. Margaret Ashton was the speaker at that meeting. Betty Powicke attended and was a participant in campaigning activities. In late April, the branch held a suffrage social attended by about eighty people. Phoebe Sheavyn, Women's Tutor at Manchester University, was the speaker, in response to Gertrude's invitation. A musical entertainment was part of the programme, and Gertrude and Betty provided refreshments.

The Reverend Frederick Powicke, Councillor Margaret Ashton, the Women's Tutor for Manchester University: these were solid professional people. The Romiley branch, like doubtless many other such groups active in the Manchester suburbs, would have launched its message in the first instance at educated, middle-class women and men. Women of other classes were not ignored or disdained, but were not necessarily reached out to. Rather, they were talked about. Some of the arguments that Gertrude deploys in her letters to Connie strike an awkward note, at least to modern ears. She does not always seem to use her own words in making these points, which, from the way they are phrased, must have been taken from pamphlets or from general discussion. This is certainly the tone in a short article on women's suffrage she sent back to her old school in 1909.[13] In her letter of 31 January 1909 to Connie Lansdell she wrote that women should have a voice in government; "we should know so much more about some things, and it would so much improve the state of the women in the lower classes – which is ghastly."

The recalcitrant nature of the movement that Gertrude and her fellow-suffragists were involved in is apparent in a far more vivid account, undated, of campaigning at some point in 1909 outside the polling booth at Glossop, where (male) voting in a by-election was taking place, presumably to elect a successor to the retiring MP. Both

Betty and Gertrude joined with fellow suffragists in seeking signatures to a petition asking for votes for women. Gertrude relates how, with mingled determination and trepidation, they set about pursuing the escaping male electors with their petition forms, encouraged "by the war-cry of the delighted spectators 'To it sufferin' suffragette – go it!'" One "elegant individual" protested that he simply adored women, but "'no, no I won't sign'". A "mournful soul" did agree to sign, but throughout kept up a "soft undercurrent [of] 'I simply loathe it'". Another man pocketed the pencil Gertrude had held out to him after telling himself it seemed a shame "'to play them such a trick'". She was told sternly that: "'Your place is at home to wash and to bake'", but when she turned to "face the foe", he had vanished. An uncomfortable exchange was had with an "icy gentleman" who refused to sign the petition, admitted to having objections to women receiving the vote, but insisted: "I presume I am at liberty to keep them to myself'". As irritating was the "creepy" facetiousness of another man:

> 'Now, yer know now, yer know *quite well*, ye're 'avin me on, yer *know* I won't sign ... Now supposin', just supposin' now, as my wife was to 'ave a vote – only supposin' now – and she went and voted Liberal, and me a Tory – just think, wot would 'appen, and '*ow* un'appy we should be – why I wouldn't ever be able to speak kindly to 'er again and then she *would* be un'appy – No, now ye're 'avin me on, yer *know* all the time as 'ow I won't sign.'

"Why didn't he tell me and have done with it", was Gertrude's feeling. "I suppose he didn't want me to miss the joy of "avin 'im on'". A band of small boys encircled her "and begged that I would get up a petition for 'Votes for Lads' – and ere long ... they proceeded to circulate among the crowd a dirty scrap of paper and a scrubby pencil with the polite request that the enfranchise should be extended to 'lads' on the 'same terms as men' – a phrase borrowed from my own rendering of our request." At length, with the polling booth closed, the campaigners started for home. "'Well miss' said the gem of a policeman who had been helping us grandly, 'You've had a pleasant run'. 'Yes' said I 'I'll be trotting home again' – but answer came there none – for he had never read Alice through the Looking Glass."

It is not evident if this entertaining draft was ever worked up into an article. Perhaps it formed the matter for a report at the Romiley branch meetings. Gertrude was ready to take the cause into whatever camp. In July 1910, she raised the issue at a Christian Union conference at Swanwick (near Baslow), and on 8 March 1912, a letter from her explaining 'Why I want the vote' was published in a local newspa-

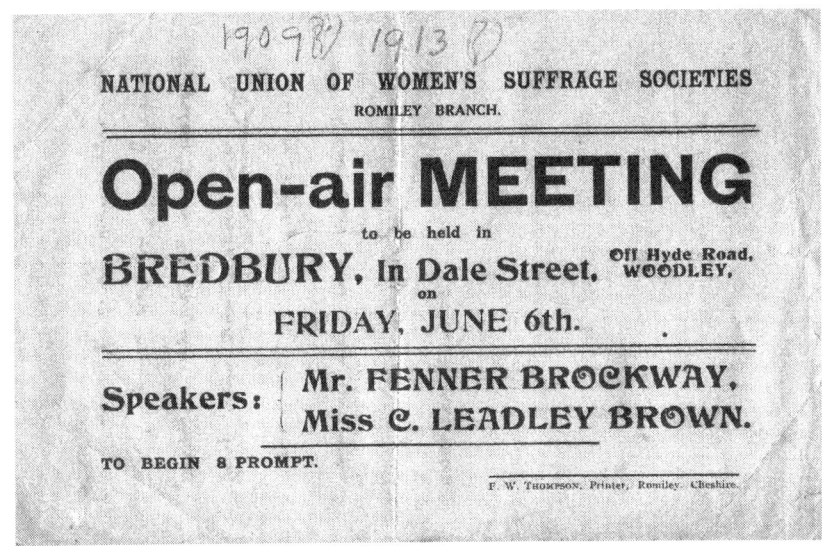

7 Flyer for open air meeting in Bredbury, 6 June 1913, organised by the Romiley branch of the NUWSS

per, the *Hyde Reporter*. It is interesting in that it is largely addressed to women readers and suggests that female reluctance or indifference was as much of an obstacle as male hostility and ridicule. Gertrude argues against the assumption that many women felt no need of the vote and therefore would not gain from it. "Now, I maintain that their gain would be immense. The very fact that they fail to acknowledge their need makes it the greater."

Gertrude's suffrage campaigning remained based in the Romiley branch of the NUWSS. She was actively engaged in the work of the branch throughout 1913 and 1914, as entries in her engagements diaries for both years show, and indeed into 1915. On 27 February 1913, the branch made a presentation to Millicent Fawcett, president of the NUWSS. On 14 April, Gertrude was made branch secretary. An open air meeting in Bredbury on 6 June had Fenner Brockway (see Biographical notes) as one of its speakers. A month later, on 5 July 1913, degree day at Manchester University was marked by a suffrage procession, for which Gertrude may have been a steward. Agnes noted in her memoir (page 26) that in the photograph of the event, "[m]ost of the women are in academic dress and Gertrude's head can be seen crowned with a mortar board and looking sufficiently serious." From 11 to 24 August, Gertrude attended a suffrage summer school based at St Hugh's College, Oxford. Subjects for protest and debate were the 'Cat and Mouse Act'[14] and 'sharp practice'. Agnes recorded further that a group photograph showed Gertrude at the end of the back row, holding a pile of the NUWSS's weekly newspaper *The Common Cause*. On 6 November 1913, Gertrude addressed a suffrage meeting at Ancoats.

Suffrage committee meetings and branch meetings continued throughout 1914, with various speakers including, again, Margaret Ashton. Two open air meetings were held in July. On 29 September 1914, Christabel Pankhurst spoke at the Free Trade Hall "on THE WAR". On the outbreak of conflict, suffrage groups halted their political activities and many redirected their energies towards the war effort and relief work. The NUWSS did not dissolve (Gertrude records three meetings in her 1915 diary, though she was able to attend only one), but instead provided registration centres for volunteers anxious to undertake some activity. The Manchester Suffrage Office became such a centre.[15]

With her departure for France with the Friends' War Victims' Relief Committee (FWVRC) on 6 June 1915, all formal activity came to an end. The issue of women's suffrage, however, was not abandoned, and indeed, was a lively topic for discussion among her new colleagues, both women and men. Gertrude had favoured the moderate strand in the campaign for the vote, but Elsie Dalglish and Gertrude Townend, a couple of new FWVRC acquaintances in Bar-le-Duc, the town in northeast France where she worked for four years, were members of the militant WSPU and had "thrilling" things to relate. Gertrude noted in her diary on 26 June 1915 that Miss Townend had been with a deputation that had tried to see the King and had been battered by the police. Some of the men with whom Gertrude discussed the question seem to have required convincing. An unofficial Friends' League for Women's Suffrage had been active in the years before the First World War. The London Yearly Meeting for 1914 (that is, the British Quakers' annual assembly) took a more neutral line. It issued a statement through *The Friend* for 19 June 1914 on the position of women which made it clear that while the Meeting upheld spiritual equality for women and men, it left the question of women's political enfranchisement and of political action to the "judgment and conscience of individuals".

Eventually, however, the issue, perhaps, even, its importance, faded away in Gertrude's diaries and letters. The immediacy and pressure of the work in France may have pushed that question and indeed much else of what was happening in Britain into the background. In any case, it was clear that the responsibilities she and other women workers in the FWVRC were carrying were equal to those of the men and were equally valued. What is surprising is that she makes no references to the first concession to women's demands, in 1918, when the Representation of the People Act, intended to widen the male franchise, included a clause extending a limited franchise to women. The bill was presented on 6 February 1918 and passed both Houses of Parliament later that year. It gave the vote to women aged over 30, who fulfilled certain property qualifications. Those with a university degree were also entitled to vote. On at least two scores, age and university degree, Gertrude should have been eligible to vote in the general election held on 14 December 1918, had she been in Britain. But she makes no mention of any of this.

Harry Pickles
None of the four sisters ever married, and only Nancy was ever engaged for a while. Gertrude's closest friendship with a man would seem to have been with a fellow-student from Manchester University, Harry Pickles. The first mention of him in connection with Gertrude is in mid-1911. He was an able student, taking first class honours in the history school in 1910, then focusing his interest on the law. He combined practical with academic training, being articled to a firm of Manchester solicitors, one of the partners of which, Mr Goulty, was a friend of Gertrude's father's, while at the same time pursuing his legal studies to graduate as a LL.B in 1913. He then continued his studies in London and passed his solicitor's examinations in 1914.[16]

Harry was one of a group of young people, men and women, who formed part of Gertrude's social scene in 1913. Like Harry, many of them had studied at Manchester. A strong bond for the group was the Historical Society and its outings. There were also dances, university functions and sport, and visits to the theatre. At some of these events, Gertrude was "seeing something of Mr Pickles", as Agnes puts it in her memoir (page 25). They went together to see the Gilbert and Sullivan opera, *Princess Ida*. They shared an interest in history and a taste for the author George Meredith. For part of 1914, Harry was studying in London; then, in response to the outbreak of war, he enlisted on 17 September 1914 as a private in the 10th Service Battalion of the Duke of Wellington's Regiment. (This regiment had long-established links with the West Riding of Yorkshire – now West Yorkshire. For Harry, a native of Barnoldswick, it would have been a natural choice.) His training was at Frensham Camp at Farnham in Surrey, and two photographs have survived showing him and a fellow-trainee in ill-fitting uniforms, posing in a studio. Gertrude's reaction to hearing his news may have been instinctive, but it served the purpose of acknowledging her interest in Harry without singling him out unduly: she dispatched a parcel of 'comforts' to his company, D Company, containing gifts for all its members. In a letter of 18 October 1914 to Nancy, she described what she had sent to the "pickled onion" – twelve helmets (presumably knitted or woollen ones), a large tin of two kinds of toffee made by her and Betty, some Mexican chocolate, small boxes of matches, and two cakes of Pears soap. The shopping list is jotted down on the inside back pages of her diary for 1914. Harry sent thanks from the whole tent, so she felt "amply rewarded". She continued to send parcels to D Company until Christmas 1914; as 'comforts for the troops' they would not have roused comment. They met over Christmas and once or twice thereafter, in Manchester. In February 1915 he was promoted to the rank of second lieutenant. On 18 March they met in Salford just before he left for France, the last time they saw

8 *Harry Pickles and a fellow-trainee, Frensham Camp, Farnham, Surrey, November 1914*

each other. They continued to exchange letters into the spring of 1915 and on 28 April she sent him another parcel.

It is impossible to tell how closely they may have been involved with each other. No letters from Harry have survived among Gertrude's archive. Gertrude herself seems to have been taken aback by the strength of her emotion. Writing to Nancy on 31 January 1915, she contrasted the state of her "imaginings" with her sister's confident relationship with the man she was engaged to, Leonard Harris. She went on: "it seems a very much bigger thing than I realised and yet all along I've known it meant almost everything to people". The general reaction to something about which she felt so tentative non-plussed her. "It's the light and airy way in which it's talked of and the inexcusable habit of teasing people (on the subject) that makes it seem so startling at first."

Reservations over the course of their friendship must have grown on Gertrude's side, as in a letter sent on 25 May 1915 after several days' cogitation, she brought it to an end. Harry replied a few days later. Her mother, in whom she may have had confided, was much relieved: "Gertrude has done the one big and right thing" (letter to Agnes, as noted in the latter's memoir, page 33). The reactions of the rest of her family are not known. However, they doubtless had been aware of Gertrude's and Harry's mutual attraction. Susan Powicke, writing to Maurice on 9 July 1911 from Hatherlow to tell him inter alia about Gertrude's graduation ceremony, says how much struck Betty was by "Mr Pickles's long eyelashes" – suggesting that the family already knew about Harry and his interest in and to Gertrude.

There was a wider context, to which Gertrude had alluded in her letter to Nancy. The country was at war, young men were being mobilised and couples were being thrown into situations where relationships could no longer develop at a calm pace. Marriages were contracted hastily, in knowledge, even defiance of the hazard that they might not last long. It is most unlikely that such would have been Gertrude's style. More importantly, she had, by early May 1915, committed herself to her own form of war service with the Society of Friends, and this engagement would, she surely estimated, require the energies of an unattached person. Harry took another course, which, in those wartime circumstances, was becoming not unusual: he got married, on 20 January 1916, a week before he returned to France with his regiment. His wife was Ada Herf, of New Eltham, on the southeast outskirts of London, and they were married in Lewisham, in south London. Although he was freed from any obligation towards Gertrude, he nonetheless wrote immediately to tell her about his marriage. She received his letter on 26 January and replied straightaway. In a subsequent letter to Agnes, she asked her to try to get hold of any newspapers for 20 January that might carry an announcement of the wedding, but to say nothing about it to the others. She told Agnes in a letter of 28 January 1916 that she would be telling "Mother and Betty and Fif [a family friend] that he is married as I think they will want to know". She assured her sister that she was getting along very well, "so don't worry…" Nonetheless, almost four lines are crossed out at this point in the letter and are pretty well impossible to read; perhaps an indication of emotions felt but finally not exposed to the record.

The most terrible test was to come. On 26 April 1916, Harry was killed by a shell exploding in his face as he leaned back in the trench to talk to the men of his company. They were on the front, at Houplines, northeast of Armentières, and were under sustained bombardment at the time. He is buried at Cité Bonjean military cemetery in Armentières. His death was announced in the *Manchester Guardian* of 12 May 1916.

Gertrude learned of his death on 9 May (it would seem through a letter from Nancy). She was devastated and particularly agonised by a lack of details. A number of diary entries for May show her distress and the continuing hold of her affection for him: "I see now that I have always hoped to see him again, that the knowledge that he was alive and that I could get at him has helped me". She sought courage in the similar sufferings of the women she worked among:

> It is true … I have found courage today, in the thought of all that my women have lost .. of the suspense they endure … I have only had my share in the toll exacted … There has come to me a feeling of participation in the sorrow and misery of the war, a feeling of initiation almost which is new to me.

She returned to her decision to break with Harry, fearful that she may have been too hard. Her only conduit for expressing her grief seems to have been through her diary and through letters to her family: "there is no-one to talk to, so fortunately I have to get along as usual." The days following were very hard, full of loneliness, homesickness and confusion: "I can see no way clear". By the end of May, she had received a letter from Harry's father, doubtless written in response to one she had sent, after some hesitation, to his mother, whom she had met. It gave her the details on Harry's death that she had longed for. A copy of Professor Tout's notice on Harry's death, carried in the Manchester University magazine, had also reached her through Dolly. She wrote in her diary on 30 May of the past year, one in which "good and bad have mixed pretty equally – I have been happy in the work ... but restless and lonely at heart. Now it is for me to be strong... I will look life squarely in the face and not go under, and may God guard me."

Harry is not much mentioned after this. She spent one Sunday morning in July re-reading such letters from him as she had with her, but with a sense of dislocation: "I do not yet realize all that has been – it is as if I read my life as the story of anothers", she noted in her diary for 9 July 1916. A few days later she received another letter from Harry's father. On leave in London in August, she visited the Inns of Court, where Harry had studied. For her, she wrote in her diary entry for 6 August 1916, they were "a place apart. Everytime I visit them I am haunted by memories. Today I remembered that he will visit them no more – last time I saw them he was alive."

Sometimes the recollection is more oblique. On 1 October 1916, she reflected that Rupert Brooke's "'war-poem' on a soldier and on Death are beautiful. 'Some corner of a foreign field that is for ever England' – I know of one such corner – and there are thousands, such." The acceptance that Harry's death was one among a multitude brought a certain comfort. At the festival of All Saints (Toussaint) on 31 October to 1 November, she was "led to think much of my 'man' – at such times one cannot but have the memory vividly before one. He is of a truth among many. There are 4,000 buried in Bar alone."

As the first anniversary of his death arrived, Gertrude expressed her longing again in her diary on 25 April 1917 (the date has been corrected to 24 April): "He has been in my thoughts almost all day and every day for the last few weeks, ever since the sun returned. Every day I have thought of him morning and night for two years – nearly three ... His Father and Mother must be feeling very sad today." A short poem, possibly her own (since no authorship is given), occupies the entry for the following day.

Thereafter, mention of Harry falls away: a short diary entry for 26 April 1918 – "Two years ago today. . La vie est brève"; then nothing. He cannot have been forgotten, but his memory had sunk beneath the unremitting demands of work, the many new experiences and constantly changing colleagues, the absorption into new tasks.

She does not appear to have become close to any other man. She did, however, correspond with another university acquaintance from her year, George W. Glover, who was a lieutenant in the Rifle Brigade. (He had also studied modern languages and graduated in 1911 with a first class degree.) News of his being wounded was announced in the

9 Christmas card from George Glover, 4th Division, to Gertrude, Christmas 1917

British newspapers, several of which were forwarded regularly to the FWVRC expedition in France, and Gertrude read it at Sermaize in July 1916. When she was home on leave that same summer, she met him in Manchester on 15 August. A month later he was awarded the Distinguished Service Order, and Gertrude wrote to him to offer her congratulations. They started to correspond, and Gertrude, following an earlier pattern, sent him several parcels of magazines and books to where he was stationed in France following his return to the front. In November 1916 he was in camp at Le Havre. "Poor man – out again", she noted in her diary on 3 November 1916. He sent her a Christmas card for 1917 from the 4th Division (to which his battalion was attached). It is a printed card based on a hand-painted original showing a 'Tommy' facing a winding road marked with military engagements.[17] Their exchange of letters was not an intimate one, but seems to have pleased both sides. It ended with his death from wounds on

1 September 1918. Gertrude learned the news from Dolly in December 1918, when they met in London, and was much saddened. "It is awful", she wrote in her diary on 12 September 1918, "I can't believe it ... poor boy. I must find out details One more good friend gone I shall miss his letters for we've always kept up with each other. I hope he got my last one. I feel as if I can't bear it."

When war broke out on 4 August 1914, Gertrude was still on the MHSG teaching staff. She had already been given leave of absence for a year to seek a post abroad. Her position had presumably been temporarily filled, so she had no assigned teaching duties to fulfil once the new session started. Her headmistress straightaway suggested she approach the Red Cross organisation, and on 9 August Gertrude duly did so. As she told Professor Tout in a letter of 6 August 1914, her intention was to volunteer for foreign service under the Red Cross, where her knowledge of French and German would be of use.[18] On return to the High School on 2 September, she met Miss Burstall and the following day was put in charge of the School's 'stores' of clothing and relief materials brought in by the pupils for distribution to the Belgian refugees who were already arriving in Britain and also to soldiers' families in need. She joined her friend Barbara Garrard in a Salford plan for district nursing and stayed with Barbara in Pendleton (in the northern part of Salford) for much of September, following first aid classes and visiting. She continued the visiting into October and November. The nursing course continued until 25 November, and on 17 December she took an examination at Pendleton and another examination in first aid and home nursing on 4 February 1915.

The pace speeded up, as she sought to equip herself with a wide range of skills in anticipation of securing some kind of war work. On 25 September her diary notes 'Mind and Memory' as she embarked on a course in Pelmanism. This system of mental exercises, aimed at strengthening and developing the mind and at expanding an individual's mental powers, was much advertised in the years before and during the First World War. An early form of distance learning, it operated through a correspondence course based on worksheets that were to be completed and returned and was backed up by instructional reading material. The course Gertrude followed may have consisted of five lessons. Her diary for 1914 shows that she paid £3.00 for the training.[19] Her reasons for taking this course are largely unexplained: it may have attracted her intellectually, or she may have felt it really would strengthen her capacity to undertake the variety of work and training she immersed herself in during the autumn of 1914 and spring of 1915. Certainly, the Society of Friends seems to have been impressed (see below).

Even though she was on leave of absence from the High School, she clearly helped out with class work, noting on 29 September 1914 that she had spent an hour in the Christie Library (of Manchester University) planning a scheme for classes. On 30 November, she set exam papers. A letter of 18 October 1914 to Nancy detailed the various activities that she, her family and friends were engaged in. Betty was "busy with good works". Agnes was much involved in the care of Belgian refugees. Gertrude herself was continuing to attend on and off to the stores at the MHSG and told Nancy they had sent off eighty parcels since the beginning of term. They had also started on splint-making and bandages needed in the hospitals. There was jam-making with her fellow-teacher Dolly Lunn for the hospitals – she reckoned they had made 2,400 pounds of jam. She was not yet "called up", but was filling in forms and gave her father firm instructions on 5 November 1914 on communicating immediately with her in Pendleton should any letter arrive for her at home from the Red Cross.

On 21 October 1914, her diary records the start of her next venture: learning to drive. She took instruction from Cockshoots garage, whose main offices at that time were north of Manchester city centre.[20] As well as servicing cars, the garage offered instruction not only in the technique of driving but also in car maintenance. From late October to late December, Gertrude's diary records being in the motor works and in the shop, as well as driving frequently around the Manchester area with a variety of instructors and sometimes by herself. On 24 October, she took the magneto to pieces and put it back again, then towed in a broken-down car from Deansgate (a short distance). On 30 October she tested a Renault in Salford. On 4 November she was in the works all day, dealing with tyres and accumulators; on 2 December she was vulcanising. An entry for 23 December notes, ambiguously, a "smash up" in Old Trafford, but does not make clear what happened. There was no requirement for her to take a driving test (which was not imposed until 1930), but she acquired a driving licence valid for a year from 28 October 1914.

She clearly decided that she should brush up her spoken French, and from the beginning of November 1914 until the end of March 1915 had conversation classes with Sœur Marie Françoise at an unnamed convent. Typing, finally, was added in late December to the skills she was determined to acquire.

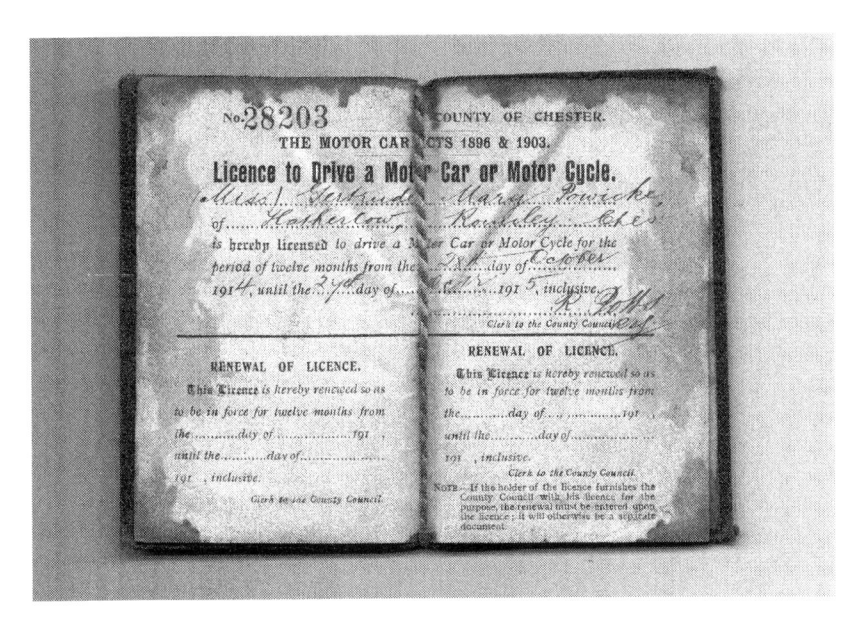

10 Driving licence issued to Gertrude Powicke, 28 October 1914

Such an outlay of effort (and doubtless expense) demanded some return, but Gertrude had to try in a number of quarters until she could find a suitable job. As Agnes noted, the period from January to June 1915 was a very unsettled time for her. Her diary for these months gives an indication of some of the possibilities she was exploring. In the London area the NUWSS appears to have suggested work in an administrative capacity or as an orderly in a hospital under women's organisation, or chauffeuring. Interpreting in French and German was another possibility. There is a reference to the Women's Automobile Club and to the French Automobile Club, the latter for women drivers in France. Other organisations she may have considered or approached in addition to the Red Cross Society were the French Red Cross Society, the Order of St John of Jerusalem, the Women's Volunteer Reserve (a uniformed auxiliary force), and the Royal Flying Corps. Agnes records that "her chief aim was to get work abroad". She made contact with the Third Scottish Women's Hospital Unit[21] and may have been offered a job with them as bookkeeper. She also approached the Friends War Victims Relief Committee (FWVRC), and a woman named Princess Bariatinsky, who seems to have been organising a private initiative. Gertrude visited the FWVRC in London on 19 April 1915, where she met Ruth Fry (see Biographical notes), its honorary secretary, and Edith Pye (see Biographical notes). Their letter of acceptance arrived on 2 May. She joined the FWVRC in a voluntary capacity, as an "ambulance driver and interpreter", as her diary records on 11 June 1915. Agnes (page 34 of her memoir) says that it was Gertrude's "knowledge of French and the capacity (gained through her Pelman studies) to cope with intricate details, that the Society [of Friends] found they could use best" in their programme of relief work. Though she never drove an ambulance, she eventually achieved her wish to drive a car; she accompanied the FWVRC trained nurses on their home visiting; and on occasion she changed dressings. Her powers of organisation and administration were stretched to the full. The methodical preparation had paid off.

The necessary arrangements for departure could now be put in place. In the course of May she was vaccinated and received two inoculations (against what, though, is not known). On each occasion she reacted badly and had to stay a few days in bed. She had to apply for a passport and obtain the necessary photograph. On 19 May she wrote to the family's solicitor, Mr Goulty, for a reference. To the modern eye, her 1915 passport has a strange appearance, since it consists of a single sheet of stiff white paper, 53 cm by 64.5 cm, bearing the imprint of a French manufacturing company, which was then folded lengthwise and crosswise until it approached the dimensions of the modern passport. Information, observations and endorsements were pasted on to this sheet. Hers was issued on 24 May 1915 and bears the signature of the then Foreign Secretary, Sir Edward Grey. She listed items she should buy: a compass, penknife and thermos, a Scout's book and Keatings powder (against fleas). The MHSG teachers gave a donation for her new work, and Miss Burstall sent a farewell letter. Finally, on 5 June, she sailed for France.

No one in her family seems to have tried to dissuade Gertrude from accepting the Society of Friends' invitation to join their relief expedition to France. They had witnessed her determined preparations for active war work and would have known that she would eventually be caught up in some sort of effort. Maurice indeed wrote to her on 9 May 1915 to congratulate her on being "required" by the Friends. The family were not pacifist – both Maurice and Will undertook differing kinds of war work, though neither bore arms, and Gertrude had been of the view, when she wrote to Nancy on 18 October 1914 that the war was exciting their father rather a lot, saying enigmatically: "He's as good as a recruiting officer just now". Nonetheless, we may suppose that they understood that element in Quaker belief and practice. They were content that Gertrude would be engaged in "good work". They accepted that she might be in danger, but were more concerned as time went on about the effects of continual hard work in harsh conditions on her health. Only when she consented to the Friends' second invitation to go to Poland in 1919 did they express disquiet, but they did not oppose her decision.

Gertrude's own thinking in the early stages of the war is revealed in the same letter to Nancy:

> It is very difficult I find to keep level-headed on the subject – I do want to be perfectly just and the only result is that I find it quite impossible to come to any definite conclusion. My one wish is that we may make it possible to come out of it with clean hands and that the war spirit *will* be quenched. I can quite see that it is, as it stands, a righteous war as far as such a thing is possible, but how long it will remain so is a question. It's no good theorizing however – only God help us – when we get to the end as well as now.

It is likely that many people wanted to see the war as a righteous one that would lead to a world without war, and hoped that Britain would acquit itself honourably. In sharing such sentiments, Gertrude could also see that the situation might develop into something far more complicated and compromising.

Chapter Two

The Society of Friends and war relief

Among the basic tenets of the Society of Friends was their desire to offer testimony against war, a wish that often brought down on them the hostility of secular authorities. By the beginning of the twentieth century, testimony against war had metamorphosed into testimony for peace, a more diffuse concept.[1] This shift in emphasis, however, did not mitigate the sharp contradictions with much of the rest of society that British Quakers experienced on the outbreak of the First World War. From a position of accommodation with the British state (full citizenship since 1870, access to the professions and all universities, nine Quaker MPs in 1906), the Society of Friends found itself again standing out against the requirements of that state. Individual Quakers might and did make the decision to enlist; but the Society as a whole, together with the five Quaker MPs then in parliament, resisted conscription and welcomed the insertion of a conscience clause in the Military Service Act of January 1916 when it finally introduced conscription for single men. The Society saw it as the duty of its members and of other conscientious objectors to claim the exemption from military service offered by the Act. Throughout the war, the Society's organ, *The Friend*, reported regularly on the operation of the tribunals set up to hear applications for exemption on the grounds of conscientious objection, and on the treatment (sometimes extremely harsh) of objectors. Not all of the latter were Quakers.

In forming its practical response to the consequences of war, the Society of Friends in Britain chose to focus primarily on non-combatants, especially those displaced in one way or another by the fighting. Its methods of work aimed to avoid all direct involvement in the conduct of the war and the military chain of command. The three organisations chiefly associated with the Society were the Friends'

Ambulance Unit (FAU), the Friends' War Victims' Relief Committee (FWVRC) and the Friends' Emergency Committee. This last was set up within weeks of Britain's declaration of war on Germany (on 4 August 1914) to assist Germans, Austrians and Hungarians in the United Kingdom, that is, enemy aliens, who might have fallen into distress. The FAU provided ambulances and ambulance drivers, medical supplies and volunteer medical and nursing personnel for behind the front duties in France, Belgium and Italy throughout the First World War until 1919. (Gertrude came across FAU volunteers in northeast France.) The French army authorities were happy to use its services, even if the British military viewed it with suspicion. However, as correspondence in *The Friend* in the early months of the war hints, some in the Society of Friends worried that an ambulance corps might find itself drawn into working with the military; some even expressed concern over the FAU's close relationship with the Red Cross. The FAU chairman, writing in November 1916 in *The Friend*, described the FAU as a civil unit of the Red Cross, receiving the co-operation of the military authorities, and FAU workers as wearing Red Cross khaki uniform. Presumably on account of such reservations, the FAU was never organised as an official Quaker group. It remained independent of the Society of Friends and operated under its own committee, though enjoying the moral and fundraising support of the Society. The FAU recruited a large number of conscientious objectors.

With the FWVRC there were no such reservations. It was set up as an organisation responsible to London Yearly Meeting of the Society of Friends,[2] with its own executive, and offices under its honorary general secretary, Ruth Fry. The initiative for the relief effort and for a visit of investigation into conditions in the non-occupied parts of France came from Dr Hilda Clark (see Biographical notes). A first meeting was held on 4 September 1914 to address the needs of non-combatants in France and Belgium. Dr Clark and T. Edmund Harvey MP (see Biographical notes) were among those who subsequently visited France, Belgium and Holland and reported on the requirements of relief work, which especially for France encompassed medical assistance and rebuilding. Authorisation from the French government and military authorities was secured in mid-October, and in early November 1914, the first group of thirty-three volunteers left for northeast France.[3] They had been preceded in September and early October 1914 by a small group of five Quakers who were permitted to take clothing and boots to distribute in villages near Meaux, to the east of Paris.

In establishing its War Victims' Relief Committee, the Society of Friends was, in fact, reviving an earlier effort. Some forty years previously, during the Franco-Prussian War of 1870-1871, the London Meeting had set up a committee with the same name to provide a measure of aid to non-combatants caught up in the conflict. A UK-based group supported a band of unpaid volunteer 'commissioners' or field workers, comprising Quakers and non-Quakers, who rotated their month-long stints on the ground, working alongside other similar relief organisations from all over Europe to distribute clothing, food and seeds. They were active in both France and Germany, where they could move with passports delivered by both countries. Funding was raised through public subscription.[4] The fighting affected much of the northeast and north of France, and memories remained among the French population there in 1914 of the Prussian invasion and indeed of the previous presence of FWVRC workers. The re-formed FWVRC invoked this earlier project from the start. The experience gained four decades before doubtless enabled a speedy decision to be made at the 4 September 1914 meeting to revive such an effort. Along with its title the committee reactivated the same symbol, the eight-pointed Quaker star in black on red, as a badge for personnel (it is clearly visible on the left arm of Gertrude's jacket in her 'official' photo – see Figure 39) and to identify paperwork and goods. The small band of frontrunners who went to Meaux obtained recognition from the French authorities for the use of the Quaker star.[5]

As with the earlier committee, the FWVRC as it operated during and beyond the First World War was organised from a London base given general charge of the work, with field units comprising teams or *équipes* (the French word was commonly used) active in projects overseas and in the main allowed to govern themselves through a committee and to arrange their own work. Nonetheless, leadership and control throughout the FWVRC remained in the hands of the Society of Friends in London. An executive committee met weekly to supervise the work of subcommittees, as outlined in *The Friend* for 29 January 1915, and leading members of the Society were present in guiding and overseeing roles in the various country programmes. In this way the Friends' basic tenet of no submission to military supervision could be maintained and their style of work with its emphasis on discussion and consensual decisions preserved. While Quakers firmly led the FWVRC, they accepted non-Friends such as Gertrude as volunteers. Decisions on the types of relief activities to be undertaken were based on visits of investigation by Friends or by members of an équipe in anticipation of a proposed project. (That was how Gertrude and two fellow-workers in Poland came to visit Eastern Galicia and Western Ukraine in November-December 1919.) Inspection visits from London to established centres aimed at keeping the work 'on message' and the London committee informed. Regular submission of reports from the équipes also permitted an overview of how work was being conducted. Lapses in behaviour among workers were few, but someone whose conduct was felt to have been blameworthy or who evidently could not cope with the work might be asked to withdraw.

The FWVRC enforced strict financial accounting in all activities. It would have judged this essential to maintaining the Friends' name for probity and responsibility in disbursing funds and goods collected through donations. Among the London office's chief functions was that of fundraiser, in which capacity it was surely successful, since according to Ruth Fry, "about one and a half million pounds went through the London books".[6] She mentions further a British Treasury Grant, which for certain countries matched with £1 every £1 collected by approved societies, an arrangement that benefited the FWVRC to the extent of £24,000 per month.[7] *The Friend* carried continual appeals for money, footwear and clothing, sometimes issuing very precise instructions on the types of garments requested in reports from the field to meet local taste, and offering patterns and directions for working up clothes for French, Belgian or Serbian recipients. A warehouse in London stored clothing and some food and forwarded it to the various fields of work. Ruth Fry valued these goods at about "half a million pounds".[8] Direct appeals for the gift or loan of motor vehicles also appeared in the journal. The sums raised by the London office did not include gifts sent direct to field units by donors such as the American Friends Service Committee and the American Red Cross. Units working in France were eligible for official French grants and supplies of material. The Society of Friends was able to benefit from the issuance of visas free of charge for all the countries in which the FWVRC worked, as well as from the grant of free travel.[9]

From an early stage it was recognised that some of the funds raised would have to go to the maintenance of relief workers. The majority of these were recruited as volunteers and received no remuneration, "though in exceptional cases, and often for doctors and nurses, an honorarium was given".[10] (Gertrude, and the FWVRC, were in effect subsidised by the Manchester High School for Girls, which continued to pay her her yearly salary of £40.) These volunteers, however, still had to be fed and housed and uniforms, in 'Quaker grey', provided. As Ruth Fry put it, "there was a sort of republic on communal lines established, where all the ordinary needs of daily life were provided in return for voluntary service".[11] She calculated that around 1,070 British had volunteered at some point, in which figure she included Irish workers, and 780 Americans. A group of 270 people assisted in the London office and warehouse. Australian and Canadian volunteers also participated (though it is not clear if they were counted among the British group), and local volunteers augmented the field units. Some volunteers could spare only a few months, while others, such as Gertrude, stayed for years. Turnover in personnel was consequently frequent.

The FWVRC's first and most extensive network of activities was in France, but it conducted relief work in several other countries and co-operated with other like-minded organisations in a number of settings. Ruth Fry's account of the FWVRC's work, *A Quaker Adventure: The Story of Nine Years' Relief and Reconstruction*, published in 1926, and successive issues of *The Friend* give a survey of the Committee's reach. Belgium, neighbouring on France, was occupied almost in its entirety by German troops, except for a small area around the mouth of the Yser river. In this unoccupied zone, the Aide Civile Belge received direct support from the Friends' Ambulance Unit and administrative support from the London office of the FWVRC. The Netherlands remained neutral throughout the First World War but agreed to let the FWVRC run projects offering care and occupation to the many refugees, largely from Belgium, who had fled there. In southern Europe, the FWVRC co-operated from late 1915 with the Serbian Relief Fund (SRF), set up in September 1914 to alleviate medical and humanitarian needs among the Serbian population and army and Serbian refugees escaping the Austro-Hungarian invasion of the Balkans. FWVRC did not send its own unit, but 'lent' thiry-four workers to support the SRF.[12] Gertrude knew several of the FWVRC workers sent to assist the SRF and on and off wished that she might join them. The Serbian allure was sharpened for her by a chance meeting on the crossing from Southampton to Le Havre on 22 October 1918 with a woman who had been in the Antwerp retreat in early October 1914 and the two Dobrudja retreats in Serbia. Gertrude told her family in a letter of 3 November 1918 that she felt that this woman "looked rather terrible, got up just like a man with short hair and military coat and cap and all the accessories. But I enjoyed travelling with her."

The FWVRC first interested itself in Russia in 1916, when a team of four men left in the spring to investigate the conditions of Polish refugees driven eastwards by the German invasions. The team visited Moscow and Buzuluk in Samara in western Russia. On the basis of their report, a unit was set up at Buzuluk to offer medical care, relief and occupation to both local inhabitants and refugees. It stayed on through the October Revolution of 1917, civil war and increasing shortages and left only in October 1918. The Friends returned to what had become the Soviet Union, joining with other relief organisations under the name of the All Britain Appeal, to give assistance in the Great Famine of 1921-22. Refugees were by then flowing out of Russia, bringing with them typhus.

Conditions were equally chaotic in Poland in 1919, and for similar reasons: refugees and typhus. The country only achieved independence, after two centuries of partition, in November 1918. Subsequent fighting in the region over control of borders climaxed in renewed war between Poland and the Soviet Union in 1920 (see Chapter Seven). Local populations lived in a state of flux, people who had been expelled eastwards from Poland during the war sought to return home, and prisoners-of-war, both captive Russians and Poles returning, brought further problems. The FWVRC unit joined first in the general anti-typhus campaign in Poland in August 1919, then continued to care for refugees and prisoners-of-war, and to undertake reconstruction where it could. It remained in Poland until 1924.

Under a new title from 1919 of Friends' Emergency and War Victims' Relief Committee, the Society of Friends sent units to Germany and Austria after the war to help with the resettlement and rehabilitation of the population.

Working in the zone of the armies
The five French armies (whose number was subsequently augmented) that faced the seven German armies drawn up facing Belgium and France in August 1914 were installed along the well-fortified border with southern Belgium and Lorraine and Alsace. The German intention was that, by pushing into France from the north with a massive right wing and outflanking, then destroying the French army, France could be eliminated as an enemy. Initially, the German attack and invasion made headway, and by early September 1914, the Germans had advanced into Picardy, Champagne and Lorraine along a line that started at Ypres, almost touched Amiens, came to within forty-eight km of Paris, encompassed Rheims and Châlons-sur-Marne and swept round to Verdun, which, however, was not taken. The French forces generally fell back, though in orderly fashion. Then, as they held the Germans in Picardy, supported by the British Expeditionary Force (BEF), the French high command under Joffre rallied. In a change of direction, the armies on the extreme right of the German advance

were swung away from the Paris region towards the southeast in pursuit of the French armies and were drawn into engagement with the French in the First Battle of the Marne (5-9 September 1914). French and BEF troops, regrouping behind the Marne, pushed the Germans east and north, but could not drive them back to the frontier. Instead, by 15 September 1914, the Germans were digging in along and beyond the river Aisne along a line well within the northern frontiers of France, in positions from which they could not be dislodged. The period of open warfare was over, and the long period of trench warfare was beginning. The French had to renounce hopes of recovering territory lost to the enemy in ten departments along the country's northern and northeastern border, as well as the principal French mining and manufacturing region of which Lille was the centre, and the Lille-Metz railway. In the occupied territories in both the north of France and Belgium, which remained under German control throughout the war, the inhabitants suffered greatly through hunger, requisitioning, forced labour, hostage-taking and deportation.[13] The zone of land lying between the furthermost line of the German advance in early September 1914 and the front line as it had established itself by the end of that month (roughly Compiègne to Verdun in the central and eastern sectors) had been left ravaged through fighting and deliberate destruction.[14]

Much of this stretch of territory caught between the lines of German advance and retreat formed the ground over which the FWVRC worked. It lay within the zone of the French armies. The Friends' mission managed to operate in this zone only through close liaison with French military and government authorities. The negotiations undertaken in London and France resulted in the French Minister of War accepting the Society of Friends' offer of help on 16 October 1914 and in the first relief party being placed under the authority of the army's Service de santé (health services) and the Directeur de l'arrière (director of the rear area). The Minister of War stipulated that the Society's workers were never to be active at the front, but were to be granted the means of organisation, accommodation and requisition where required.[15] They were specifically prohibited from any form of proselytising, so there could be no promotion of peace or pacifist arguments. The FWVRC was placed under the direction of the Directeurs des étapes et des services (DES) (primarily concerned with logistics).[16] This 'patronage' seems to have lasted through the war. If FWVRC workers were to get anywhere near to their chosen areas of activity, they had to be equipped with the necessary military authorisation. Only with such consent could non-com-

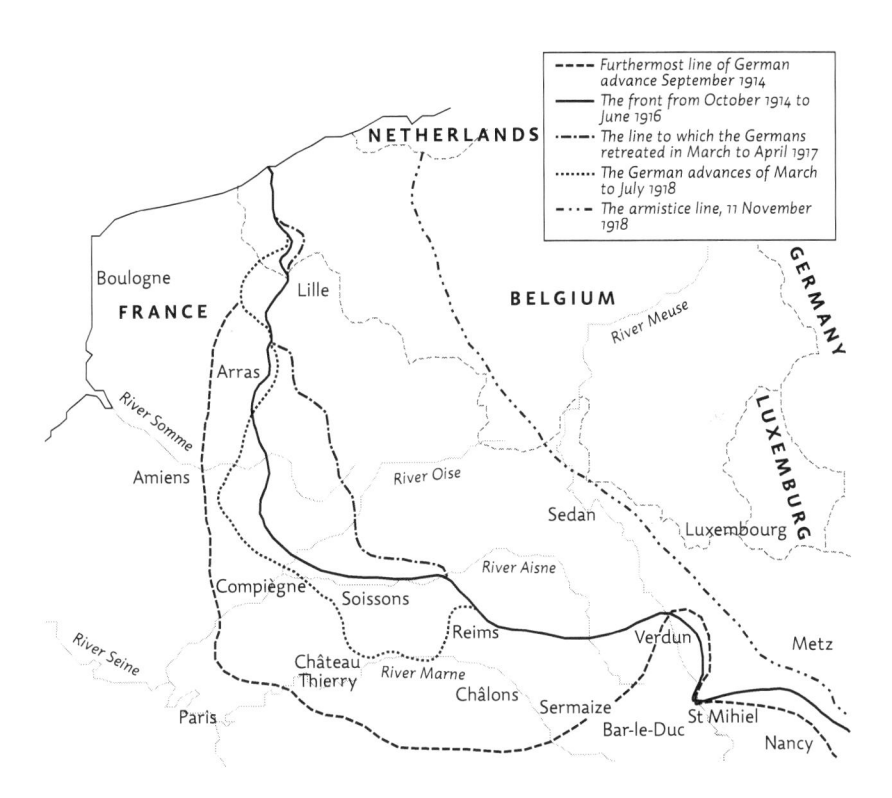

Map 1 *Western front, 1914–1918, showing German advances and retreats*

batants live, work or travel in the zone of the armies.[17] A formidable system of safe conduct passes, *carnets d'étranger* (foreigner's permits) and other permits ensured adherence to the restrictions in place.

Most of the FWVRC's teams were set up in the zones of the French third, fourth and fifth armies, that is, in an area running west from the Verdun–Bar-le-Duc line to the Fismes–Chateau-Thierry line, in districts that had been ravaged by the fighting of the first six weeks of the war. Military needs in these districts prevailed over those of local people and relief workers, and troop movements might mean that travel permits were temporarily withheld. Even with the initial acceptance of the Society's offer of assistance, tortuous negotiations continued to be necessary to secure clearance of FWVRC workers. Correspondence between T. Edmund Harvey, who represented the Society to the French authorities, and the London Committee shows that he had to intervene with the French army general headquarters and even on one occasion with President Poincaré. This appeal to the president was prompted by the threatened withdrawal of permits from FWVRC workers in early 1917, thought to be attributable to Joffre's successor as commander-in-chief, General Nivelle. Supported by Monsieur Léon Bourgeois, senator for the department of the Marne, head of a French parliamentary group representing the occupied territories and champion of the Society's work, and advised by Sir Henry Austin Lee (see Biographical notes) of the British embassy in Paris, Harvey was received by Poincaré on 3 March 1917. The president undertook to place the matter before Nivelle, and the threat receded.[18] The gravity of the situation was generally known among FWVRC workers, and Gertrude's diary for 3 March 1917 records a discussion on the problem.

If military authorities had sometimes to be convinced of the usefulness of the Friends' work, so too did some government departments, and here the Society drew on the contacts it had nurtured with influential figures. (Edmund Harvey's standing as a Member of Parliament would have helped here.) Foreign Office officials in Paris, including the ambassador, Lord Bertie, and Sir Henry Austin Lee were supportive. Thus, when the French Customs sought to charge duty on goods imported by the FWVRC, the difficulty was resolved through discussions between the French Ministry of Finance and Sir Henry Austin Lee and authorisation issued on 5 February 1915 to the Society to import a range of relief goods.[19]

More disquietingly, doubts over the value of the FWVRC's activities and over its volunteers' style of life persisted even into 1916 and affected the granting of permits. The British Committee of the French

Red Cross acted as sponsor for FWVRC volunteers in obtaining permits and indeed was described by Ruth Fry as having been "placed *in loco parentis* to our work by the French Government".[20] It became aware of complaints and in November 1916, sent out two British military officers, Major A. W. Mayo Robson, who was on the Committee's medical council, and Lieutenant-Colonel Sir W. Hutcheson Poë, to inspect the FWVRC's centres of operation and talk to its workers. Gertrude encountered these two officers when they visited her *ouvroir*, or workroom, in Bar-le-Duc in late November 1916 and questioned her closely but to their satisfaction, as she noted in her diary for 20 November 1916. Their report appears to have seen off suspicions.

Once established in France, FWVRC teams had to work with the civil authorities, ranging from national ministries such as the Ministry of the Interior, which incorporated a Service des réfugiés et des Blessés – the section handling services for refugees and the wounded, down to departmental *préfets*, or prefects, and town and village *maires*, or mayors, on whom responsibility for refugees at a local level had devolved.[21] The prefect, in his capacity as representative of the national government within his department, and his assistant *sous-préfets*, or sub-prefects, held considerable powers of initiative and were able to disburse state funds. Thus in 1914, the prefect of the Marne requested the FWVRC to organise a maternity hospital for refugees at Châlons-sur-Marne to care for the needs of women and babies from among the refugee population of the department.[22] Gertrude herself dealt with local civil servants in the course of her work at Bar-le-Duc and even with the prefect of the department of the Meuse, Monsieur Piette, as when he sought her views on the evacuation of villages north of Bar in the face of a possible German advance in June 1918 (as she noted on 12 June 1918). The invaluable element the FWVRC could bring was skilled man- and womanpower.

The FWVRC was by no means the only foreign voluntary organisation working in France. Through the American Relief Clearing House, established in Paris in November 1914, the United States channelled considerable aid to France. The Red Cross in its various national groupings – particularly the French, American and British – interacted in various ways with the Friends' mission in France. FWVRC workers maintained contact with French Red Cross workers. The American Red Cross (which set up a hospital in Paris and was particularly active in anti-TB work) was a big donor to the FWVRC, and from late 1917 onwards, Gertrude encountered and worked with their personnel on French soil. The British Red Cross had FAU staff on its hospital trains. The Young Men's Christian Society (YMCA) was also present in France, where, as in Britain and other posts abroad, it provided hostels, canteens and recreational facilities for British and later American troops.

The FWVRC enjoyed the support and co-operation of a number of French welfare groups and of religious leaders and institutions in such areas as the provision of care for the aged. At the individual level, local people, particularly middle-class women, gave their support, both practical and moral, to the FWVRC équipes. Gertrude formed close friendships with several such ladies. Considerable scope existed for private initiative (as it did also in Britain). Those with a large property, in the countryside or a village or near a town, might offer the house and its grounds as a hospital or reception centre for the duration of the fighting, while they themselves withdrew to safer areas, undertook some kind of war work or merely trimmed back their presence. The FWVRC found itself several times the beneficiary of such arrangements, notably at Bettancourt and Sermaize, where it was able to set up convalescence and hospital services in vacated properties.

The path of the FWVRC's activities in France moved broadly from west to east through the swathe of territory devastated in the first weeks of the war by the German invasion and retreat (see Map 1). The first group of thirty-three volunteers with four vehicles and supplies left on 5 and 6 November 1914 to work at two sites in the department of the Marne: the maternity hospital for refugees at Châlons-sur-Marne, and at Esternay, where teams of men embarked on the construction of temporary wooden houses to accommodate those who had lost their homes in the fighting. Early in 1915, the volunteers moved east to Fère Champenoise and Vitry-le-François. Mobility and flexibility were features of the FWVRC's approach, and once a need had been met and a job completed, a team moved on, especially in such activities as house-repair and house-construction. In the main, in the early stages efforts were concentrated in an area straddling the departments of the Marne and the Meuse and centred on Sermaize-les-Bains. By early 1915, a team was in place at Sermaize, which became and remained the regional headquarters for the mission's work in the surrounding villages and small towns until early 1919 (see section on Sermaize). By August 1915, *The Friend* for 13 August 1915 estimated that the FWVRC's work was spread over a corridor sixty to seventy miles in length, though much less in width.

Access was from the west, by road or by the railway line linking Paris to Nancy, still in French hands. Movement to the north or northeast was not possible without running into enemy lines (see Map 2).[23] Visits to the front were made with (sometimes without) army authorisation. The American writer Edith Wharton made several tours of the Argonne, Verdun and the Vosges in 1915 to inspect and publicise the situation as part of her support for French refugees; and on 10 May 1916, Gertrude recorded a visit to the équipe in Bar by a French woman journalist who with two women companions had managed to reach forward points in the Argonne beyond Ste Menehould the previous year. Conditions were very rough, and they were questioned by security police. Such adventures were not for the FWVRC volunteers.

Within the angle formed by the front in this region of France, the FWVRC teams were scattered over a number of villages and small towns. Initially, the area that could be visited was closely limited by military restrictions that applied to all forms of transport. (Gertrude's carnet d'étranger is a good example of the precisely delineated boundaries of the district that could be covered.) Gradually the area they could operate in was widened, as in October 1916. No real expansion of the mission's remit in the Marne and the Meuse was envisaged until very late in 1917, when several of the FWVRC's leading members in the French expedition toured the area to the west of Verdun in December, at the invitation of the sub-prefect of Verdun. The purpose was to study the possibilities for rehabilitation in that district, in anticipation of allied victory. The moment of deliverance was severely threatened by a renewed German offensive in the spring and summer of 1918 along long sections of the front, and once again, villages and towns had to be evacuated. By September 1918, however, the German offensive had been broken, not least by the arrival of American troops. The armistice of 11 November 1918 allowed the FWVRC to put into operation its plans for reconstruction in the Verdun region.

The Society had outposts in other localities. FWVRC teams were sent to departments in the Picardy region in mid-1917 to help those who had returned to their homes following a German withdrawal from the area in the early spring of 1917 (even if they had to evacuate again in spring 1918). At Dôle, in the department of the Jura, a heavily wooded region on the border with Switzerland, and at Ornans, in the department of the Doubs in the eastern Jura, centres were set up in 1916 and 1917 respectively for the construction of pre-fabricated houses, *maisons démontables*, using timber supplied by the French Ministry of the Interior. These houses were dispatched by rail and lorry to where they were needed.

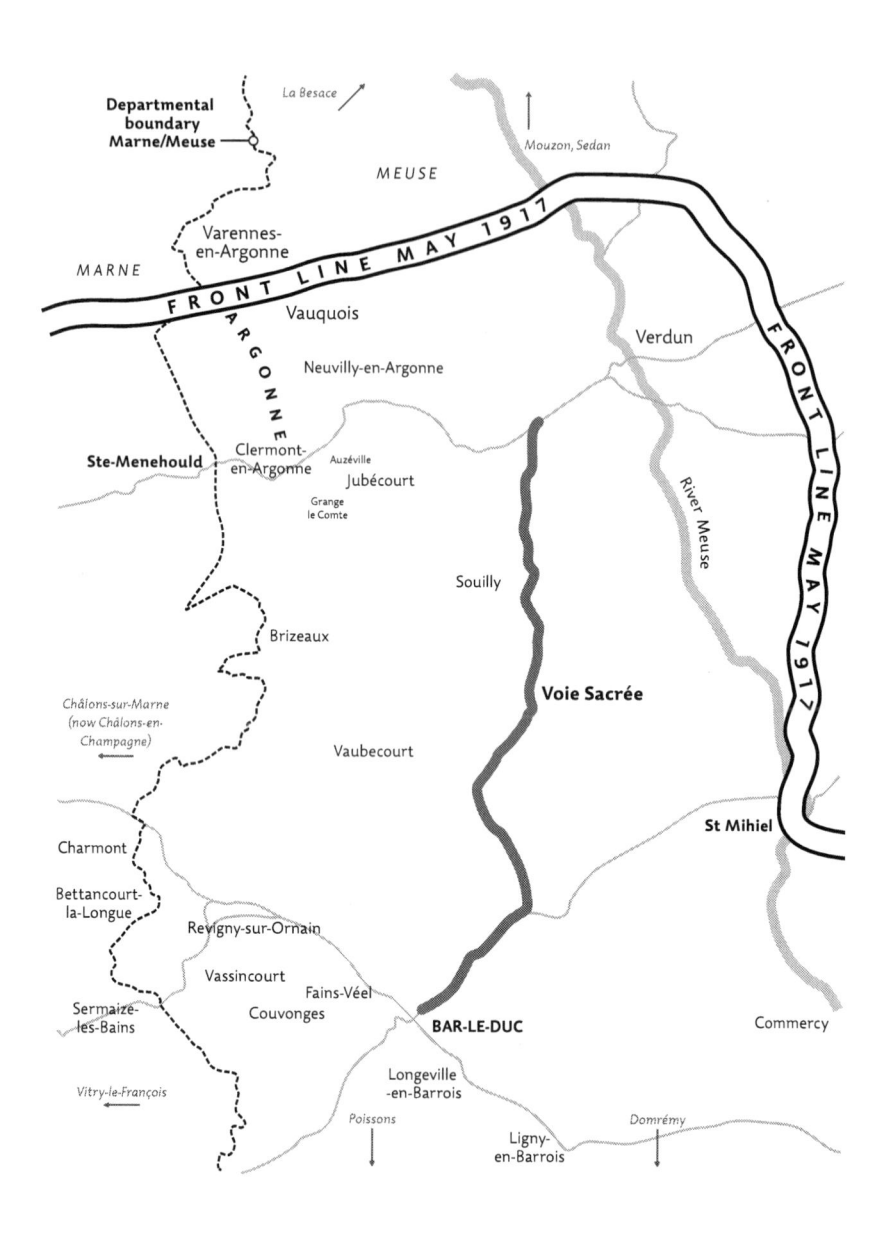

Map 2 *Area north and east of the FWVRC's main area of activity, showing the front line, May 1917*[23]

Another project that took shape in the eastern part of France was the convalescence centre at Samoëns in the department of the Haute Savoie. This was initially conceived in the spring of 1916 as a place for those needing medical care among the mass of the French population expelled from the occupied territories as *bouches inutiles* – unproductive elements – back to France via Belgium, Germany and Switzerland. Many came from the departments of the Aisne, the Marne and the Ardennes.[24] This group of people formed the category of *rapatriés*, the repatriated, which was largely comprised of the very young and their mothers, the elderly and the ill. Some who could pay for their passage out were assisted to leave, the impoverished were expelled in forced journeys that continued until the end of the war. Once in France, they were treated as refugees and generally became a charge on municipal authorities.[25] Samoëns was not far from Annemasse (on the French-Swiss border just east of Geneva), through which large numbers of repatriated passed. Some of these people went on to Samoëns for recuperation, but eventually the centre was run primarily, until December 1918, as a care and convalescence home and received many tuberculosis cases. A second similar home was opened at Entremont in the same region in 1917.

The FWVRC had two other important centres, at Troyes and Paris. Troyes, and the department of the Aube of which it is the capital, had to cope with a large influx of refugees in 1914: about 5,000 in the city and another 15,000 scattered throughout the department. To these were added a further 3,000 in the spring of 1918, as the Germans mounted their final offensive. A FWVRC team worked in the city from the autumn of 1915 to relieve the poor conditions in which many refugees lived, providing clothing, furniture and bedding at reduced prices and eventually renting houses to let out to refugees and erecting some of the pre-fabricated homes.

Early on, the FWVRC recognised the need to establish an office in Paris to handle dealings with the French authorities, co-ordinate the work of the two Quaker centres involved – London and later Philadelphia – manage the financial side of the operation, make purchases and receive goods sent from Britain for forwarding to its centres of work in France. An audit and finance section was set up under a treasurer, who received the accounts from the various posts and made visits of inspection. The mission's headquarters was at the Hôtel Britannique (was it chosen for its name?), 20 avenue Victoria, in the first arrondissement close to the Hôtel de Ville – the city hall – of Paris.[26] The hotel still flourishes under the same name and at the same address. FWVRC workers passing through Paris put up at the

11 *Plaque in the foyer of the Hôtel Britannique, Paris, commemorating the Society of Friends' use of the hotel as its headquarters, 1914–1920*

Britannique on their way to and from post, and Gertrude stayed there on many occasions.

Paris had its share of refugees, who were often crowded into the poorer quarters where tuberculosis was prevalent. Such people were candidates for recuperation at Samoëns, and the Paris office helped others with accommodation. The German push in the spring of 1918 brought Paris within range of long-distance bombardment and produced a fresh influx of refugees who arrived in Paris by train. Forty thousand were said to have passed through the Gare du Nord and the Gare d'Ivry on their way from the war zone.[27] They were fed by the French and American Red Cross organisations, the YMCA and the FWVRC and given a night's lodging before being sent on the next day to destinations in the south and west of France. Wilfrid Shewell, secretary to the FWVRC mission in France, noted that they brought with them numerous babies in prams and family pets and small livestock.[28]

FWVRC activities
The FWVRC's report dated March 1915, 'Behind the battle lines in France', gives a succinct and sobering account of the damage inflicted in the German advance in the Fère Champenoise region in the department of the Marne:[29]

> (1) Total destruction of houses and farm-buildings by incendiarism and shell-fire; (2) damage to buildings, making them unsafe and insanitary; (3) burning of stock, agricultural implements, harvest, and seed-corn, &c.; (4) loss of standing crops in August and September, owing to the mobilisation and to the fighting over the farms; (5) loss of clothing, furniture, &c., by pillage as well as fire; (6) great scarcity of male labour and of horses to work the farms; (7) overcrowding in the remaining houses in villages only partially burnt, as well as overcrowding by influx of refugees from the North, from territory occupied by the Germans.
> Many homes have already lost their breadwinners, some through death or severe wounds in the war, while in some cases civilian hostages have been carried away into Germany.

This brief list encapsulates three of the four main areas of activity regarded as essential in the FWVRC's programme: reconstruction of housing, agricultural rehabilitation, and relief of personal hardship. The fourth activity selected, medical aid, was also urgent. Often help was needed simultaneously in more than one direction and had to be co-ordinated. The list also makes the official distinction between those who had lost homes and livelihood in their villages and those who had fled from their villages in occupied territory, as well as hinting at the fate of civilians captured by the enemy.[30]

For the first category of people, those who had been burned out of their homes and farms, help in reconstruction of damaged buildings and provision of temporary shelter for humans and animals was urgent. New temporary wooden housing was developed, starting in workshops at Vitry-le-François, where French carpenters, some of them Territorial soldiers, fabricated wooden shelters which were then carried to neighbouring villages and erected by FWVRC men. Among the latter were several architects. The necessary timber was supplied by the department,[31] departmental architects offered co-operation, and local skilled labour might be authorised. The model of standard-pattern, portable wooden housing was adopted widely by the FWVRC from early 1915, based on designs by a British architect, Granville Streatfeild (see Biographical notes), who himself joined the team working in the department of the Marne in November to December 1914.[32] Different types of housing could be made available

12 *One of the FWVRC's pre-fabricated houses on display at the Exposition de la cité reconstituée, Paris, summer 1916*

to meet size of family and individual taste. Frames, walls and floor were all of wood, and roofing was at first tarred felt, later on tiles. Furniture was supplied by the Bon Gîte (Sound Shelter) association or by the departmental prefect. With the approval of local prefects, the Friends' mission extended its activities eastwards from Vitry and worked in building and agricultural reconstruction in ruined villages between Vitry and Sermaize. Gertrude visited some of them in 1915.

The need for both patching up and temporary housing was considerable: *The Friend* for 23 April 1915 stated that over 3,000 houses had been destroyed in the department of the Marne. The situation was clearly judged to have improved over the following fourteen months, since *The Friend* for 2 June 1916 was able to report that the task of rehousing and reclothing and of agricultural distribution in the departments of the Marne and the Meuse was almost completed. The practice of small scattered teams was terminated and, as seen above, the production of pre-fabricated wooden houses was centred at Dôle and Ornans. This particular activity lent itself well to concentration and rationalisation, as *The Friend* for 23 March 1917 explained, and allowed the FWVRC to aim at building up a stock of housing that could be distributed in the occupied areas, such as the department of the Ardennes, when this became possible.[33]

The house-building scheme produced two interesting offshoots in 1916: participation in an exhibition in Paris on the theme of the reconstituted city (Exposition de la cité reconstituée), held at the Tuileries gardens from 25 May to 15 August 1916, and the creation of a small 'garden city' at Sermaize. (See section on Sermaize for a discussion of this project.) The two concepts were related, in the context both of international engagement with the development of rationally planned and socially beneficial urban spaces, and of the work of small-scale rehabilitation that the FWVRC was bound up in. Officials such as departmental prefects were themselves anxious that villages should be rebuilt on more hygienic and spacious lines.

The FWVRC's report of March 1915 (see above) summed up the immediate problems in the agricultural sector: the destruction of farm buildings, machinery, livestock and supplies, the loss of standing crops, and the scarcity of male labour and farm horses. Those left to work the land were often women and elderly men. The mobilisation of essential village members, such as blacksmiths, might deprive villages of their source of repairs. A less expected threat to farmland was the arrival of wild boar, some of them driven south by fighting in the Ardennes. (On 29 August 1915, Gertrude recorded seeing wild boar, "a line of silvery-grey creatures pass[ing] in single file", in the forests northwest of Bar-le-Duc.)

The lack of machinery and of seed corn made it difficult to prepare and sow for the next harvest. The FWVRC agricultural unit made these two deficiencies priority concerns, together with the restocking of farms. Again, the work spread from west to east. In the department of the Marne, the provision of seed corn, manure and agricultural implements was undertaken by the French Ministry of Agriculture,[34] so the FWVRC turned to a yearly distribution of vegetable garden seeds to those able to use them and of seed potatoes. Sermaize became a centre for raising seedlings and breeding small livestock and chicks for distribution to families. *The Friend* for 8 October 1915 reported an initiative to rehabilitate animal husbandry in one village that involved the gift of "one of King George's rams" to the village shepherd – no further details are given! The bigger problem concerned the provision and use of agricultural machinery to supplement what may have been available from French government sources. FWVRC purchases of machinery were augmented by further equipment paid for through voluntary contributions and by donations of machinery. In its issue for 7 July 1915, *The Friend* reported that twenty reapers and binders presented by the Royal Agricultural Society of England were to be consigned to the French government. The harvesting and threshing seasons, which ran consecutively from the late summer of one year to the spring of the next, were times of high demand for machinery, horses and labour. In 1914 and 1915, the French military authorities granted soldiers special leave to help in the harvest or hay-making or released teams of men for farm work. T. E. Harvey wrote in April 1915 of a French military territorial 'agricultural battalion',[35] while Edith Pye, writing in *The Friend* for 12 February 1915 about a visit to Rheims, gives a poignant picture of "soldiers in uniform tending the vines". By 1916, however, the French army was less willing to make such concessions, and the FWVRC agricultural unit had perforce to send some of its members out to join in the work. Gertrude reported in her diary for 14 October 1916 that another fellow-worker had a sore throat from "so much threshing". One American Quaker, Walter Bowerman, related how the male threshing team would move from village to village with its machinery, "often sleeping in the same room with the entire peasant family".[36]

His observation highlighted what many of those involved in the FWVRC's agricultural work regarded as a problem: control over equipment and the perceived unwillingness of many French farmers to work jointly with their neighbours. For the mission the difficulty was not just that of a wasteful practice, but had a moral aspect. The Quaker ethos put high value on co-operation and compassion, and members of the mission, both British and American, frequently deplored what they saw as the individualism of the French peasant and his refusal to consider the needs of less fortunate neighbours. Another source of frustration to the outsiders was French farming's inefficient use of land through sub-division and adherence to what were seen as unscientific practices. Walter Bowerman found the villages "overcrowded, ill planned and unsanitary", reflecting the ancient patterns of their formation. The American soldiers who arrived from mid-1917 were more forthright. They found French farmers' methods well out of date and the villages filthy and deplored the French peasants' attachment to their dung heaps.[37]

The state of the land and of farming in the Marne and the Meuse became quite problematic to the FWVRC agricultural unit. Edward West, the then head of the unit, reported in *The Friend* of 20 October 1916 that the land and the people's spirit were deteriorating. He evoked the need for a good centre and constant staff for the unit and as a start, advocated the renting of a derelict farm as a centre. A year later, *The Friend* for 5 October 1917 detected a similar note of doubt, even weariness, surfacing in the agricultural unit's report for 1917. The harvests from 1914 to 1917 had all been poor, in the first year because of the invasion and subsequently because of bad weather. The style of farming, using laborious hand methods in scattered fields, and the prevalence of village feuds continued as problems. Still the unit strove after reconstruction as more important in the long term than first aid. Only from late 1918 was it able to start working as it wished to.

The plight of those caught up in the conflict could be very terrible. Dr Hilda Clark gave this account:[38]

> They left their homes suddenly, sometime losing their friends and relations, sometimes leaving them behind, sometimes seeing their homes burning as they left. Those who had a horse and cart might save a few clothes, but they have had difficulties in feeding and lodging the horse, and generally have to sleep beside it in the stable. The majority fled on foot, expecting to return in a few days. Many who remained behind were taken prisoner into Germany, and one of the patients in the Maternity hospital [at Châlons-sur-Marne] to whom this happened ... states that all the women in her party whose babies were born while there died, and all the children under ten.

Of the FWVRC's projects, that of bringing relief to people uprooted by war could demand at times the speediest responses and the greatest flexibility, but also imagination and ingenuity.

Strategies were put in place by the French government to deal with the refugees. Immediate assistance, such as food and shelter, was provided by the departments, municipalities and communes where they ended up. Thereafter officialdom aimed to disperse them to other regions of France, despite their reluctance to move too far away from their original homes or native region.[39] In the Marne and the Meuse, many refugees crowded into towns such as Troyes, Châlons-sur-Marne and Bar-le-Duc or settled in the surrounding villages to join those who had returned to their devastated homes. Though there were heavy concentrations of refugees in places, there seem to have

13 FWVRC distribution of bedding at Couvonges, Meuse, 1916

been no camps. French government allocations to refugees and the families of prisoners-of-war enabled the recipients to buy food and pay small sums for lodging.

The FWVRC thus was not called on to provide emergency feeding, except where conditions demanded. It was not the Committee's policy to give out food or money, though it clearly did make one-off distributions, as when forty refugees from the Verdun area arrived at the équipe in Bar-le-Duc in February 1916 looking for help, as Gertude noted in her diary for 21 February 1916; they were given tinned beef and footwear. As people were re-accommodated, their other needs for clothing and furniture became clear. Many had fled in their summer clothes and were in need of warm garments. The FWVRC expended both funds and personnel in home visits to families both in the towns and in outlying villages to assess their situation and to deliver parcels of clothing, footwear and bed-linen. The mission's premises also served as distribution points. Gertrude wrote in a letter to Professor Tout of 6 December 1915[40] of handing out blankets and quilts from the Bar-le-Duc équipe in the cold weather to shivering refugees. Much of the clothing came through collections back in Britain of used garments or clothes sewn by supporters. Furniture and beds were distributed according to a scale of needs. In preparing their lists of recipients, relief workers, who were almost entirely the female members of the équipe, were often guided by the leaders of the local French communities: the mayors, parish priests, police inspectors and village school teachers, as well as by French district nurses.

In places crowded with refugees, such as Bar-le-Duc and Troyes, one of the most pressing needs was for care of and occupation for the large numbers of women and girls. For both groups, workrooms were opened where their skills in sewing and embroidery could be utilised, and they were paid for their work. The finished garments were taken up by the FWVRC for distribution to other groups of refugees, were sold to the women themselves at cost price, were sent for sale in Paris and London, or were made to private order, with all proceeds going to the FWVRC. As important as the occupation was the companionship.

Another of the FWVRC's policies was to encourage those among whom they worked to make whatever financial contribution they could for the goods and services offered to them, on the principle that to do so encouraged self-reliance and restored their dignity. One way of achieving this was through the opening of 'shops', as at the Bar-le-Duc ouvroir (see Figure 35).

The drafting of many French civilian doctors into the army and the diversion of civil hospitals to meet military needs cut into the provision of medical services for the civilian population. In particular, the masses of refugees were left largely without medical care. This lack prompted the FWVRC from the outset to include some degree of medical and nursing services among its activities. In accepting the Society of Friends' offer of assistance, the French Ministry of War had stipulated that its doctors were not to take the place of civilian French doctors where these were still working;[41] but in the event, not many civilian doctors remained in their practices. The inclusion of a sanitation inspector in the first group to go to France reflected the mission's awareness of the urgency of public health.

The maternity hospital at Châlons-sur-Marne (see above) was housed in one wing of the town's asylum, and departmental funds paid for the necessary alterations, the general domestic equipment and the maintenance of patients and staff. The Friends' mission provided the staff and medical equipment.[42] In July 1918, the town came under such severe bombardment that the maternity hospital had to be evacuated further south for six months. The building it occupied was damaged and later renovated, but in 1922 was replaced by a new maternity hospital. During the five years of the FWVRC's management of maternity services at Châlons, 981 births were recorded.[43] The matron for much of that period was Edith Pye, who in 1919 was made a Chevalier of the Légion d'honneur.

Much effort went into caring for the many children among the refugees. Classes were arranged to allow them to receive a little schooling. The delicate ones among them were sent on convalescence, some to Samoëns, the sturdier ones to holiday camp. Children who had endured the bombing attacks on Rheims, which lay within range of the German artillery for most of the war, were a special cause for concern. Many babies and children in need of recuperation were placed in the mission's home at the château at Bettancourt, a little north of Sermaize. (The French word 'château' connotes far more than a 'castle' and is sometimes best translated as 'large country house'.) The aristocratic owner of Bettancourt, the comtesse de Morillot, lent her home to the Friends' mission, which entrusted it to the writer E. V. Lucas and his wife (see Biographical notes). They in turn equipped the institution, supported it at their own expense and managed it for at least forty patients with the assistance of their daughter for a year from mid-1915. An anonymous donation, possibly from the playwright J. M. Barrie, who was a friend, helped their work.[44] Bettancourt continued its work after the Lucases' departure, largely maintained by another English donor. Later in the war it became more of a hospital and convalescence centre and had a doctor in attendance. Gertrude, going there in March 1918, found it full of nurses.

Sermaize-les-Bains, the hub of the FWVRC's work in the Marne-Meuse region from early 1915, supported two small hospitals, where a nucleus of doctors and nurses was brought together. The first hospital was constructed by FWVRC workers, the second was installed in a neighbouring 'château', again lent by its owner, and specialised in surgical cases. When the Château hospital closed in mid-January 1919, some of the equipment was taken to a new hospital further north at Brizeaux, which in turn was finally transferred to Varennes.

Nurses were as essential as the medical staff. Out of the first party of thirty-three people who went to France in November 1914, ten were trained nurses.[45] They were deployed in the Châlons maternity hospital, but as importantly in home visiting, in which they were experienced, having all been district nurses in Britain.[46] From Châlons the practice of home visiting spread to Sermaize and to Bar-le-Duc. Other nurses were active in the villages in the FWVRC's area of operations, particularly in the eastern section. They also cared for German prisoners-of-war, where the need arose, and for the mission's workers.

The FWVRC mission was able to recruit two dentists, who in 1917-18 provided much-needed treatment sessions to people who had been long deprived of dental care. Robert Tatlock, a long-term FWVRC relief worker, was an expert in "optical matters" according to Ruth Fry. (She does not specify if he was a trained optician.) He may have been qualified to examine eyes, since Gertrude reports in her diary for 4 September 1915 that he had "taken to eye-testing" and was very tired after seeing forty-seven cases that day. He was certainly in demand for replacement of lost spectacles and for spectacle repairs. Serious eye cases were treated at the Sermaize hospital.

The doctors, both male and female, nurses and orderlies recruited by the FWVRC went to France for varying lengths of time, some staying for only a few months, in one instance as a 'summer job'. Several might have already served in other relief organisations, such as the Scottish Women's Hospital Units. Some, such as Dr Hilda Clark and Edith Pye, were members of the Society of Friends. The Society was prepared to forgo its voluntary principle for its doctors and nurses and often offered them an honorarium, possibly as an inducement, possibly in recognition that they had taken leave of absence to join the FWVRC. They certainly were viewed as an essential element in the FWVRC's programme.

Chapter Three

Work in Bar-le-Duc

On 5 June 1915, Gertrude crossed via Folkestone and Boulogne to Paris. The Channel, she noted in her diary entry for that day, was full of "mine-sweepers and torpedo-boat destroyers". From Boulogne the train went down the coast past Etaples with its "large base hospital, close to the railway lines",[1] then through Amiens. After Amiens, it passed through Creil and Chantilly, to the north of Paris, "and over the bridge (newly repaired) which was blown up to prevent the Germans' advance on Paris. We saw the small temporary bridge which had been used as a substitute till this week." She added that the Germans had occupied Chantilly for about two days, but had departed precipitately on receiving sudden orders to leave. During this first weekend in Paris, she noted on 6 June 1915, she had tea with a woman who lived near the Eiffel Tower and who

> told us all about the time when Paris nearly taken – and of Zeppelin raids – very near them because of wireless station in the Eiffel Tower. When Government removed to Bordeaux all well-to-do left – stations packed. Food scarce – no paper money accepted – very little cash. Everybody preparing for a siege.

By contrast, the mood nine months later, in June 1915, was much lighter. The French capital struck her as lively and gay. She observed on 5 June that "[t]he soldiers have very picturesque uniforms and give a festive air to the streets, otherwise I should not remember we were in a country invaded by the enemy." From Paris, she and Ernest Montford, a friend she had first met in 1914 at a weekend school at Woodbrooke, who was also working with the FWVRC as a sanitary inspector, travelled to Vitry-le-François by train. From there she went on by car to Sermaize, on the border between the departments of the

14 View of Bar-le-Duc at the time of the First World War

Marne and the Meuse. The drive showed her the reality of the ravaged countryside. Villages, factories and churches had all been damaged or destroyed.

At Sermaize she was lodged in makeshift accommodation; "in a little bare room far away in the top storey of a theatre – with a bedstead and a blanket and a tin basin – and huge mosquitoes buzzing round", is how she described it in her diary on 7 June 1915. The room appears to have been the theatre manager's, since the door bore the announcement "Chef du theatre – Frappez et on vous ouvrira!" Meals were taken "in what was probably the pit" of the theatre. The building was also shelter to a number of people bombed out of their houses.

The Friends' mission in Sermaize decided that Gertrude should be sent to Bar-le-Duc in the department of the Meuse. Bar, a small, historic town, lies on the river Ornain and the Marne-Rhine canal. It is constructed over two sites, one a steep escarpment, the other the narrow valley at the base of this cliff, and is thus divided into the upper and the lower town, with steep streets joining the two parts. The FWVRC had had an outpost in Bar since April 1915, and on 10 June Gertrude went there, again by car, with a colleague driving. She found several fellow-workers in place: two had arrived in April, another had come in May and a fourth came shortly before Gertrude arrived.[2] The size of the Bar équipe appears to have generally been kept to four to five people at any one time. It lived for at least two and a half years at 99 boulevard de la Rochelle, in the lower part of the town towards the centre (see Chapter Six for a fuller account). Boulevard de la Rochelle

15 Corner bend from boulevard de la Rochelle into the rue St Mihiel, First World War. No. 99 is one of the houses on the immediate left

was, and remains, a main thoroughfare. It was formerly lined with trees, alas, all cut down by the summer of 2012 (see Figure 38). At its southern end, at a short distance from number 99, the boulevard turns the corner into the rue St Mihiel, which leads directly towards St Mihiel and Verdun. In 1915, it was used by the army as well as civilians, with traffic passing constantly, even during the night. From 4 am every morning, about fifty army lorries roared past, waking Gertrude up. She would sit and watch the procession. By day it was crowded with soldiers. "[I]n the evening it is their promenade and they crowd under the elm trees in blue and red and khaki", Gertrude told her mother in a letter of 14 June 1915.

The immediate needs of the refugees who poured into Bar-le-Duc in August-September 1914 were met after a fashion by the municipal authorities; but quite quickly these authorities, aided by leading citizens of the town, put more effective measures in place to sustain the new residents. The FWVRC's équipe in Bar thus took its place alongside a range of other similar initiatives.

Its programme concentrated on relief and medical assistance. The first took the form of distribution of clothing and bed linen, home visits within Bar and in twenty-six of the surrounding villages, the sale of furniture, bedding and materials, and the provision of gainful occupation for the many refugee women and girls. Clothes, boots, sometimes food, requests for medical attendance and provision of work were dispensed to a continual flow of visitors to the équipe's premises. True to its practice, the FWVRC sold furniture, materials and manufactured goods at below cost price, paid the women for their work, and sold many of their products to raise funds for its venture. Gertrude was soon participating in all this work.

The first two FWVRC workers, who arrived in April 1915, were Gertrude Townend, a trained nurse, and Eliza Dalglish. They were active in relief work and sanitary and medical work, well aware of the close connection in Bar between the two strands and of the need to tackle the poor conditions in the town.[3] In this they would have been aided by Ernest Montford, who in mid-1915 was dividing his time between Sermaize and Bar. The two women were responsible for re-opening the municipal dispensary in the spring of 1915, after it had been closed during the early months of the war, and for organising home visits.[4] Earlier, *The Friend* for 25 June 1915 had reported that 320 cases had been dressed at the dispensary, forty-nine home visits made and milk, food and medicines supplied.

Within a few days of arriving in Bar, Gertrude was undertaking home visits with Miss Dalglish among the refugees, to assess needs. The people they visited were often accommodated in insalubrious housing in frequently squalid conditions with cesspits for sanitation. Many were crammed into the old houses of the upper town. Susanne Day, a fellow relief worker who arrived towards the end of June 1915 (see Biographical notes), described the air as "solid with smell".[5] Fleas were another hazard. Gertrude was forthright, in her diary for 14 June 1915, about a day spent in a bad quarter in this part of town:

> Some doubtful characters, some very nice people mixed up amongst them. Sanitary arrangements too appalling to describe. Very difficult to get at real truth. I cannot help admiring the courage of even the worst of them – they have lost everything and will probably never see it again – many of them have husband and sons at the war and they sit and wait in the most sordid, filthy holes, with no furniture, very few friends and often very unsympathetic neighbours. There is little to be done for them. I've had some fine lies told me too, and enjoyed looking 'simple' – by Jove they do pile it on if you look as if you believed every word. One old woman offered to give lessons in French, English and German!

After visiting, case papers had to be written up and an assessment of need made before parcels of clothing were made up for distribution to clients. Home visits took her to houses in all parts of Bar, its outskirts and beyond. Refugee families often had to live packed into one room. Some managed well with the problems: Gertrude was impressed by a

16 Rue de l'Horloge in the upper town, Bar-le-Duc, First World War

family visited on 29 July 1915, when, as she noted in her diary, she saw "all the children in bed – such nice clean little beggars". Others had great difficulty in coping. On 18 August 1915, Gertrude and another worker visited a family living twelve in their room. She recorded that:

> they are miserably housed, on dirty straw mattresses with black coverlets, swarming. It was repulsive and yet very sad. They all sleep together in a sort of medley. Mme is very ill, worn to skin and bone and with no comfort, not even ordinary decencies. In one corner a dreadful looking old woman was taking off her chemise – three small boys were curled round each other, on a mattress, still dressed.

Putting further pressure on the confined space, some women took in washing and hung the steaming laundry out to dry in their rooms. Firewood was expensive, and people gathered wood in the forests. Daily necessities were also dear.

Gertrude continued with home visiting in the town and in surrounding villages throughout her years in Bar. She went to assess need, to visit the sick among the équipe's cases and her ouvroir girls, to arrange convalescence or recuperative holidays for delicate children or sanatorium treatment for the elderly. In October 1917, in the wake of German bombing of the town, the équipe was involved in sending off a party of children to Brittany to be under the care of the Féderation des instituteurs et institutrices (Federation of Primary School Teachers). She visited in hospital and once, on 18 August 1915, on the boat where some clients were living, probably on the canal. "There was a jolly smell of tar on the boat", she recorded. She found a job in a café for one of her girls. One of her most unusual tasks was to help in the arrangements for the funeral of a person she did not name. This involved much to-ing and fro-ing between the secular authorities and the priest and a trip to the cemetery to check that the grave had been remembered. She found the grave, with a small boy in it who invited her to help them. "It is apparently the most difficult thing imaginable to get buried decently and in order" was her comment on 3 November 1917.

The need for preventive health work in Bar-le-Duc remained high. One of the great fears was of the spread of tuberculosis. By the spring of 1916, charge of the dispensary had been handed to a religious order which may have been organising it before, and the nurse's work was directed to visiting and home nursing among the refugees and in particular to seeking out tuberculosis cases for referral to the mission's doctors. Gertrude often accompanied the nurse (Mrs Jackson to begin with, once Miss Townend had left, and then Mrs Jackson's successors) on her evening visits in Bar-le-Duc. She may have been required to interpret, but it becomes clear from her diary that she helped where necessary and that from early 1916 she was doing dressings: a girl with an abscess, an elderly man with a bedsore, a deep cut, "almost to the bone" that the butcher at the Maison des parents had inflicted on himself, as she noted on 15 February 1917. Later on, she acted as assistant and driver to the mission's medical staff ("Monsieur le Dentiste! I being Infirmiere spent the day at his elbow, occasionally emptying teeth etc.", was her comment on 4 June 1918). She also had responsibility for checking the medical cupboard at the Bar équipe. Gertrude was not a trained nurse, but as part of her preparation for war work had taken examinations in first aid and home nursing, so she was not without qualifications. (Had she done war nursing, she would have been taken as a VAD – Voluntary Aid Detachment.)[6]

Interpreting for her colleagues was among the duties expected of Gertrude when she joined the FWVRC, and she was introduced to the mission as an interpreter. The first half of the description of her work, however, of "ambulance motorist", was far from true, and she had to wait a couple of years before she was entrusted with any regular driving. The big task she was handed on arrival was supervision of the ouvroir, the workroom.

The ouvroir

The concept of ouvroirs as a means of providing occupation and raising funds was well established in France by the First World War. Their organisation appears to have lain largely in the hands of voluntary bodies, though some might be instigated by a local authority. Their output generally took the form of bedding and clothing, and their labour force appears to have been exclusively female. These two factors were, of course, closely linked, since at that time most women, of whatever class, would have known how to sew and embroider. The preparation of fine household linen was a question of pride for many. Drawing on this tradition, the FWVRC opened the workroom in Bar as an obvious way to offer occupation to some of the women refugees and encouraged the creation of others in smaller places. Within Bar-le-Duc itself, the mission's ouvroir was not the only one. On 12 June 1915, Gertrude mentioned the "town ouvroir". For the FWVRC, the Bar ouvroir was their most important one, and they publicly applauded Gertrude's successful management of it in *The Friend* for 17 September 1915. The region between Verdun and Nancy was renowned for its fine embroidery in both white and coloured cottons, some of it executed on frames (*métiers*), as described by Gertrude's fellow-worker Susanne Day.[7] Before the war, a network of Paris shops had sustained embroiderers in this area through orders placed through middlewomen, but these links were severed by the fighting, when the middlewomen might themselves become refugees. The FWVRC offered itself as a middle link to the embroiderers and was able to commission work, provide free cotton, pay the women and market their output both locally and overseas. Rachel Alexander and her sisters Jean Alexander and Emily Dinely (see Biographical notes) were much involved in this initiative. Embroidery centres were set up in the region (Gertrude writes of four), stimulated by embroidery contests and exhibitions. Women who could not leave their houses did such work at home, collecting orders from the Bar équipe.

Gertrude did not open the ouvroir, she took it over. One or other of the FWVRC workers already in Bar had started it up in April 1915, before she arrived. When Gertrude took charge of it, the workroom was housed in three rooms in the municipal dispensary, probably the one from which Eliza Dalglish and Gertrude Townend were operating. (The fact that all three of these women were gathered near the entrance to a building to be photographed suggests this might have been so. Gertrude, indeed, describes the building as the ouvroir in a note on the back of the photograph.) Here, sessions were held from Monday to Saturday from 1pm to 4pm. As premises for the ouvroir,

17 *Bar-le-Duc, 30 June 1915. From left to right: unidentified nun, Gertrude Townend, Eliza Dalglish, Gertrude (on far right)*

the dispensary was not convenient. Everything that could not be locked away when the day's activity was over had to be carried backwards and forwards to and from the équipe's living quarters. Moreover, as women felt encouraged to attend, it became very crowded. In mid-September 1915, Gertrude sought the help of the mayor of Bar over new premises. In response, the town architect and director of municipal works, Monsieur Charles Boller, offered a room at a former barracks – *caserne* – situated in the town. He took her to view the premises on 16 September 1915. Gertrude accepted the offer, and Monsieur Boller undertook to get everything ready for its use. Margery Fry (see Biographical notes), as Gertrude's immediate supervisor, agreed to the move and sent one of the men based at

Sermaize to help with fitting the workroom out. Gertrude purchased lamps and sewing machines (there was a Singer shop in Bar-le-Duc) and found matting for the floors.

She went back to Britain for a short holiday from 6 October to 1 November 1915. On her return to Bar, the final additions and alterations to the new workroom were made, and on 6 November, a Saturday, the move from the old to the new ouvroir took place. Furniture, material, lamps, stove, stools, trestles and a table were brought in and installed In her diary for 6 November, Gertrude described how "[e]ventually order began to shape itself". The lamps, which were acetylene fuelled, caused Gertrude, and Monsieur Boller, great anxiety, since it was feared they might explode. The stove was also to give trouble, since it smoked, and later had to be replaced. Nonetheless Gertrude was pleased. All the materials required for the workroom were gathered in one place and stored in cupboards and pigeonholes. She herself had a small office for her use. The following Monday, "her women" arrived for their first session in the new room and expressed their satisfaction. The ouvroir received its formal opening on 24 November 1915, with coffee, a violin performance and singing.

The building housing the ouvroir that Gertrude refers to as the caserne Oudinot was more properly the former Oudinot barracks. The new barracks of the same name were located in the area southeast of the town centre that had been developed for the use of the military and was home to the town's regiment, the 94th RI (infantry regiment). Both old and new barracks bore the name of one of Bar-le-Duc's illustrious sons, Marshal Oudinot (1767-1848), who served under Napoleon. The former barracks were around the corner from 99 boulevard de la Rochelle, thus adding to the convenience of the new arrangement. During the First World War, they provided the municipality with an invaluable space, firstly for one of the feeding stations set up in August 1914 to provide meals to the poorest sections of the town's population, and later to some of the refugees. The buildings were used to offer a simple and immediate shelter, sleeping on straw, to the refugees arriving throughout the early autumn of 1914. They could also be fed at the caserne.[8] This previous use of the barracks would explain why Monsieur Boller arrived in the early hours of 9 March 1916, as Gertrude recounts in her diary, to tell her that 300 more refugees had just arrived in Bar and "could they be lodged in the Ouvroir", i.e. back in the barracks. Other charitable activities operated out of the barracks: a shop offering re-cycled clothing for the benefit of refugees, and another benevolent group that received donations of food and clothing for dispatch to prisoners-of-war and soldiers at the front.[9]

The barracks were later demolished and the fire station erected on the site. The buildings remain, covering a large area (they would have included the firemen's accommodation), and may still be used by the fire service, but the fire brigade's headquarters are now out of town.

Gertrude was organiser, supervisor and accountant of the FWVRC ouvroir in Bar-le-Duc. Her colleagues might help out on occasion, and she had the assistance of several French ladies, but generally she was on her own. She seems to have been given a free hand in how she managed the workroom, on the understanding that it ran along agreed lines and was financially accountable. The aim was to provide occupation and some supplementary income for the refugee women in Bar and, as a subsidiary goal, to raise funds through their output. The ouvroir did not offer training. From Gertrude downwards, some competency in sewing was assumed, and only the girls might need some guidance.

The workroom produced sheets and pillowcases, shirts, chemises, petticoats, undergarments (*pantalons*) and dressing-gowns, skirts, blouses, babies' jackets, aprons and pinafores, and bags and sacks. Much of the work was what would have been called 'plain sewing', but in September 1916, Gertrude introduced 'fancy work' – embroidery. Much sewing was done by hand, but sewing machines were installed. Materials for the workroom came from various sources, some 'from England', including a parcel of sewing materials and cloth sent by the Manchester High School for Girls in December 1915. Gertrude purchased some in Bar direct from the local textile factories, at wholesale prices. Soft linen sacking might be used for simple sheets, as for the beds the FWVRC donated to the refugee accommodation in the town's covered market. Stuff bought in the town tended to be expensive. Gertrude notes visits to the shops of various of the mill owners, sometimes with one of her 'ladies', to make purchases and settle bills. Such shopping often constituted the morning's task for her. The afternoons were given over to the sewing sessions.

Careful oversight was practised of the materials bought or received. Thus cutting out (from a pattern) was largely entrusted to Gertrude and to some of her French assistants. Others were chosen from among the women attending the ouvroir. Despite the vetting, some of them failed in the job, and Gertrude noted bitterly on 27 July 1915 that one of them had "torn up 15 pillowcases wrong, and it means a dead loss to the Ouvroir." Another time she was thwarted in her own plans when "they" cut up the wrong material. She handed out the work to be done, dispensed thread and buttons, demonstrated the construction of tricky garments such as pantalons, and helped the girls with such points as cutting buttonholes and tacking hems. She also supervised the quality of the work and on occasion, when she was being 'difficult', as she acknowledged in her diary on 29 January 1916, insisted the women undo what they had done. Attempts to deceive her generally failed. She reported on 10 July 1916 that she had caught one old lady in the act of pocketing a reel of black cotton: "She sits next to my table and apparently looks out for spoil." Calm sometimes had to be imposed when the women chattered too loudly, and Gertrude once had to ask two women who were disputing use of the sewing machine to "finish it outside", she noted on 3 November 1916.

The women were paid by the piece for their work. Their products were sold through a variety of outlets. Much of it went, at cost price, to the FWVRC's headquarters at Sermaize and to others of the mission's outposts for distribution in their districts. Local orders might come from hospitals or from the Secours national (National Assistance) organisation. Some of the orders were for large quantities of goods, such as the unspecified one for 1000 bags, 100 shirts and 80 pinafores, to be ready within a fortnight, as Gertrude recorded on 8 December 1916. Some of the output was sold in Paris. Individual purchasers placed orders. Eventually the women themselves were allowed to buy some of the work they had produced, at under cost price, and were able to commission clothes to be made up. Gertrude herself got dresses altered and garments made at the ouvroir, such as a blouse she mentioned on 6 May 1916, cut out by herself, sewn by one of her women and embroidered by another.[10] She also handled orders from further afield, from family and friends in Britain, and took small objects, such as tray cloths, back with her on leave to sell. Thus on 24 March 1917, she told Professor Tout in a letter that she hoped Mrs Tout had received her letter about the embroidery, since they needed the "right measurements" in order to proceed with her other orders.[11]

During the early functioning of the ouvroir, the Society of Friends assisted it with a monthly grant of 400 francs; but eventually, possibly by mid-1916, it became self-supporting through the sale of its output and through income brought in by sales of second-hand clothing sent from Britain and the United States, organised at the workroom, with Gertrude as *marchande* – shopkeeper, as she styled herself in her diary on 20 October 1916. These sessions seem to have been popular with the women, who "fingered and haggled and criticized", as Gertrude put it on 22 May 1917. The sales raised large sums of money for the ouvroir: 150 francs on 1 February 1917, then 1,041 francs in

March 1917 from sales to the refugees alone. The women were able to enrol in a club, the Cercle de couturiers, which allowed them to save money for purchases at the sales of ouvroir products and of second-hand clothing. Donations from Gertrude's family and friends at home arrived now and again for the ouvroir, and in December 1916, the MHSG magazine carried an appeal from her for funds for the work in Bar.

Attendance at the ouvroir, which was entirely voluntary, fluctuated throughout the couple of years she ran the workroom, on one occasion rising to sixty, on another dropping to six. Fewer women came on the days they went to collect their government-issued allowances. School holidays also seem to have reduced attendance. When work was available for the women, as it was during the summer of 1915 at the factories making the *confiture*, or preserve, for which Bar is celebrated, fewer came to the ouvroir,[12] and as the girls got jobs in the town, they fell away from the workroom.

Gertrude's first reaction to taking on responsibility for the ouvroir was unenthusiastic and she regretted on occasion that it tied her down when she would have liked to get about more, but in time she became deeply involved with the women and girls who attended it and with their wellbeing. Several of them are mentioned often in her diaries, perhaps because they were long-term participants at the workroom, perhaps because of their colourful characters, as she developed a closer interest in them. Of course, she had to run an efficient and productive workroom, but she also sought to provide a sociable space where "her women" could find companionship, a change of surroundings and a measure of regularity in their lives. The ouvroir became, in her words, a sort of club for them, a place for exchanging news, but also for vying with each other in the retelling of their stories of flight and disaster. Through them, Gertrude learned much about the effects of the German advance and occupation of villages. Her assessment of the state of mind of many of these women living under the shock of displacement is sympathetic and penetrating. In a letter of 31 July 1915 she told her mother how the women

> describe all they have lost, down to the smallest details of their wardrobes, and generally break down over a pig or a hen, it is queer how stoical they can be over a great calamity – and how inconsolable over some small details in it

and suggested in her article in *The Englishwoman* for June 1918,[13] that nothing could give a sharper idea of the early days of the war than these "odd disconnected tales told by the women." It is clear that, while at times their behaviour irritated her, she respected greatly their stoicism in the face of loss and bereavement.

Gertrude put thought and effort into providing an attractive environment for the women and girls. The workroom at the former barracks was kept clean and refurbished. Curtains and pictures and posters (railway posters brought from England) were put up. In January 1916, Gertrude brought beech leaves and black berries in to her office and placed pussy-willow and catkins on the work tables. She worried about the women's safety during bombing raids, since there were no cellars at the barracks, and, as she noted on 21 February 1916, the FWVRC's petrol was stored in the yard there. To enliven the sewing sessions, she introduced a gramophone and records for half-an-hour's music each afternoon, to the women's satisfaction. The repertoire included 'The Rosary', 'Tipperary', and the 'Tales of Hoffmann'. The care Gertrude put into supporting "her women" was noticed and appreciated, and shortly before she went on leave in July 1916, they asked her to choose between a brooch or earrings as a gift. She opted for the former and on 26 July, as she noted in her diary, was presented with "a little gold brooch, the thistle and cross of Lorraine – Souvenir de Lorraine". The three oldest ladies gave her bouquets of garden flowers and then asked if they might kiss her. "So we kissed and all looked on with beaming faces."

Wherever they were, British hospitals and relief organisations during the First World War liked to put on a good party at Christmas. The FWVRC too focused its biggest efforts on entertaining the refugees on Christmas and the new year. In Bar-le-Duc, the preparations for the 1915-1916 festivities were lengthy and exhaustive, to judge by Gertrude's letters home and her diary for January 1916. Eleven parties were held for the children, adolescents and women among the refugees. Gertrude boasted to her mother on 7 January 1916 of having fed around 1,700 people on chocolate, coffee and buns over four days. For these gatherings over two hundred toys were bought and many dolls dressed. The équipe hired a magic lantern and slides, as well as a piano, borrowed a gramophone, decorated the ouvroir and put up a Christmas tree. Gifts of three forks and three spoons each were prepared for the women. Gertrude coached her girls in a play and dialogues. Notices and tickets were printed and distributed. The only sour note seems to have come from some of the French ladies who helped at the ouvroir, who questioned "the advisability of having all the émigrés to our Christmas parties. They were against it, as they say we shall have such a number of undesirables." Gertrude, noting this in her diary entry for 9 December 1915, was

"was much too weary to argue", but conceded that she felt "they certainly had reason on their side"; so admission to the parties was by ticket. The parties went off well and evidently brought much pleasure. One of the French ladies dressed up as Father Christmas and distributed the presents.

Gertrude records much less about the parties held in subsequent years, perhaps because the preparations were less elaborate, perhaps because they followed the same pattern as the 1915-1916 festivities. They did, however, cater for similarly large numbers. Those arranged for the 1916-1917 and 1918-1919 festive seasons were held at the Foyer du soldat (see Chapter Four below), which may have offered more space and had a stage. The two parties held in Bar for Christmas 1917 gathered in 1,200 guests and provided them with a "cinematograph entertainment". That same year Christmas parties were also held in two nearby villages, with guests entertained with a Christmas tree and a magic lantern. The two final parties in Bar-le-Duc, in January 1919, each brought in 700 guests, some from six neighbouring villages. They had a "cinema entertainment" courtesy of the local outpost of the American YMCA and all – men, women, older boys and girls and children – received a present.[14] Bar was outdone by the Sermaize équipe, however, which, in its relief report for January 1919, claimed twenty-two parties organised for around 2,000 guests.

The intake at the ouvroir was quite mixed in terms of age, with adult women, girls (i.e. teenagers) and children all present. Initially, separate sessions were held for the women and the girls, but these were eventually merged into a daily workroom group. The children, one must assume, came because their mothers had nowhere else to leave them. How to care for the children and interest the teenagers was a cause of concern to Gertrude, and she initiated several schemes during 1916 in attempts to meet their needs. None of them was long lived. The heavy bombing raids on the town in June 1916 may have sent families moving, and the numbers of girls diminished all the time as they found jobs in Bar.

A mention in her diary on 4 May 1916 of "an incessant stream" of children the whole afternoon suggests that the ouvroir at times served as a kind of crèche. If Gertrude was on her own, as happened on 14 August 1915, she "had to run around all [the] time". In May 1916, as she told Professor Tout in a letter of 8 May 1916, she was able to take over an attic room at the former barracks for "the children to play in and have drill." She and a group of fellow-teachers, who may have included some of the French ladies already involved with the ouvroir, instituted "a very premature and elementary series of classes" for these children. Even if the teaching may have been of limited success, the children were kept occupied – "for which their parents are grateful". On 16 May 1916, she recorded in her diary, she took her turn in the school: "Had much difficulty in teaching Arithmetic – but discovered what not to do. The children very good and nice. Gymn. was a great success." On 6 June 1916, it was not so good, in fact was "rather a nightmare: I must try and rearrange it so as to get the little ones more looked after" was the note in her diary. A month on, classes were held in the yard, presumably of the barracks. And with that, all reference ceases to the school.

With the teenagers, it was a matter of providing some stimulus. Sometimes it was hard going with them. On 1 February 1917, Gertrude complained to her diary that the girls were "so young and averse from working. But I kept them fairly well at it." She accordingly tried to arrange activities that might appeal to them. From September 1916, she introduced embroidery, which the girls found more interesting than plain sewing. On their afternoons, her French friend Wanda Bungener might read Perrault's fairytales aloud to them. From an early moment she organised an English class for the girls, twice a week after their ouvroir work. About sixteen girls joined and made good progress, she noted in November 1915. In letters home in March 1916, she reported that they were getting on well. In May 1916, they were learning 'Tipperary', after which, Gertrude told herself in her diary on 2 May 1916, she "must give them some decent poetry". In January of the same year, she was active in setting up a library for the girls, but admitted in her diary on 28 February 1916 to doubts about some of the books chosen: "Have read several of the books for the jeunes filles – all the triangle – so I suppose they won't do." But thereafter there is no further mention of the library, nor, from mid-1916, of the English-language lessons.

She proposed a more energetic activity to the girls in the shape of a garden that would focus on vegetable-growing. The idea may have come to her from the example of yet another committee set up in Bar-le-Duc, this time to encourage the cultivation of allotments. The secretary of this committee was one of the town notables, Monsieur Collot, whom she consulted on 27 March 1916 over the possibility of the ouvroir's having a piece of garden. The town was sympathetic, and on 25 May Gertrude was shown two plots, the first at some distance from the centre of Bar at a site near the river Ornain which she rejected as being "too public and not what I want for the girls". The second site, which she chose, was on a slope on the other side of the canal, up beyond the cemetery, near trees, at the top of a lane leading out of town. "The drawback", she noted in her diary on 25 May 1916, "is that it is so difficult to get water". Two days later, on 27 May, the garden was opened. "[T]he girls all trooped up to the hillside outside the town – very happy and excited and I gave them each a plot and told them about the prize for vegetables. They are all as keen as mustard about their 'Proprietés'!" Mignonette and nasturtium seeds were distributed and planted out during June. On 10 July, she tidied up the garden tools and seeds and gardened all morning. The girls themselves worked at their plots on the summer evenings. They kept everything they grew and many of them produced quantities of beans, peas and salad vegetables.

Later in July 1916, she went on leave, and the garden does not receive any further mention until 13 April of the following year, when she and one of her girls and her mother visited the garden "where they dug and I labelled". A letter to Nancy of 6 May 1917 described a day of hard work at the garden in blazing sun, without shade, working on dry soil on a slope. She was able to report progress to her mother in a letter of 15 June 1917: "My garden is getting on very well. I have sixty potato plants and lots of beans and other vegetables in small quantities. So far we've only had radishes from it and a microscopic portion of spinach we ate today. I get up every Saturday morning at 5. and work before breakfast."

From other diary entries, it would seem that by the summer of 1917 it was the FWVRC équipe and their friends and not the ouvroir girls who were principally tending the garden. It had lost its initial support, but had perhaps fulfilled some of the town fathers' hopes for a profitable use of spare land.

When Gertrude returned to Bar from leave on 20 September 1917, she reopened the ouvroir on 25 September, but, in a composite diary entry starting 20 September 1917, she lamented that

> it didn't live long alas, for the following Sunday [Sept 30th] the bombardment was such as to drive nearly all my women from Bar. We arrived back really to behold our work completely changed in character. My ouvroir is a mere matter of empty tables and cupboards – now it has received its 'requiescat' and I'm a bereaved soul.

She took comfort in the thought that she had never "had to hand it over to someone else – it ended mine, and I'm the 'demoiselle de l'ouvroir – la patrone – la directrice' – So I can feel glad for that." Some activity did continue, but not through the medium of the workroom. Women who wanted to keep on with the plain sewing now worked at home, coming chiefly from neighbouring villages to collect their order. Completed work was picked up three times a week.[15] By late October to early November 1917, Gertrude was finalising the ouvroir accounts and stock-taking. With the completion of these tasks on 5 November 1917, she relinquished responsibility for the workroom, apart from a decision on the disposal of the money.

Released from the daily obligation to manage the workroom, Gertrude had her eye on another area of activity – motoring. She had come out to France with the understanding that she would be a chauffeur. That scheme was very slow in being realised, but her insistence that she should be allowed to drive seemed on the point of being met.

Cars and driving
Gertrude clearly had a taste for things mechanical. This extended beyond motor cars to the military technology she came across from time to time, which she examined with interest despite her revulsion for the effects it might cause. On 19 August 1915, she and Susanne Day visited two of the villages immediately to the northeast of Bar, in company with the parish priest. There they saw some of "the great 75ᶜ guns, with the ovens (like a small hand cart)", together with the horses that pulled them.[16] Gertrude noted in her diary that she and Susanne "were allowed to look at the 'sighter' and to see how the range was found" and were shown "the shells in their cases, and how the screws are fixed. etc." The visitors were also shown two of the new trench mortars, the 'crapouillots', in a garden. Gertrude described them as "little squat machines, with the acorn-shaped bombs pointing upwards". Later that same year, as she noted on 30 November 1915, she heard from a French private, met at a social gathering, how "the little machine guns, which go in the front-line trenches" operated.

The same fascination with how things worked later caused Gertrude a minor mishap, when she split her new glove trying to turn a handle of a piece of enemy equipment on display in the place de la Concorde in Paris. She and her new-found American cousin Wilmer Powick, when they met up in late October 1918, had gone to look at the "Bosch guns and tanks etc.", trophies of war lined up in the centre of the French capital, as she told her family in a letter of 3 November 1918. Wilmer himself, writing to his family the same day, recorded the same incident (see section on Gertrude and Wilmer in Paris).

The nature of the mission's work tasks required independent means of transport. French train services still functioned fairly regularly, and FWVRC members used them for long and short journeys; but for visiting and working far into the countryside motorised transport was essential. In the early days, the FWVRC appealed to British

18 Bicycling permit, issued to Gertrude on 22 March 1916

Friends for the donation or loan of motor vehicles. Some men who were car owners brought them over to France with them when they volunteered, or drove cars their family had donated. Others came with their motorcycles. As relatively few of those joining the FWVRC had learned to drive, a number of men, who were sometimes as young as seventeen, were recruited as chauffeurs. The mission had a strict line on the use of cars, which were to be taken only on work visits, not for 'joy-rides'. A large vehicle, known as the 'bus', drove équipe members between Sermaize and Bar-le-Duc. The FWVRC's main garage throughout the war was at Sermaize, where chauffeurs and those driving themselves maintained and repaired vehicles in a workshop.

Far more prevalent was the use of bicycles, some brought by FWVRC volunteers when they came over, and Gertrude was able to take one over from a departing fellow-worker. A bicycling permit from the military authorities was obligatory, and moreover required frequent renewal. One of these permits, issued to her on 22 March 1916, has survived. It was valid for one month within the zone of the Third Army and detailed the area inside which she might circulate. Sermaize and Revigny were within bounds, and she and colleagues sometimes cycled from Bar to Sermaize across part of what had been the Marne battlefield or rode in the forests on Sunday afternoons; while on a Monday morning she would sometimes rise early and bicycle back from Sermaize to Bar along the canal. Cycling in Bar could be hazardous, as when she was knocked off her bicycle by a soldier. In her diary entry for 22 May 1917 she described how he had tried to force a way past her on his bicycle as they both crossed one of the bridges in Bar between two carts, and succeeded in hurtling her under the wheel of a cart. For a week she felt "sore and miserable". Later in the same year, she reported in her diary on 25 October 1917, she came off when her bicycle skidded on a muddy street. Neither accident seems to have put her off bicycling.

Her great wish was that she might be allowed to work as a chauffeur and so make good the time and energy she had expended in learning to drive in Manchester. The training had involved familiarising herself in the workshop with the workings of the motor engine and other functions of a car, an aspect of motoring that she enjoyed. She frequently detailed the types and makes of car she came across in both France and Poland (and of motorcycles, though she reached no further than trying one out).[17]

In England she had done a little driving by herself. Almost as soon as she arrived in France she "had a lesson" on 1 June 1915 on the Sermaize Ford, which she found easy enough to manage, and she told her mother in a letter of 14 June 1915 that she had driven a car, but unofficially – "only on the Q. P." Then, on 12 September, Hilda Clark asked her to drive her in her car, a Belsize, while a group of them were out bathing near Sermaize. Gertrude's account of what happened is not clear, but it seems the car may have started to roll, Gertrude applied the brake and the car turned over, trapping both her and Dr Clark inside it. The vehicle had to be lifted off them, but neither of them was injured. The car engine was not damaged, and the car was back on the road within months. Still, the episode had presented some danger, since they were on a bank above the water of a lock. In her diary entry for that day Gertrude reproached herself bitterly, both for having put Dr Clark's life at risk and for spoiling her chances of driving. "I had been given an opening and had closed it to myself." Hilda

Clark certainly did not forget, since she raised the incident, however gently, in a letter of 11 January 1920, written to Gertrude's mother after Gertrude's death. She told Martha Powicke that she was in France when Gertrude came out and "feel her death as the loss of a friend – She and I were nearly killed in a motor car once – I wonder if she ever told you about it – very likely not, for fear it would make you anxious." (Indeed, Gertrude made no mention of the incident in her letters home.)

Whatever the reasons, and this episode must have cast a negative light, Gertrude had to wait a further two years before the question of her driving for the mission arose again. From the moment of her arrival in Bar-le-Duc in June 1915, she was fully occupied with the ouvroir, accounts, and participation in the various war work schemes set up in the town. Moreover, FWVRC's demands for driver recruits appear to have been met, in spite of the impact of military conscription from March 1916. In fact, as Ruth Fry pointed out,[18] almost all of the FWVRC's male workers outside Britain were conscientious objectors, many of whom had offered themselves as volunteers before conscription came into force. Some were willing to accept the British government's condition of exemption from conscription that they remain in the voluntary work overseas in which they had enrolled. At all events, as late as February 1918, Gertrude was lamenting to her father in a letter of 11 February 1918 that "at present there are men to chauffe and they need me for accounts and the Relief work."

During the long period of waiting, Gertrude managed to keep her hand in. In her diaries she detailed the behaviour and roadside breakdowns – a fickle radiator that needed humouring on a cold day, a puncture, a dirty jet, a change of tyre, a lost starting-handle – of cars she was travelling in, and more serious problems, such as a broken back axle. At some point, she put in a strong plea to be allowed to drive, and in October 1917 those in the mission responsible for transport decided to reconsider her for that task. While her head of équipe, Sophia Fry (see Biographical notes), was nervous at the idea, Rachel Alexander had no such fear. Three days later, on 26 October 1917, Gertrude went over to Sermaize to see how she got on with a second-hand Hupmobile. On 24 November 1917 she noted that she had been at Sermaize as a garage hand for over a week. She had made several outings, seemingly with one of her colleagues, John Ransome. He was "very nice, but shouts a lot for a teacher, made me get nervy, but I didn't let on."

Of her new car Gertrude said only that it had a hood, a leather lining and a paraffin lamp. What is almost certainly the Hupmobile

19 Gertrude's dog Peter, in what was probably the Hupmobile, 1919

appears in a snapshot of her dog Peter, who is seen hanging out of the front seat. The car shown there can perhaps be identified as a 1914 Model 32 Touring Hupmobile. (Such is the view of Brian Spear, librarian of the Hupp Club.)[19] Gertrude's delight in being able to join at last in what was clearly a constant process of maintenance is clear. Such enthusiasm was necessary. The Hupmobile was a difficult vehicle, heavy and temperamental, though possibly not more prone to breaking down than the other makes of car available to the mission's workers. That said, its ailments fill the entries in her diaries: punctures and wheel changes, tyres and rims bowling off, blocked jets, dirty sparking plugs, defective oil and petrol pipes and water casket, and more than one breakdown, as well as more serious repairs. Replacement springs and other spare parts had to be brought from Paris. She learned how to humour it and diagnose its problems; and remained largely loyal to the car, which she called the Hup, Huppy or "la petite", until she came to part with it in June 1919.

She was told her driving permit would be applied for, but the whole venture was nearly cancelled when the Hupmobile performed badly in an expedition in early December 1917 over icy roads to the Verdun area, where it skidded badly. Gertrude was not driving, but one of the consequences of the car's mishap was to leave Edmund Harvey, one of the passengers, "in a blue fit" over her being allowed to drive it. A tense moment ensued when he told her she would not be permitted to do so. Gertrude, both angry and grieved, refused to accept this decision. She prevailed, as she reported in her diary on 2 December 1917. "[H]e just had to give me my way to some extent and I'm to have a Permit."

Anxiety over Gertrude's ability to control the Hupmobile clearly persisted for a while. One or other of the customary drivers accompanied her on her early outings. Their concern showed itself in "shouting", issuing "multitudinous directions" and on one occasion seizing her wheel as she was braking, to her great irritation. It is unlikely to have been a case of male condescension, since driving was not viewed as the prerogative of the men in the various équipes, and other women did drive and tend the cars; but Gertrude nonetheless had to bear a certain amount of teasing. At the same time, her male colleagues in the garage and elsewhere came readily enough to her assistance when the Hupmobile needed attention, probably because she did not play the helpless woman. Out on the road she had to mend punctures and attempt repairs on her own, often under the eyes of small boys or passing soldiers, who might or might not be helpful.

She did not have an opportunity to take the car out again until late March 1918, when she began to visit villages around Bar, driving with a colleague to distribute seeds and collect embroidery orders. She also acted as a kind of ambulance, to convey sick or elderly people to or from hospital. In the immediate term she had to grapple with the question of petrol and its storage, and on 28 March 1918 noted in her diary that she had got her *bon d'essence*, her petrol voucher, that day from the local military, who oversaw the distribution of petrol. The petrol itself was obtained from a supplier in the centre of town. On 4 January 1918, the relevant army office had issued a note, written in an elegant hand, authorising the Friends' mission to draw up to 200 litres a month from the petrol depot in Bar-le-Duc. On 29 March, she had to haul away the full ration of 200 litres, a tiring task, as her diary entry recorded. Both the petrol and the car had to be kept at a house in the upper town where the équipe had taken extra accommodation, since the house at 99 boulevard de la Rochelle was not insured for the storage of petrol.

Conditions on the roads around Bar-le-Duc were very variable. Driving in the dark on 2 December 1917, she noted in her diary that she had "had [a] near shave along the Revigny-Bar road with carts unlighted slowly ambling along on their wrong side. Ran gently into a man on a bicycle". A trip on a route nationale south of Bar in June 1918 encountered "quantities of hens and ducks and dogs, quite their day out". The Verdun road, open again to civilian traffic, was, by contrast, "some road", where on 9 May, her diary for that day reveals, she could make record time, though she had to watch out "for military cars whistling round the many curves". On another good road northwest out of Bar she reached ninety km on 21 May 1918 and incurred the attention of a gendarme. "[We] were nearly clapped into gaol, but I deftly turned the gendarme's thoughts in new channels", was her diary entry for that day.

The car was put severely to the test in the summer and autumn of 1918. From June to mid-July 1918, Gertrude used it between the Verdun region and Poissons, a small town south of Bar-le-Duc in the neighbouring department of Haute-Marne, firstly to convey elderly or infirm refugees away from areas that had to be evacuated anew and then to take them back home once the danger had passed. In November of that year, she was active in relief work in the regions immediately south of the area of fire, then, when the armistice was declared, north of it. Driving in what had been a battleground presented a great challenge to the car's mechanism and solidity but even more to Gertrude's skills. It also placed her in considerable danger at times. Roads had been mined and were full of craters that might stretch from side to side – "holes as big as a house – some full of water" that necessitated going through the fields or risking a temporary bridge. "[T]he emergency bridges are logs, and are just wide enough to cross and no more. And you approach them over deep ruts, so that it is a toss up whether you will land on the bridge or in the hole" – so runs her diary entry for 18 November 1918. The troops that filled the countryside were generally helpful. On her first trip to Sedan, soldiers (it is not clear if they were French or American) had to lift the car out of the mud three times, "for poor Huppy stood and spun with her hind legs getting in deeper and deeper". American soldiers twice supplied her with petrol. Her worst experience remained an incident on 25 November 1918 in Varennes, when a lorry backed into the car, damaging its steering and causing it to hurl Gertrude six times into the ditch.

It was patched up and again conveyed Gertrude as she drove people back home, sometimes with their livestock, but suffered further, minor damage from being taken out on bad roads. In March 1919, Gertrude sprained her wrist trying to crank the car up. She was able to take the Hupmobile, newly repaired, to Luxembourg in May, where she left it and continued her journey to Germany by train (see section on Luxembourg and Germany, May 1919). On the return journey, a burst tyre caused her to swerve into a tree and break the back axle. A replacement Ford car was not very satisfactory; but by mid-June 1919, Gertrude was starting to plan her departure from France.

She was reluctant to let go of her Huppy, and when she heard that there was a chance of buying the car at a low price in several months' time to bring it to Britain, she asked her sister Agnes, in a letter of 13 July 1919 (written from Heaton Moor), if she might be in a position "to lend me something till I get wealthy". Agnes agreed to help, and on 1 August, in a letter from Paris as she prepared to leave for Poland, Gertrude thanked her and said she was not prepared to pay more than 500f[rancs] for the car. "I haven't any answer yet. They've not started to mend her up yet either. SO there'll be time for us to fix things up." Time, however, played them short. In her final letter to her family of 3 December 1919, Gertrude passed on a "sad" message to Agnes that "[t]hey've been and gone and sold the Hup, because some Frenchman offered to buy her without repairs and offered a fabulous sum too. So where did yours truly and her widow's mite come in? Isn't it a shame."

Accounts
These were the bugbear of Gertrude's work in France and she railed against them as "maudits" – accursed. Against her will she eventually found herself with responsibility for a number of separate accounts: workroom, embroidery, relief, medical. The structure of the FWVRC enterprise in France (and elsewhere) was underpinned by meticulous reporting of both activities and expenditure. (The Society of Friends' relief operations relied heavily on public support, particularly from its members, and an exact account had to be rendered of what was spent.) Gertrude must have shown some ability in accounting, though she had never had any formal training or experience, beyond being treasurer of the Romiley branch of the NUWSS from 1908 to 1913. That may, however, have been sufficient, when compared to what may have been the utter lack of experience or interest on the part of other colleagues.

She started off in June 1915 with the ouvroir accounts. These would have included a note of expenditure on materials and presumably of payments to the women and of sales of finished products and second-hand clothing. She spent many evenings, at the end of the other work of the day, in 'doing the books'. The weekend was another time for getting to grips with them. The accounts seem to have been required on a weekly and monthly basis. On 2 September 1915, she recorded that she "[d]id accounts violently with Miss Fry" for much of the day. (Miss Fry, probably Margery Fry, doubtless had to sign them off.) It was not an easy job. On 30 November 1916 she reported: "Last day of November – am wrestling with accounts and am much out. Generally am first time I go at 'em – sleep on it and voilà." Every so often the finance officer at the FWVRC's Paris office would mount a visit of inspection. Gertrude's accounts were generally accepted, but on one occasion in early April 1916 they were found wanting, when it transpired that Gertrude had let herself be cheated in a purchase and had to refund the 40 francs involved.

By November 1916, she also had responsibility for the medical account, which appears to have included charge of the medical cupboard (Agnes Powicke, memoir, page 75). An unwelcome development came in February 1917. Susanne Day, who had worked on the embroidery projects in four centres, left Bar on 20 February at the end of her tour with the FWVRC. As Gertrude related to her mother in a letter of 11 February 1917, Miss Day was to leave her "as heritage a mass of accounts, a regular net-work of Bookkeeping. I remember that I hesitated to take on the job of bookkeeper to the Scottish Women's exped. and lo, I find it thrust upon me on this." Wanda Bungener gave her a hand in April 1917, but she even had to take them with her on leave to clear a backlog. Writing on 31 July 1917 to her sister-in-law Susan Powicke, she describes her room in the new family house at Heaton Moor as "so quiet and easy to work in. I've still lots of accounts to finish for the society and need to be calm as a lake before I start on them."

One source of such labour ended with the closure of the ouvroir in November 1917 and finalisation of its accounts. These were replaced by the accounts for the various relief projects, while the embroidery and medical accounts still remained to her charge. The prospect of "endless muddled accounts" did not please Gertrude, as she complained in her diary on 2 December 1917. The pace seems to have been relentless. Writing to her father on 11 February 1918, she told him that she had done very little that month except accounts. Before going on leave in June 1918, she informed her family in a letter of 30 June 1918 that she had to spend "one full day" in Paris with Philip Meyer, financial officer for the FWVRC's French enterprise, "for the wearial purpose of adding two and two and then subtracting them with 'Brother Philip' – the ill-fated purse-bearer of the Mission". Responsibility for the embroidery accounts at Bar ceased only in May 1919, when the équipe at Bar-le-Duc was finally closed down.

It was understood that volunteers with the FWVRC should accept the work allocated to them by their country organising committee, and it was in this spirit that Gertrude took on the task of dealing with so many accounts: "I have to do what is most needed", as she explained to her father. The fact that she was able to get on top of this job and was, as she described herself, a stickler for method doubtless led others to ask her continually to extend this work; but one also has the feeling that her willingness and capability were being taken advantage of. By late 1917, she felt she had almost had enough. She had been passed over for the position of next head of équipe in favour of an older colleague and felt she was being relegated – such was her complaint in her diary for 31 October 1917. "I see myself with simply tons of work to do accounts galore and no scope. It seems to me I go on sticking here and people come and go and 'cos I'm always the youngest I never get a move on."

In the event, her determination to hold out for the chance to be a chauffeur saw her through, and the threat of a life dominated by accounts receded.

The first year
The months following her arrival in France were a period of reaction to a new situation. The job itself, though challenging and often tiring, was full of interest and variety and is unlikely to have unsettled her. More difficult was the need to develop good working relations with her colleagues. She had been in a similar situation before at the finishing school at Schwerin and had found a way to cope. She had been a member of staff for three years at the MHSG, where there was a similar need to get on with fellow-teachers. The pressure and pace of work at Bar, however, probably sharpened the atmosphere. She was often the youngest among her immediate colleagues and had come from lively family surroundings into a setting that was in many ways demanding and austere. The effects of temperament, both her own and that of others, fill a number of entries in her diaries, particularly during the first year.

With some people there were sparks, for Gertrude could flare up. She particularly disliked those whom she judged to be overbearing, patronising, officious or underhand. On 8 September 1915, she noted in her diary, she and Eva Gilpin, who had arrived the previous month, had "a fierce quarrel" that only subsided after the two of them had taken two turns up and down the boulevard de la Rochelle, with Miss Gilpin clinging to Gertrude all the way. The exact cause of this exchange was never revealed. Three days before, as her diary for 5 September 1915 recorded, another member of the équipe, Margaret Bulley, had irritated Gertrude by her "consequential" manners, though what she had done to make Gertrude feel that she "could have driven a hat-pin up to the hilt in Miss Bully [sic] today at lunch" is again not stated.

Gertrude valued an understanding of what constituted good manners. Among her first colleagues when she arrived was Elsie Dalglish – she and Gertrude Townend had been the first relief workers in Bar-le-Duc. Miss Dalglish was also faulted for an overbearing style and lack of breeding. "I have to keep pulling myself up not to contradict everything she says because she says it so peremptorily", Gertrude told her diary on 10 June 1915. She and Miss Townend left Bar in July 1915 with their "pioneering work" acknowledged in the pages of *The Friend* for 30 July 1915. Alas, they were not so impressed by elements of the FWVRC and in September one of them contributed a press article written "against" the Friends.[20] Despite the absence of a signature to the article, the FWVRC attributed the remarks to the two women. Gertrude noted in her diary for 2 October 1915 that it "simply caddish" of them to have done so. She claimed she tried not to gossip, but even before the incident of the press article had been indulging in a running critique of Miss Dalglish's ways, regaling others on 6 August 1915 "with tales of Miss Dalglish and Co" and on 17 September 1915 with stories of "the Dalglishian period", as her diary entries for those dates reveal.

In August 1915, the members of the Bar-le-Duc équipe were Mrs Jackson (the nurse), Gertrude, Susanne Day and Mary Staveley (a history lecturer at Bristol University). Over the weekend of 7-8 August, they all four abandoned Bar for a visit to Domrémy. They travelled by train for part of the way, having secured the necessary permission, and then two of them bicycled and two walked the rest of the road. They slept all in one room in an inn in a neighbouring village, with "a milk-jug for a washing-jug". On Sunday morning they joined soldiers and civilians at mass at the church in Domrémy. This trip into the Vosges much impressed Gertrude, who felt very moved to be in Joan of Arc's birthplace, even amidst the wounded and the soldiers crowding the street. She writes beautifully of the surrounding pine forests and the silence of the road, broken by the distinct sound of guns. On their return to Bar late on Sunday evening, they passed a small group of tired, silent soldiers waiting to start off for the front.

Another aspect of the work that she found unsettling in this early period was the constant need to adjust to departures and new arrivals. Many volunteers stayed for only a few months. Thus on 23 September 1915, she noted in her diary, she had to take farewell of Mary Staveley, of whom she had become fond: "I'm so sad – for it has been a treat to have her". On 11 February 1916, the diary entry lamented, another good colleague, Helen Proctor, was posted to the mission's convalescence home in Samoëns: "It is rotten without her. The whole place seems different". Taking up work again after leave in the autumn of

1915 seems almost to have felt like starting all over again, she told her mother in a letter of 1 November: "everything has struck me as so strange and, in a sense, primitive". As time went on, however, there was less passion in Gertrude's judgements on those around her. Before long, she had adjusted to the circumstances of the work, accepting the need to get along with people and also doubtless acquiring some perspective on the flow of new colleagues.

Chapter Four

Bar-le-Duc at war

Bar-le-Duc was never taken by the Germans. At its eastern tip, the First Battle of the Marne raged around Bar, and the enemy came close to the town – at times to within six km – near enough for people living in the town to feel the vibration in the streets and to hear the deafening noise of the cannon, which continued for three days,[1] but it was spared. Troops of the French Third Army, which included some from Provence, managed to hold off the German attempt to force the line at Revigny, and on 10 September, the enemy withdrew to the northeast (see Map 1). The defence of Bar came at great cost. Villages lying to the west, northwest and north, such as Vassincourt, took the brunt of the fighting and were left largely in ruins. Casualties on both sides were high, and bodies were buried in the countryside. The German Fifth Army led by the German Crown Prince had sought to move southeast against Verdun and the Meuse valley, but the forts around Verdun held, and the citadel never passed into German hands. Against that, the Germans captured St Mihiel on the Meuse in mid-September and retained it until almost the end of the war.[2]

Bar-le-Duc thus remained intact and in the ensuing war of attrition was to fulfil an important logistical role for the military. It was already a garrison town. Its mainline rail connections to Paris and Nancy remained in place, and retention of this vital rail link allowed the French military authorities to bring up reserves to the line of fighting. Bar-le-Duc, at thirty-five km from St Mihiel and fifty-six km from Verdun, was near enough to the front to serve as a military administrative base and a staging point for French troops. With its integration into the local narrow-gauge railway system and the existence of a road linking Bar with Verdun, the town's role as a hub was particularly important during the siege of Verdun in 1916, when the double means

20 *Café-restaurant des Ruines, Vassincourt, Meuse*

of transport for both men and supplies allowed Verdun to be constantly relieved (see section on Verdun, Figure 52). An already existing airfield to the northeast of the town served as an air base.

Problems and coping strategies
The war confronted Bar with severe problems: the general effects of hostilities on living standards in the town, the influx of refugees, the presence of large numbers of soldiers in transit and equally in need of hospitalisation or temporary support, and the arrival of the families of wounded soldiers to visit their family members in hospital. Under the initial danger of early September 1914, the town's response faltered in some areas. The hospitals that had already been set up were evacuated with some of their personnel, and the many casualties of the fighting outside of Bar who arrived in the town were dealt with at the station, which became an evacuation post staffed by an inadequate number of doctors and nurses, supported by civilians.[3] The town's provision for the growing numbers of refugees it had to receive was also slow to get going. Within weeks, however, some of the hospitals were re-installed, and during the autumn of 1914, the first of various relief initiatives were under way as the town rallied its resources to cope. A system of bread vouchers and the creation of popular kitchens

21 *Soldiers and townspeople in the rue Oudinot, Bar-le-Duc*

or feeding stations were set up at the instigation of Pol Chevalier, a former mayor of Bar-le-Duc (see Biographical notes), to feed the poorer sections of the town's population.[4] He later opened a market to ease the impact of commercial prices and help consumers in difficulty.

Refugees began arriving in Bar within weeks of the outset of war, forced out of their devastated villages by the invaders, or evacuated by the French army. From being relatively few at first, as the autumn wore on they started to arrive in convoys of sometimes forty to fifty people, by train, sometimes by horse-drawn cart, sometimes on foot, when they might spend up to six weeks on the road. They had fled from the north of the department of the Meuse, from neighbouring Ardennes and Meurthe-et-Moselle, from Luxembourg and Belgium and from frontier villages. Some came in from areas surrounding Bar that had been destroyed in the fighting. Pol Chevalier estimated the

22 Refugees passing through Bar-le-Duc, 1914–15

number of refugees the town had to cope with throughout the war at a little over 3,000.[5] (The FWVRC put the figure higher, at nearly 4,000 towards the end of 1915.) Whatever the exact figure, it had to be absorbed into a pre-war population of 17,000 to 18,000.

In accordance with official requirements, responsibility for dealing with the refugees fell to the prefectural and local authorities. The prefecture had its 'contrôleur des émigrés', i.e. of refugees, and the municipality had a dedicated 'service des réfugiés'. Within the zone of the armies, the commune was obliged to meet the immediate need for food of refugees without means; the costs were borne by the state and reimbursed through the prefecture.[6] When sufficient warning was received of an impending exodus, the existing arrangements for feeding and accommodating these people overnight were adequate, but struggled to cope if, at an hour's notice, a group of fifty, 100 or 200 required feeding. From 1 January 1915, the government-authorised allowances for the families of mobilised men, of 1.25 francs per day per adult refugee and 50 centimes for each child, were distributed in Bar, thereby assuring a small income to refugees. A number later found employment. But their longer-term needs required more thought and organisation.

Early provision for the refugees was inadequate and makeshift. Chevalier records that they were camping out in sheds, outhouses and workyards and notes a police report of 17 October 1914 which spoke of a lack of assistance, with refugees existing on bread and the remains of soup they had begged from the military – *du pain de soldat*; the greater number among them had no change of linen or footwear; there was a need to replace the straw on which they lay, disinfect the places [where they slept] and provide them with blankets for the night.[7] The most urgent requirement for those who stayed in Bar-le-Duc was for accommodation. Collective housing was seen as the speediest way to help them, and they were installed in houses belonging to the town, in public buildings such as schools and the magistrate's court, and in large buildings lent by private institutions and owners. Some of this housing was already in a deplorable condition. Efforts were made to keep people from the same or neighbouring districts together, such as the village of basket-makers from east of the river Meuse who had fled en masse led by their mayor and were placed, some forty of them, in one large room where they carried on their trade. (Both Pol Chevalier and Susanne Day wrote admiringly of the tenacity and industry of this group.)

These were conditions of severe overcrowding, and the local committee of support acting on behalf of the municipality had to impose rules of order and hygiene. It visited the premises where refugees had been placed twice a year. Observers such as Gertrude and Pol Chevalier could note extremes of good and bad household management. Bedding, heating and cooking appliances, fuel and household equipment had all to be provided at the outset. Medical attention was available free on the basis of public assistance. An office staffed by three refugees opened in the town hall of Bar-le-Duc as a liaison point. With the distribution of government allowances, refugees were eventually expected to pay for their accommodation, heating and food. Their needs for clothing (many were still in summer clothing), occupation and healthcare were met by public and voluntary organisations, of which the FWVRC was one, and by private groups and individuals. Many of the town's middle-class women, 'the ladies', volunteered in the various schemes or developed their own initiatives. The refugees were never entirely welcomed, and some were frankly regarded as undesirable, but they were never turned away.

As it became clear in February 1916 that a German assault on the fortress city of Verdun was imminent, the districts east and west of Verdun were evacuated, often at such short notice that it was not possible to make relief arrangements along the way.[8] Pol Chevalier relates[9] that on 11 February word arrived in Bar that 400 refugees should be expected the following day. Some made the journey on foot (Gertrude recorded that one couple had walked forty km to Bar). The policy indeed was to disperse them, but those arriving still had to be offered immediate relief. The municipal authorities directed them largely to the *marché couvert*, the covered market, in the centre of the town. This building, now demolished except for an entrance on the boulevard de la Rochelle and the small area behind it, occupied a considerable space. It was constructed on two floors, with an open balcony running at first-floor level round an open central well. This balcony area received the refugees, while the market continued below.[10] Dormitories, a refectory and a kitchen were created within this space.

The number of people crammed into this area at the peak of the exodus from around Verdun was enormous: in diary entries for 8 and 9 March 1916, Gertrude noted estimates of 1,000 to 1,200 refugees. People could arrive in the middle of the night, and in the small hours of 9 March Gertrude was asked to accommodate over 300 refugees in the FWVRC's workroom. Conditions at the covered market were rudimentary and insanitary. People were sleeping on straw in promiscuous confusion. The air in the dormitories was thick and fetid. The

23 *Entrance to the covered market, August 2012 (all that remains after demolition of the building)*

FWVRC Bar équipe had offered assistance to the organisers of this temporary shelter and on 13 February, took basins, soap and towels as well as buckets to the covered market, since, in Gertrude's words, there were "no arrangements". The équipe was able to donate beds and a quantity of bedding for the use of the elderly and invalid among the refugees (the gift was warmly acknowledged by the local press on 19 March). Thus an 'English dormitory' (*dortoir anglais*) was created. Gertrude was determined to devise a *petit coin* or lavatory/washroom where the women could retire. A space was found and the équipe handyman fixed up a framework to which sacks were nailed and where a table with basins and other necessities was installed. The arrangement was much appreciated, even if it was known as *le petit coin des dames anglaises*.[11]

Meals were constantly required, sometimes for hundreds of people, and sound to have been more than adequate. Susanne Day wrote of the hot three-course meals with soup and meat prepared for them.[12] Gertrude and her colleagues spent much time at the covered market serving up this food, then washing up in cold water, sometimes working through the morning or staying until after midnight. Some of the refugees seemed unable to comprehend their situation and, as if in a restaurant, complained about the service. Gertrude took a humorous line in her diary entry of 9 March 1916:

> "On est bien mal servi ici!" – this from an irate man at the M[arché] C[ouvert]. Who had had to wait many minutes while I served five tables – It was natural – but what can be done with over 1,200 emigrés jostling you and the soup and their bundles and all with one accord asking to be fed and quickly too. I overheard many amusing remarks. "Demandez à la bonne de se depêcher!" – was one. One lady swept up and ordered "bouillon pour 4 et une poule!" – and another later ordered a "fricassée de poulet" – poor dears – they were all moithered and bewildered and they thought they were at an hotel. I saw one man trying to get Miss Day to accept a tip. They slept in every available corner of the dortoir – sitting on the sides of the beds and along the passage, the other room was packed and in the eating room they leant against the tables – on them, under them – outside, on the staircase – a hopeless numbed mass – too tired to do anything but sleep. Miss Alexander and I stayed on till 1.30 – all the time feeding them – serving washing up, cleaning away on and on. Then another 300 arrived and it began again and nowhere to put them. The inner room was too thick and close for words – how anyone can sleep there I don't know. But there was no time to do anything but feed them – some were almost starving and begged with tears in their eyes for bouillon or café.

Other refugees tried to cling to their routine or to hold to some kind of order. The situation was complicated by the arrival of babies and elderly people and sick, demented or handicapped refugees. Throughout those days German bombing raids added to the tension. At last, as the military confrontation in the Verdun area settled into a months-long siege, the flow of refugees diminished, leaving the beds and floor of the dormitory "in a filthy condition" and "[t]wo poor children left behind purposely by their mother", Gertrude noted in her diary for 12 March 1916.

The refugees, once placed in accommodation and assured of a minimum standard of living, settled into a kind of alternative existence; some found work, their children went to school. It was not easy to prise them out of this life. Even on grounds of military demands or of hygiene, people were reluctant to move elsewhere.[13] In the end, the German bombing raids on Bar-le-Duc, which were especially heavy in the autumn of 1917, provided the impetus for refugees to leave.

The military in Bar-le-Duc

Another group of people who found themselves involuntarily at Bar-le-Duc were the *poilus*, the many soldiers who were garrisoned in the town or passed through on their way to and from the front. They filled the existing barracks, were billeted on the population, thronged the streets, paraded, and were constantly at the railway station. Their bands filled the air with music, while in mid-evening the call to return to barracks sounded out.[14] Lorries and ambulances were parked in all the main squares and often on the pavements. Some soldiers were quartered in wooden huts in the forests near Bar. Gertrude and Susanne Day out on a Sunday walk on 2 February 1916 met some of them "gathering leaves for salad" and saw their "big hut", as Gertrude noted in her diary for that day.

The town had its share of military pomp, as when General Joffre, chief of the French general staff, Lord Kitchener, British secretary of state for war, and the then French minister of war, Alexandre Millerand, visited Bar-le-Duc on 17 August 1915; but also its starker ceremonies, as Gertrude recorded in her diary for 3 August 1915, when two amputees received medals that same day, almost on the équipe's doorstep. Sometimes the scene was rousing, as when on 2 November 1916, "[t]roops came down from Verdun very gay – with German helmets and flags flying", or when, on 3 October 1916, as her diary reports, a "regiment of Senegalese with kitchen-baggage, and band passed this morning ... looking picturesque but very tired". One of the most stirring moments for Gertrude came on 31 March –

24 Military lorries parked on the place Reggio, Bar-le-Duc

Easter Day – 1918, as her diary noted, when she saw "hundreds of men tramping thought Bar all afternoon, for the first time since I was out here I heard them singing ... they sang in parts – one company taking it up as the other stopped. All down the Boulevard the same song ran 'Madelon' – it was just magnificent."[15]

As often, what she saw was far from cheering, and she notes with compassion the exhausted soldiers she encountered, their sky-blue uniforms[16] brown and dingy or in tatters. Many were hungry. On 2 October 1915, her diary recorded, several regiments passed through Bar. "All look tired and grey, some limping, some cycling some on horse back. They were buying 'couronnes' of bread and hanging them round their neck – though some of them were so hungry that they tore at them on the spot." As the German assault on Verdun intensified in late February 1916, so did the pace of military activity in Bar. In the evening of 26 February, Gertrude and Rachel Alexander had to escort a small party of refugees to the railway station to catch the train to Paris. They left their charges in the waiting room and set out for home, as Gertrude related in her diary entry for that day.

> It took time to elbow our way back through the crowd again. All along the Rue de Sebastopol – and down the Rue de la Gare were camions which had brought the Territorials from Verdun – they (the Ts) were waiting for the Paris Train. We had got as far as the Bld.

25 Soldiers' huts in the woods

when an agitated militaire accosted us – or rather me – because of my badge and asked if we knew of any Boulangerie which would be open. All the men from Verdun were almost famishing as they could get no bread and had had only soup all day and that in the morning. All the bread had been bought up. We consulted together and led him to the M[arché].C[ouvert]. where we commandeered a 'couronne' and a big box of our tinned meat. He and Miss A. carried the box between them with much interchange of advice as to the best way to carry it and with very many pauses for breath. I had the better part with the bread and various oddments. He insisted on our accompanying him to his company – or rather 'camion' – so nous voilà – at 10. pm – trailing along with a soldier – carrying food – pushing past crowd after crowd of soldiers and penetrating in amongst all the camions till his select crew were disinterred. Then – having finished our share we bade him a hasty farewell. He was very much excited and rather weak as he could not manage the box at all .. We felt very bold and bad as we made our way back through the crowd.

To strengthen the town's hospital capacity, at least four schools or colleges had had to be surrendered to army medical needs for varying lengths of time during the war, in addition to the central military hospital in the barracks area and a civilian hospital-hospice, which was turned over to army service. The numbers involved were considerable: 5,000 beds, with 3,500 alone at the central military hospital. Other military hospitals were installed in at least two villages to the south of the town. Further off, near Revigny, was the British Urgency Cases Hospital, the only British hospital in the Meuse, working under French army regulations.[17] An infirmary operated at the railway station as a triage and evacuation point for wounded or ill soldiers in transit. It was first housed in the station's goods hall, but was later transferred to seven wooden huts constructed in the passenger forecourt and in the buffet garden. For a while, the hospital trains loaded up on the passenger platforms.[18]

The situation of soldiers passing through the town to or from the front rapidly became urgent. Many were unattached, in the sense that they had no local units to which they could turn, and were reduced to hanging around the station as they waited to move on, lacking sustenance and sleeping where they could in all weathers. Their immediate need was for refreshment and rest.

From the first days of the war, the station had established itself as a focal point for these men and as a place of contact between the military and civilian spheres. From the outset, a canteen in one form or another operated at the station to provide refreshment first for the wounded and later for those in transit or going on leave. It eventually came under the care of a voluntary group, the Société de secours aux blessés militaires, which in February 1916 had two huts on the station forecourt[19] and in mid-June of that year set up another canteen for soldiers in transit in Marbot, a suburb of Bar on the Verdun road. Several Bar-le-Duc ladies among Gertrude's acquaintance were busy at one or other of these canteens during the spring and summer of 1916. Also in Marbot was the centre, described by Pol Chevalier[20] as a purely military initiative, launched by Commandant Zivy (Major Zivy) and known as Zivy's camp. Gertrude visited both camps on 27 September 1916 in company with her friend Madame Bungener, recording the visits in her diary of that day. There she extended her knowledge of French soldiers' slang, when she had a *roupie de singe* or some 'rubbish',[21] which was possibly coffee (*jus*), and "read all the directions as to the sale of 'Pinard'" – red wine. Commandant Zivy, with whom Gertrude was acquainted, also organised an officers' mess in the town. It functioned from July 1916 alongside a similar mess for non-commissioned officers. The two establishments enjoyed the services of a military maître d'hôtel supported by several cooks and military waiters or town waitresses, as reported by the *Echo de l'Est* of 30-31 July 1917, all of which suggests that the French Army, could, when the need arose, find a certain surplus of personnel.

26 Interchange between lorries and trains: the station at Bar-le-Duc

Some of the FWVRC équipe in Bar took turns to serve in the station canteen from the winter of 1915-1916. In a letter of 7 January 1916 to her mother, Gertrude described it as the 'Hut', where, she tells her, they "are still busy" and she was learning to "shop-keep", selling ham and sausage. Such work lay outside the mission's avowed spheres of activity, but as a recognised relief agency in Bar, the équipe clearly felt that this was a need it should address. A note in Gertrude's diary for 8 July 1916 indicates the team's concern: "I hear that a lot of the men who came back from Verdun 'en repos' had to sleep on the pavement – it is terrible. We have made enquiries and found that the town was taking steps. But I am afraid they're slow steps." The équipe's involvement grew to such an extent that in November 1916, with the backing and assistance of the local military authorities, it opened its own station canteen, or subsumed the existing canteen – the exact sequence is not clear. The aim of the new building, which was known as the Foyer des alliés – the Allies' club – was to provide an enclosed shelter and in that it differed from its predecessors, which were open-fronted booths.[22] A site was chosen close to the station canteen, and funds received from "British friends", according to Pol Chevalier (not necessarily solely the Society of Friends) for the building itself and for the acquisition of equipment. The new canteen was intended for soldiers in transit and for *permissionaires* – soldiers going on leave – to whom it sold food and hot drinks at modest prices. It proved popular, an officers' room was added, and in the summer of 1917, the premises were enlarged, with walls decorated by soldier-artists from the local camouflage workshop.[23] A dormitory was even envisaged. The local French command pressed the Friends to maintain and expand their foyers, particularly in 1917, when evidence of discontent and poor morale and episodes of mutiny among French troops led to great anxiety within the high command and attempts to improve conditions for ordinary soldiers; and staff from the Bar canteen opened up three new premises in the department of the Marne.[24] The Foyer des alliés at Bar carried on through enemy air raids directed at the station and continued its service until the end of the war and possibly beyond.

In a letter dated 3 December 1916 to her sister-in-law Susan Powicke, Gertrude attributes the initiative of the Bar canteen to her colleague Rachel Alexander; and Pol Chevalier credits Rachel with inviting Agatha Batten to come from London, where she had been managing a YMCA canteen, to organise the Bar-le-Duc establishment.[25] Miss Batten and several colleagues arrived in Bar in early November 1916 and were interviewed by Rachel and Gertrude. Alas, Miss Batten's tenure was not a success. She spoke "awful" French, in Gertrude's judgement, and seems to have proved difficult to work with. Things got so bad that Rachel Alexander had to sack her at the end of March 1917. Nonetheless, she and her party were among the first in a succession of around thirty women, both British and American, who, between late 1916 and early 1919, came for varying lengths of time to work alongside the FWVRC workers and the local French ladies. The numbers of American volunteers increased from mid-1917 as the United States entered the war.[26] Their participation was essential, for the scope of the work would have otherwise been beyond the powers of the Bar équipe. The volunteers were accommodated in various flats around the town. On 6 May 1917, Gertrude, using the French military term, noted that a *popotte* – mess – of English ladies had been set up in a neighbouring street and that Rachel Alexander was endeavouring to obtain another flat elsewhere in the town.

The indications are that Rachel Alexander and the Bar équipe were regarded as having a general, perhaps formal, responsibility for the Foyer des alliés. Gertrude drew up a shift timetable for the staff when, in May 1917, things had got into a muddle, and on 2 October 1917, after some particularly heavy nights of enemy bombing of Bar, stepped in to open up the foyer a couple of mornings. Nonetheless, the role of the Society of Friends in this particular venture is nowhere stated and is far from clear.[27] Gertrude, who worked alongside the volunteers, records appreciation and irritation in equal measure in her diaries. She was particularly fond of two youngish British women, Lila Sampson and Bertha Johnson, whom she describes as artists, who arrived in Bar in December 1916 from a munitions factory. They worked at the foyer for five months, Bertha as manager, and returned in 1917 for a further stint.

The pace of work could be intense and the hours very long. Troop trains arrived at all hours, sometimes in the very early morning, disgorging large numbers of soldiers. The canteen was open from 7 am to 11 pm, she told her sister-in-law in a letter of 3 December 1916, but a train often arrived at 11.15 pm and it was 11.30 before the men had been fed. On 15 November 1916, she noted, she was there from 9 to 10 am, from 6.15 to 7 pm and again in the evening for "three or four mad hours", from which she "slunk" in at 12.15 am. Six days later, on 21 November 1916, she recorded the following scene:

> Time: midnight – Scene the station square – at the side door of the Foyer des Alliés. A great crowd of tired mud-stained hungry men, clamouring for food and drink. They are just down from Verdun, – and their train arrives an hour late, just after the Foyer has closed. They knock at the windows and try to follow the advice: "Entrez, Ouvrez la porte." pasted on the window.
>
> I've opened the door, and it was pathetic to see them; they were so grateful for what we gave ... I poured out cocoa, coffee and soup steadily for about half an hour – there seemed no end to them – no sooner had I filled some six or seven "quarts" then seven others appeared and more and more, thrust under arms, over heads round shoulders – at all angles, and always "Merci bien Madame" – Behind me R.F.A. [Rachel Alexander] distributed 'petits pains', and eventually waved sausages aloft and bread – for they begged us to sell them food for the journey. We closed definitely at 12.20. The boulevard was empty and deserted as we came along and crept into the house.

The demand continued into the following months. On 17 January 1917, Gertrude noted snow and frost again, in which she "[h]utted fast and furiously till 11.am". The volume of soldiers could be enormous, with the counter "four deep". Then on 7 July 1917, she reported that the Foyer kept open all night, with a "mob" continually present and hardly enough supplies.

The members of the Bar FWVRC équipe who helped at the Foyer des alliés did so in addition to the other tasks they were engaged in, in Gertrude's case the ouvroir, accounts and home visiting. From October 1916, along with other members of the équipe, she had also been helping one evening a week at the Foyer du soldat (see below). Gertrude had never gone every day to the canteen, but in face of her heavy workload, Sophia Fry, who was directing the work of the Bar équipe, advised that she should give up the morning stint at the Foyer des alliés, and her attendance slackened off.

Even though the press of soldiers could be daunting at times, she clearly enjoyed the feeling of being in the thick of things, the varied situations and the occasional strangeness of the scene. On the whole she liked the men. Some tried out their English on the foreigners or gave their life history. Some of her descriptions have almost a touch of romance about them, as she noted on 29 November 1916: it was a "red-letter" night when

> the men gave an impromptu concert started by one man who began to recite – others followed suit and we had a gorgeous time – they all did so well. Then they sang – the latest songs on Verdun and songs evidently composed and sung by the men "out there" – with choruses. It was a splendid sight, all these men singing and enjoying themselves – the room was packed, the men standing six deep at the counter.

At times the conviviality – the need to shake off the memory of terrible events – got too much. One noisy evening yielded "several 'drunks' – two of them lifted a form by its end ... between their teeth, till it was horizontal. – it made mine ache to see them", she noted on 24 November 1916. Susanne Day describes an "unbridled" night of "wild revelry" on new year's eve 1916-1917, marked by singing and a speech of protest against the capitalists responsible for the war, which ended with a call to fellow soldiers to lay down tools. The speaker's appeal was rebuffed on the spot, but the French military authorities, alarmed by what they heard, conducted an inquiry.[28]

The women helpers' presence in the foyer elicited a variety of responses. Gertrude received various nicknames, a new one being Bébette; on 10 March 1917, "one old horror said he'd marry me 'après la guerre' – Merci"; soldiers who knew her embarrassed her by being comic to her; and on 1 December 1916 she noted that she and Susanne Day had received an offer of an escort from two men who followed them "for a bit of the way but Miss Day told them off". The counter, the sometimes furious activity in the canteen and a few well-chosen words generally provided the necessary barrier.

The Foyer du soldat – soldiers' club – was launched in October 1916 to provide distraction for the growing number of men garrisoned in Bar-le-Duc. The initiative involved civilian and military co-operation and, as described by Pol Chevalier,[29] had a strong feminine element. Impetus was given by Madame de Rieux, a vice-president of the Union des femmes de France, who had visited the Maison des parents in Bar (see below) in company with Madame Poincaré, the French president's wife, earlier in the year, and by Madame Krug, wife of the town's Protestant pastor. Madame Krug strongly urged that management of the club should be in the hands of women, or ladies, a proposal that Pol Chevalier endorsed on the grounds that feminine action could only have an improving effect on the soldiers' education. General Goigoux, the local commander, took a blunter line, according to Chevalier, since he "wished to see established in our town a club where non-commissioned officers and soldiers would find drinks that were both wholesome and cheap, as well as entertainment that would keep them from dance halls and unhealthy behaviour of every kind."[30] The unstated aim of all parties, as Chevalier fully and ironically understood, was to keep the soldiers away from strong drink and bad company.

The Foyer du soldat was consequently placed under a set of general regulations. Although a private and civilian initiative, it functioned under the surveillance of the local commander. As one of his preoccupations was to nip any expression of dissatisfaction or defeatism that might spread among a gathering of soldiers, any kind of political or sectarian propaganda was forbidden. Gambling was not permitted, nor was bad or familiar language. A non-commissioned officer was to maintain order. The only alcohol to be served was beer, to a maximum of two glasses. As agreed, a committee of ladies was once more set up to manage the club. The committee, numbering thirty-five, included Gertrude and Rachel Alexander (in response to Pol Chevalier's solicitation), and an evening was assigned to the FWVRC. The ladies officiating at the club were requested to wear white tunics and caps embroidered in red with the initials F. S. (it is not certain that this uniform was wholeheartedly adopted). The launch ceremony held on 22 October 1916 was attended by General Goigoux, who announced an opening donation of 500 francs to the club's funds. After his departure the foyer opened for the first time to the soldiers, of whom 800 turned up.

If the regime governing the club's existence appears austere, it seems to have been more relaxed in its actual functioning. To begin with, such was the shortage of available spaces in Bar that it was installed in novel premises, in two superimposed foyers within one of the town's theatres, in the avenue du Château. Even to achieve this arrangement, a number of railway workers and refugees who had all

27 The café in the soldiers' club, Bar-le-Duc

been sleeping in the foyers had to be shifted around. The lower foyer, which seems to have kept its original decoration, served as a café, the upper as a reading and writing room. As well as books, magazines and writing materials, games and musical instruments were provided. Mrs Griggs, an American lady who had attended the opening ceremony, arranged for a New York lady to send a "superb" gramophone together with 700 needles and fifty records.[31] A programme of lectures on very diverse subjects – military themes, national history, medical problems that might confront the poilu (syphilis and alcoholism) and travelogues – invited mental reflection; while a series of concerts and drama entertained the soldiers. The culmination of the cultural programme was a gala fund-raising evening on 19 March 1917.

Gertrude's diary comments on the foyer suggest that she drew amusement from her connection with it, from the hurried preparation of an embroidered 'nurse's blouse' and borrowing of a veil from one of the local hospitals for the opening ceremony, to working the gramophone and taking in her own records in preference to the "rotten American records – chiefly ragtime" that were there. Some of the soldiers tried out their English on her, and eventually she got to know some of the habitual visitors. The absence of 'Miss' and the gramophone in the summer of 1917 (when Gertrude was on leave) was noticed by some of the men, as Madame Bungener informed her in a letter of 31 August 1917. And then she had to say goodbye to "old pals" when they were posted elsewhere. Some of the entertainment was impromptu and not always enjoyable, but on 21 December 1916, she attended a concert and theatre at the foyer, from which she returned at 12.15. She was interested to see how the audience was seated: "The officers in the body ie. pit, the poilus in the gallery and us – ie. the infirmières, big pots and Monsieur le Préfet etc in the Dress Circle. Some style."

On 26 February 1917, Gertrude was asked if she would take the part of the English girl in the play, *L'anglais tel qu'on le parle* ('English as it is spoken'), which was being rehearsed by the foyer's drama group. She declined outright: "It would be great fun, but hardly comme il faut... and Miss Sophia's hair would rise". Even though she was assured that the male actors were very respectable gentlemen, Gertrude did not see how she could. Instead, she attended rehearsals and helped with the English, and felt she was "well out of it". The part she had been offered appears to have been taken by another British woman not connected with the équipe. The first performance of the play was on 15 March, with a further performance at the gala evening on 19 March. Gertrude noted in her diary for 15 March 1917 that she and another helper had "very good seats in the 'fauteuils' opposite the stage" for the first show.

> The place was packed and 300 militaires had to be turned away. The performance was amusing, it was great fun watching the men in the gallery when the "comics" came on, they literally rolled with laughter. 'Nellie Martyl' (Mme Scott) sang – she is very pretty and sings well – but I find her voice very metallic. She sang the Marseillaise finely. I can see why they send her up to the front to sing to the men. I liked "avec mes sabots" best, I think.

Nelly Martyl was a star of the Opéra-Comique, whose rendition of the *Marseillaise* was renowned. Throughout the war she served as a nurse, for some of the time in Bar-le-Duc. She was married to the artist Georges Scott, illustrator of the convoys of soldiers travelling up to Verdun (see section on Verdun).

The Foyer du soldat was open every evening, from 5 pm to around 8 pm. The numbers attending do not seem to have diminished, and a third space was eventually fashioned out of the balcony overhanging the lower area, with the assistance of army engineers. For their Christmas parties over 1916-1917, the FWVRC were allowed to use the club's premises. From autumn 1917, the foyer opened up to a fraternal set of soldiers, the Americans, who had a local base at Ligny-en-Barrois, south of Bar, and Independence Day was celebrated in the club on 4 July 1918. The model of the Bar-le-Duc club spread to neighbouring villages and other towns. It continued in service until the end of August 1919. Gertrude was clearly still taking her turn to help in June 1918.

In the wearing conditions of war – episodes of tension and danger interspersed with periods of waiting and monotony – the foyer provided simple, cheering, uncomplicated activities that were unlikely to get soldiers into trouble. Yet they were offered only to the soldiers of the local garrison, whose welfare was already relatively assured. The contrast with the hurried, sometimes rowdy setting of the station canteen where frequently exhausted men crowded for refreshment and temporary shelter must have been very clear to the women, French and British, who found themselves serving in both places over the same months.

The presence of so many hospitals in Bar receiving sick or wounded soldiers brought in yet a further group of people, the relatives of those in hospital. They came sometimes from considerable distances – in her diary on 6 April 1916, Gertrude noted people from Cantal and Auvergne in the centre-south of France, from Marseille and from Cherbourg in Normandy. Unable to find affordable accommodation, like the soldiers they were spending the night at the station, or on seats in the boulevards or in churches, in a state of considerable distress. The idea of offering them some form of lodging and extending moral support was first mooted towards the end of 1915, Pol Chevalier relates, by General Goigoux and Dr Pasteau, chief physician at the military hospital at the Lycée, but the project was delayed by a lack of suitable premises.[32] The problem was solved by capitalising on the conversion work that had already been carried out at the covered market to provide a reception area for the refugees from Verdun. By March 1916, refugee numbers had fallen away, and it was possible to consider using the space already available – the balconies and a large room on the first floor – for a form of hotel. Those who had been involved in helping to run the refugee shelter were invited to join in the new project.

Gertrude thus attended a meeting on 17 March 1916 in the mayor's office to discuss the setting up of the hotel. The town architect, Monsieur Boller, and a doctor, probably Dr Pasteau, were among those involved in the planning, as was Pol Chevalier, who was elected president of the Maison des parents de malades et blessés – residence for the families of the sick and wounded – as it was called. Many of "the beau monde of Bar", as Gertrude described them in her diary on 17 March 1916, were there, from among whom a management committee of ladies was organised and volunteers sought to help with the running of the hotel. Those assembled then visited the covered market, where the "dortoir anglais and cabinet de toilette were much eulogised". At a further meeting on 21 March, Gertrude was invited to be secretary of the committee but declined, as she had no time to spare and felt a French person would be much better. The chair was to be Madame Salmon, an acquaintance of Gertrude's whom she did not much like. The FWVRC équipe was assigned two evenings a week. The meeting passed detailed regulations on the management of the hotel, including the daily menu, and recorded further thanks to the Society of Friends for its donation of beds and bedding to the covered market (and for undertaking to launder the bedding).[33] A grand opening ceremony was held on 26 March, which Gertrude described to her mother in a letter of 27 March 1916. It was attended by the prefect and the mayor, the premises were inspected, the menu was discussed and Monsieur Chevalier recited a poem he had composed for the occasion. Admission to the hotel was to be on presentation of a printed note issued by the chief physician of the hospital where a relative was being treated, and the hotel was to be advertised in the hospitals. The maximum length of stay was to be three weeks.

The use of partitions formed by fabric stretched on wood to form separate bedrooms was continued in the space at the covered market. The FWVRC's 'English dormitory' was scrubbed out and divided up into six bedrooms, each capable of sleeping five people, and a sitting room. Gertrude told her mother in the same letter how "[w]e have left the beds we had put there for the émigrés – and it has been great fun arranging the rooms – nailing up pictures – stuffing pillows and mattresses and doing the most varied jobs." Meals were served in a dining room. Reading and writing materials were provided in the sitting room. Electric lighting was installed at the rate of one (overhead) light per two rooms, and to that end the cloth partitions did not extend right to the ceiling. Heating was a problem in a building not designed for human habitation. In the end, stoves were placed in the dining and writing rooms and guests were kept warm in bed through the provision of hotwater bottles (these last were supplied by the ever-constant British Committee of the French Red Cross).[34] Equipment, coal and foodstuffs were donated by a variety of benefactors, some within Bar itself, others within France, London or even New York (the last through the intervention of Mrs Griggs). Chevalier raised funds from official sources. Some six weeks after its opening, the accommodation had to be extended, such was the popularity of the hotel. It was extended a second time, finally to provide eighteen rooms for guests, with twenty-two military camp beds lent by the local army com-

28 Dining room at the Maison des parents

mand.[35] The level of staffing, both paid and voluntary, was increased. The hotel had all its windows on the street side of the covered market shattered in the air-raid of 1 June 1916.

Management of the hotel was in the hands of Madame Colardelle, a resourceful woman who cooked a huge *pot-au-feu* (boiled beef with vegetables) for 300 refugees expected at the covered market in early April, as Gertrude noted in her diary for 5 April 1916. (Refugees continued to arrive and were fed the same menu as the guests in the pension.) Gertrude became friendly with Madame Colardelle and on occasion relieved her in reception on a Sunday afternoon. Among the other staff was Dédé, the butcher at the popular market, also located in the covered market, who doubled up as night porter, and a supposedly young messenger boy, Monsieur Jacob, who in the event was far from young and was known as 'grand-père'. When 'grand-père' had to appear at the opening ceremony, Gertrude was able to kit him out in a fine new shirt, as she recorded on 26 March 1916.

The volunteers' duties at the Maison des parents consisted again of serving meals and looking after the rooms. The pace and style of work was quieter than the approach needed for handling the refugee crowds, but brought with it the difficult and painful requirement to deal sensitively with people who might have suffered great loss. Some days could be very hard. On 6 April 1916, Gertrude related in her diary, the pension was full – "one poor woman lost her son today, she started crying at dinner and set them all off, it was terrible." On 5

29 Sitting room at the Maison des parents

October 1916, her diary records, a good many guests were there:

> one poor group had come from the far south only to find the son and husband dead. The third son lost in the war. There was one woman who had lost six. There is an element of tragedy in the Maison terrible in its downright simplicity.

In such circumstances, the greedy and insensitive could be very irritating.

Gertrude's attendance at the Maison des parents seems to have tailed off by the spring of 1917. The Maison des parents was finally wound up in May 1919, and in April of that year Gertrude recorded a couple of trips to the covered market to retrieve the beds and other equipment the FWVRC had lent for its functioning.

The Society of Friends may not have wished to advertise any connection with the Foyer des alliés, but acknowledged the assistance given by the Bar-le-Duc équipe to the Maison des parents in 1916.[36] It was more closely involved in a similar hotel at Revigny, northwest of Bar, which had a military hospital. Once again, Rachel Alexander seems to have been the moving spirit. In October and November 1916, Gertrude recorded her discussing with the Sermaize équipe how to "fix up" the new establishment. One of the FWVRC building teams helped in its construction.[37] Revigny itself had been badly damaged in the Battle of the Marne, and it is unlikely many houses were left intact. In January 1917, Gertrude and Rachel went to Revigny to arrange rooms for Emily Dinely, Rachel's sister, who was to manage the hotel. The ladies were "very graciously received" by the Commandant d'étapes (in charge of logistics), as Gertrude noted on 21 January 1917, were given all they asked for and finally sent in the Commandant's car to see the Maison. A month later, diary entries for 23-25 February 1917 record that Gertrude was spending the weekend with Mrs Dinely at Revigny. The trip included a call at the Intendance to see about provisioning (for the hotel) – a further indication of the local military command's interest in the initiative – and visits to the military cemetery and the nearby prisoner-of-war camp, where all Gertrude's German "fled" from her.

Over the last weekend of April 1917, she relieved Rachel Alexander, who was managing the Maison des parents at Revigny during the week in her sister's absence on holiday. In a letter of 29-30 April 1917 to her mother she described the work as "very interesting – only the catering is difficult these days. I seem to spend my time cycling in and out of the village with bread slung over my handle-bar and potatoes and onions rolling all over the place." Marie, the maid, had to be goaded into action. Rachel had been giving English lessons to a French doctor at the hospital, and Gertrude had to take over: "He turned up promptly on Saturday and I had to do my bit too, much to my amusement." She ended her letter with a return to the catering: "It's time I nipped into yon village which was once a town, and buy meat and bread and eggs."

Emily Dinely was still at the Maison des parents in Revigny in March 1918 and remained in the Bar/Sermaize area at least until March 1919. A report for February 1919 by the FWVRC Works Department indicated that the Maison was being dismantled and the constituent parts sent to Clermont-en-Argonne for further use by the mission.[38]

Bombing raids

Bar-le-Duc and its surrounding district may have been considered to be in the rear and out of range of firing, but the sound of the guns nonetheless was frequently audible, sometimes faint, sometimes heavy like "a continuous thunder", as Gertrude noted on 19 December 1915. The noise of the shelling at Verdun carried over a great distance, and firing from the direction of St Mihiel could be heard clearly in Bar.

The town was more vulnerable from the air. For German aircraft it was not so distant, and for three and a half years, from May 1915 to October 1918, Bar and its surroundings endured bombing raids, French sorties to drive off the intruders, and anti-aircraft gun activity.

Pol Chevalier (whose chapter 11 in *A Bar le Duc pendant la guerre* on the bombardment of Bar has provided much of the information in this section) was of the opinion that the air-raids were "demonstrations" that had little bearing on any general and sustained fighting, taking place, as they did, at a certain distance from the line of fire established along a static front. The town was of interest to the Germans because it was an important point for revictualling and mustering troops. If the German aim was to damage Bar-le-Duc's logistical capabilities, it is doubtful, however, that much was achieved. The supply routes between Bar and Verdun were largely kept open. Among the casualties, including fatalities, that the town suffered through bombing, the proportion of military to civilian seems to have been three to two, but the total figure of all casualties was probably no more than 300.[39] The total for alerts over the years 1915 to 1918, as reported by Chevalier, varies between 210 and 250. Dumesnil states that at least 600 bombs or torpedoes were launched over the town, destroying seventy buildings and damaging 150.

The Germans deployed both Zeppelin dirigibles, which were fuelled by gas-filled bags contained inside the airship (they had a Zeppelin base at Metz, ninety-seven km east of Verdun, within the German-annexed part of Lorraine)[40] and Taube and Gotha aeroplanes. (Taube, meaning 'dove', is a misnomer, even if the plane had a graceful profile.) The first Taube attacks on Bar came in May and September 1915. They did little damage, although two soldiers were wounded, and Gertrude's account of the one on 9 September 1915 sets the tone of novelty:

> Before breakfast a Taube dropped bombs on us – a tremendous noise – I heard the whirr of the aeroplane – then a great swish and then a roar – Great interest and excitement but no trace of panic. Five altogether, the ones we heard fell in the Rue des Grangettes and in the Lycée garden.
> Miss Day and I went up to see the former. It's a miracle that no one was killed, for there the émigrés are packed as closely as sardines, and the shell fell in a small courtyard, not five feet from the walls of three houses. It made a fairly large hole, and cracked the walls of two houses. The chimney fell in in one and just by chance the woman had decided not to dress the baby near there and was at the other side of the room ...We were allowed to nose round in the courtyard and searched cheek by jowl with a commandant, for traces of the shell itself, but no success.

The use of bombing raids as an arm of warfare was still at an early stage, so much so that people treated the first German sorties over Bar as a kind of air show and stayed on the streets "to see", with disastrous consequences. Conscious of this, the mayor of Bar issued advice on 20 September on how citizens should behave in the event of bombs dropping that included instructions not to gather in public areas or to "gawp" and to walk "sideways", as Gertrude noted on 21 September 1915.

Whatever relative lightheartedness might have prevailed came to an end the following year. The German assault on Verdun, launched on 21 February 1916, was accompanied by a morning air-raid on Bar that same day, which smashed the station roof, burnt part of the nearby evacuation hospital "to a cinder", as Gertrude's diary for that day recorded, and caused several deaths. Gertrude and Rachel Alexander found themselves in the middle of an extraordinary scene. They were handing out tins of beef and sabots to a group of refugees when several bombs fell. The refugees continued to clamour for the footwear until the two women led them down into the cellar.

> There from bring a pushing rather repellent crowd they became a quiet impressive group of people, huddled together in the far corner and chanting the Litany and ever the refrain "Jésus, priez pour nous misérable[s] pécheurs" – one woman chanted the main part and the rest responded.

As soon as the bombing ceased, they started again to demand their sabots. Throughout, the équipe handyman "continued to chop and saw in the breakfast room – he refused to come in when I asked him – saying that he preferred to die 'les yeux ouverts' – to being buried in a cellar." Later that same day, the staff went to the covered market to serve lunch to the refugees piled in there, and in the afternoon Gertrude presided over the ouvroir. Bombs could not be allowed to disrupt the day's tasks, and so it continued throughout the campaign of air-raids.

Revigny and Sermaize were also attacked on 21 February, and colleagues at La Source, the FWVRC base at Sermaize, watched the duelling aircraft or even dodged the shells. During the night, a Zeppelin was spotted in the searchlights at a height of 2,000 m, doubtless aiming for the railway lines near Revigny, and was hit by French shells. The Zeppelin's contours glowed red and then it came down in flames; the projectiles it had been carrying exploded and the entire crew of twenty-six was killed.[41] Those at Sermaize had a close view of the episode. The young French boys being cared for in the hospital reacted in defiant style, bursting out with the *Marseillaise*.

On 26 February 1916, thirty Taubes were sighted at lunchtime and people were directed to the cellars. The mayor "was almost dancing up the street, sending people in and making the shops put up their shutters", Gertrude noted that day. The streets were "full of or rather edged with people peering out from their doorstep – to see the Taubes coming – very much 'on tiptoe for a flight." A warning system of sirens, which could be used only for that purpose, was installed at three points around the town and activated by the military once enemy aircraft had crossed over the front line. The sirens were augmented by factory hooters, bugles and the tocsin, or warning bell, at the old clock-tower in the upper town. On 27 March, the mayor issued instructions on taking shelter in vaulted cellars and on blackout precautions.

Despite the cautioning, people still came out on to the streets "to have a look" when enemy aircraft were spotted. In that way, the double daytime bombing of Bar-le-Duc on 1 June 1916, Ascension day, brought a large number of victims, as residents left their houses to see what was going on, then rushed to find shelter. Thinking the raid was over, they came out again, to once more be struck down when the aircraft returned after ten minutes to make a second raid. A toll of sixty-four dead and around one hundred injured was recorded and damage was caused in many parts of the town. Refugees, children, soldiers and railway porters were among the victims. A public funeral ceremony was held on 3 June, presided over by the bishop of Verdun, Monsignor Ginisty, who had withdrawn to Bar-le-Duc, and attended by Madame Poincaré. At the cemetery, André Maginot, National Assembly deputy for the Meuse, joined the mourners. Gertrude's diary entry for 3 June 1916 suggests that she attended the ceremony.

The raid of 1 June was the deadliest that Bar experienced. It prompted a formal notification from the mayor, dated 5 June 1916 and reported in *Echo de l'Est*[42] on 9 June, on the designation and accessibility of cellars as air-raid shelters. The press reiterated the message against staying out of doors when bombs arrived, since bomb splinters and falling debris could inflict serious damage, especially on a group of people. More raids and an increasing tally of alerts followed throughout the summer, disrupting work and sleep. The workshop had no cellars to retire to, and the girls had to go to the Gendarmerie opposite the barracks. Gertrude was away from Bar on leave in the summer, but recorded continuing raids on her return. Ouvroir sessions had to be halted, but she noted on 10 November 1916 that "the women have much more nerve than in June".

The following year was to try everyone's spirits. The number of alerts, if not of raids, increased to around 150 (after an estimated four in 1915 and forty-eight in 1916).[43] On 26 May 1917, German aircraft

30 *Effects of the bombing raid of 30 September 1917, corner of rue du Cygne and rue Notre Dame, Bar-le-Duc*

targeted hospitals in Bar. Rumours of poisoned sweets and of alarmist talk about future bombings of Bar-le-Duc circulated and were reported in *Echo de l'Est* on 15 May and 9 September 1917. The year's tribulations climaxed in September. Three consecutive days of bombing on the 4th, 5th and 6th that caused deaths and damage to municipal, military and commercial premises were followed on 28 September by a raid that smashed the station glass again and destroyed the nearby dormitory for soldiers going on leave, damaged a cotton mill and hit the barracks area. Four soldiers were killed. Even greater damage was inflicted in night-time bombings on 30 September and 2 October. Both caused a number of deaths and injuries among civilians, soldiers and prisoners-of-war. The first of these two raids flattened a section of housing forming the corner of two streets, rue du Cygne and rue Notre Dame; Gertrude wrote on 30 September 1917 of forty houses burnt to the ground and continuing to smoke "for more than a week". Among the spectators on that occasion was André Maginot.[44] The second raid destroyed the Crédit Lyonnais bank and neighbouring houses in boulevard de la Rochelle. In addition, Gertrude reported on 2 October 1917, six bombs fell on the town hospital, several in the upper town, and torpedoes elsewhere. Firefighters were drawn from the town garrison, supplemented by a detachment of Paris firemen who had been sent to Bar with their equipment as soon as the situation became serious.[45] The

31 Damage to the Crédit Lyonnais bank, boulevard de la Rochelle, Bar-le-Duc, following the bombing raid of 2 October 1917

injured were conveyed to hospital by a fleet of 'American ambulances'.

Gertrude's accounts of 28 and 30 September 1917 of the équipe's experiences of the nights' raids shows how uncomfortable and hazardous the situation was.

> On Friday 28th 10. p.m we were shot out of bed by the sound of bombs dropping and the sirène sounding at one and the same time … We clapped on a few garments and collected valuables and popped downstairs. R[achel Alexander]. and J[ean Alexander] got to the cellar but the guns began firing and the bombs dropping so rapidly that Sophia [Fry] and I didn't much care to cross the verandah and yard – so we stayed crouching under an eiderdown in the hall – with the whiz-bangs going off all round and the flashes under our noses almost. As soon as a pause came we went down, and found the others. We stayed till midnight.

Two nights later, on Sunday, 30 September,

> at 10.30 the alarm went, we skipped down and bombs began to drop and the guns to boom before Sophia and R. were down. Jean and I had a horrid time thinking of them up in the hall … We stayed down for about an hour – then came up to go to bed. I undressed and had a

nice hot bath – and was just getting into bed when whiz – bang – at it again. I clapped on a trouser and a coat and took my eiderdown in one hand and my bag of valuables in the other and sped down again – the others were there – and there we remained in druid form till 4. a.m. At first we stayed in the first cellar, but ere long a beastly smell of acetylene gas penetrated and we removed to the second where we sat, two with handkerchiefs soaked in water applied to our nose and mouth – two with a corner of Rachel's white petticoat applied likewise. It was rather funny to see. I finished the Count of Monte Cristo and smoked a few cigs. The noise was terrific. Houses seemed to be crashing in on all sides – the noise of the Gothas was very distinct they came down almost on a level with the roofs to shoot at the firemen and the people burning [sic] out of the cellars of the burning houses. The rat-tat-tat of the mitrailleuse was very much part of the programme. The torpedoes had a peculiar whirring sound, as they fell, fortunately many of them were aimed from too low an altitude and didn't burst.

Gertrude and her fellow-workers escaped the bombardment of 2 October by dint of spending the night at the house of the woman who supplied them with eggs, in Longeville, a village some five km southeast from Bar. It was an exhausting business, as she related in her diary for 2 October. The party walked all the way, tried to sleep on a bare floor and returned on foot to Bar soaked from a heavy drenching. During the night Gertrude "sat out in the village street talking to some French women for nearly two hours – I read but I didn't sleep." They arrived back at boulevard de la Rochelle to find it "in a sorry state".

From 1916, the town council had extended the anti-bombing protection available to its citizens with concrete-roofed air-raid shelters installed at nine points in the lower town and twenty-two tunnels dug into the base of the rocky promontory on which the upper town is built and into the hillsides that rise on either side of the narrow valley enclosing Bar. The work was undertaken by military engineers. One of the tunnels, constructed under the upper town, opened up a network of vaults dating to ducal times. (They have all now been blocked up, and the air-raid shelters destroyed.) The cellars created were required to be open to all.

By then, however, morale among those living in Bar was unravelling – something that would have been among the German objectives. People were already being worn down by the disruption of alerts and the illness often brought about by nights spent in cold, damp cellars. The triple bombardment between 28 September and 2 October 1917 broke their resilience, and the town began to empty as residents applied for permission to leave. The FWVRC marked the exodus by the number of sugar ration cards returned and estimated that about

32 Concrete bomb shelter constructed in place Exelmans, Bar-le-Duc, 1918

900 refugees remained in Bar after the bombings.⁴⁶ The mission helped in the evacuation of children and the elderly and set up a house at Charmont (Marne) for the aged which became included in the Bar équipe's work. In the hurry to get to an air-raid shelter, families had sometimes had to leave the bedridden where they were. Gertrude noted on 23 October 1917 that there were "very few children left in the streets". On 25 October, she noted in her diary, she counted the shops shut up as she came along the boulevard de la Rochelle: "in the end I decided to count those left open. It is extraordinary what a number are closed. Today the Magasins Réunis announces that it has shut – except for 'Couronnes' – of which we may stand in need. Ghastly I call it – to put that up – wreaths indeed!"

During the heavy bombardment, many of those remaining in the town would leave at dusk to sleep in nearby villages, in the woods and even in the open, returning to Bar in the morning to work. Others found space in houses in the upper town, where cellars were fashioned three storeys deep into the rock, "regular old ducal wine-vaults" as Gertrude called them. From October onwards the Bar équipe did the same and took to sleeping when necessary with a French family living in the upper town. Nights were uncomfortable, whether spent in the cellar in the lower town as on 19 October, as Gertrude recorded in her diary, when she "dropped [her] knickers on the stairs and was very chilly" in order to escape what turned out to be two "lost" Zeppelins,⁴⁷ or crowded into a room in the upper town where it was not possible to undress, wash or do one's hair. Those nights when the weather prevented a raid could be spent at 99 boulevard de la Rochelle and a good sleep, a bath and a change of clothes ensured. But even the household there had become like "bedlam", Gertrude complained to her diary on 20 October 1917. The good news was that the gas supply was to be restored. It was an unsettling time, with the Bar équipe and the group of helpers at the Foyer des alliés having to move between two sets of accommodation. Gertrude found relief through sleeping on and off at the house of her French friends, the Bungeners.

These were equally difficult times for the people of Bar. As the end of October approached, people began to look nervously at the moon as it brightened. Some decided to join the flight. Stories of escapes from bombing circulated as a way of coming to terms with what had happened, or might have happened. On a more positive note, the courage of some was publicly acknowledged in a ceremony in the place Reggio, in front of the prefecture, on 23 October. Several of the British relief workers and their French friends went to see their acquaintance Charlotte Dyckoff decorated "for fetching babies from the Maternity Pavilion when the bombardment was going on", as Gertrude put it in her diary for 23 October 1917. (Charlotte had been nursing at the town hospital in Bar.)

Alerts continued on and off, but the few bombs dropped on Bar for the rest of 1917 caused no great damage. This state of calm persisted through much of the following year, though raids resumed briefly on 15, 16 and 19 July 1918, without inflicting any casualties; and terminated in a half-hour bombardment on 23 October that swept the town. Thereafter, as Chevalier comments, the next round of explosions came on 11 November from the guns fired into the air by American troops as the armistice arrived.[48]

For its fortitude under bombing, Bar was awarded the Croix de guerre with palm on 30 July 1920.

Chapter Five

Change and movement

1917

By early April 1917, Germany had completed a strategic withdrawal from a middle section of the front stretching from Arras to Soissons, with the aim of shortening the front and recovering a reserve force. The German defences nonetheless remained strong, as was demonstrated by their ability to repulse the French at the Chemin des Dames, a ridge running twenty-five km east between Soissons and Rheims in Champagne, where they had dug themselves in. The French attack, launched on 16 April 1917, broke itself on the ridge under German fire. Casualties and loss of equipment were enormous, and the operation was halted by the first week in May. It had been the initiative of General Nivelle, commander-in-chief of the French armies since 16 December 1916. Its failure led to his dismissal in mid-May and the installation of General Pétain in his place.

The French inability to pierce the German defences and the scale of losses shook French morale and was the trigger for a wave of discontent among the troops, wearied by what they saw as senseless slaughter. Their action has been described as mutiny and was treated as such, but Keegan suggests that it marked, rather, a refusal to "return to the trenches" and a reluctance to engage in fresh assaults, while still being willing to hold the line against enemy attack.[1] Further complaints centred around poor living conditions – food, accommodation – and meagre leave. Courts-martial and the carrying-out of around fifty death sentences brought resistance under control, but Pétain took steps to meet the soldiers' grievances on conditions and leave and instituted training in new techniques.

Much of this colours a long entry in Gertrude's diary of 7 July 1917.

It represents her most extended review of the war situation in France and can be taken to reflect the reactions of those she discussed the failed French attack with among her FWVRC colleagues and her French acquaintances in Bar. From late 1916 onwards, moreover, she had been in frequent contact through the Foyer des alliés and the Foyer du soldat with ordinary French soldiers and had some idea of how they lived.

> I am continually being told of the bad "morale" of the French troops ... Yet at the Foyer they are usually cheery – 'gaillard' in fact and it is unusual to hear seditious talk. Last Saturday I must say the men going up to Verdun in the camions were crying "à bas la guerre" – "vive la revolution" – etc. but they were nearly all drunk. It is the fiasco of the Champagne offensive that has done the mischief and deliberate enemy intrigue ... There's no doubt that the French are utterly weary and depressed, but it doesn't mean that they will let the Bosch walk over them. "On les aura – ils ne passeront pas".
>
> General Goigoux ... and his staff (and most other generals methinks) have suddenly realised the necessity of attending to the needs of their men. It is incomprehensible that they never thought of it before, for there is nothing tells on men's spirits so much as neglect of their physical comforts and indifference. Up till now it has been wretched for them – no food, no possibility of getting it – no beds and no place to rest, very indifferent treatment at many hospitals and sometimes utter neglect of sick and wounded ... Now the men have had enough of it, and are worn with three year's fighting plus all this lack of attention...

On 6 April 1917, the United States declared war on Germany and immediately started to build up its combat forces both in the US and in France. (Individual Americans had enlisted voluntarily in the Allied armies before that date.) General Pershing, commander of the American Expeditionary Force that arrived in France in June 1917 and later of the American First Army, formed in August 1918, was insistent that the US forces should not act in a subsidiary role to the Allied armies, but as an independent unit. In the autumn, the US First Army was assigned its own battle front in the Meuse-Argonne area.

Pershing's command was based at Chaumont in the department of the Haute-Marne. A local command was established at Ligny-en-Barrois, south of Bar, and American soldiers quickly became a common sight in the town, to the point where Pol Chevalier insisted that "we were literally drowned in the Americans and in their material".[2] With the troops came the services that catered to them, notably their YMCA. American soldiers directed the traffic at the principal intersections and entertained themselves by hauling their lorries up to the top of one of the steepest streets in Bar to drive them down. American Independence Day was celebrated in 1917 at the Foyer des alliés and in 1918 at the Foyer du soldat. Signs in English proliferated. As a measure against profiteering, in early August 1917 the municipality announced exchange rates for the dollar and the pound against the franc and warned shopkeepers against making a charge when they received payment in British or American money.[3] Chevalier's tone is not spiteful, rather, one of amazement at the cultural clash he was witnessing. He was disturbed by the colour segregation among American soldiers (such distinctions were not so strong between metropolitan and colonial French troops). His judgement on the Americans he saw was that "taken altogether, their civilisation had not evolved in the same way as ours".[4]

Gertrude was on leave from July to September 1917 and consequently made no mention of the arrival of American troops in the Bar-le-Duc region. She had various sightings of them and of American officials in the months after her return. On 11 May 1918, she noted in her diary, General Pershing was lunching in a private room at the Hôtel du Commerce in Bar, where Gertrude and her colleagues were also eating. To her glee, "[w]e had his car shifted to let the Sunbeam in!!" Later that month, on 20 May, she "nipped out to see Americans pass by on way to Champagne". She too hinted at the racial segregation among the American troops, noting "[l]ots of Americans on the road and blacks" when she was driving in the Verdun area in late November 1918.

For the FWVRC, the American presence in northeastern France extended well beyond the military to encompass the arrival of American Friends. Some had been supporting the FWVRC financially since the outset of its operations, and a few had joined in the Friends' ambulance work in France.[5] The arrival of the American Expeditionary Force in June 1917, however, allowed the American Friends to register their participation in relief work, and from late 1917, many more came to volunteer in what became a joint mission. Their input had a marked effect on the scope of the FWVRC's work especially in France, where they were quite numerous, since they brought not only fresh manpower and funds but new equipment, new ideas and a rejuvenation of spirits. In September 1917, a group of fifty-four American Friends led by Dr James Babbitt (who was to head the medical team at Sermaize) joined the thirteen already in France and were welcomed at the American Red Cross headquarters in Paris. The coming together of the two groups was seen as a way of uniting the "experience and standing" of the British Friends with the "enthusiasm and personnel" of the Americans, as *The Friend* for 28 September 1917 expressed it. Edmund Harvey, head of the FWVRC's work in France, reminded the newly arrived Americans of the particular nature of the work – no preaching, but impressing by example, and they were urged to leave any preconceptions behind. Just as the FWVRC was the formal responsibility of the British Committee of the French Red Cross, so, initially, all civil relief work undertaken by Americans in France, including the Quakers, came under the official charge of the American Red Cross.[6] The activities of the combined group of Friends were supervised jointly by the FWVRC and the American Friends' Service Committee – the London and the Philadelphia committees. Eventually the combined British and American effort in France stood on its own and by the beginning of 1918 was known as the Anglo-American Mission of the Society of Friends.

The American element was in many ways more focused in its preparation and organisation. *The Friend* for 24 August 1917, for example, reported that a group of 102 young men had been in training in the US during August 1917 as part of a reconstruction unit. (Many of them were deployed at the two house-construction worksites in the Jura region of eastern France.) Administration of the mission's work passed largely into American hands, and the impact of a new approach was quickly felt in the various centres. By October 1917, a group of American male workers were installed at Sermaize, some active on the agricultural side, others in stores or the garage. Gertrude found their company and that of the American women workers congenial. Many were in their twenties, and their exuberance and comparative youth cheered Gertrude up, who had sometimes found herself the youngest among her colleagues. She appreciated the American-style fudge parties (whatever they did to their teeth) and liked the "jolly moonlighty songs" some of the Americans sang on the way home from a picnic in May 1918. She was particularly fond of Margery Scattergood, daughter of Henry Scattergood, the American Friends' Commissioner with the American Red Cross Commission for France, who, she told her sister Betty in a letter of 27 January 1918, was teaching her "common vulgar songs. Last night it was re a mother in law who got shut up in a folding bed. I'll save all up for your edification on my return." Two other good friends were G. Cheston Carey, called Ched or Cheddy, and Edward Lownes Webster, known as Webby. Gertrude came to regard them as "special pals". Webby had a motorcycle, on which he drove Gertrude down and up hill in Bar-le-Duc, as on 5 April 1919, "to see how it ran". He and Ched entertained

33 Refugees in the department of the Oise leaving their village

her in Paris in July 1919 where she was waiting to leave for Warsaw and were among those seeing her off at the Gare de l'Est on 1 August 1919.

1918
By spring of 1918, Russia was no longer in the war following the October Revolution of 1917. The Bolshevik decision to withdraw from hostilities freed Germany to concentrate its forces for a final campaign in Western Europe. Aware of the build-up in American troops in France, it hoped to be able to strike before these troops were ready for battle and the balance of strength between it and the Allies shifted in the latter's favour. In a consecutive series of campaigns mounted from north to south along the western front, starting in late March in Flanders and culminating in mid-July along the Marne, it advanced again into the territories it had abandoned a year earlier, again menaced Paris, threatened areas in the northeast of France and forced the evacuation of Rheims. In the end, the gamble failed, not least because of the volume of American military manpower massed against Germany, French and British superiority in tanks, and the exhaustion of its own reserves.

Among the first members of the mission to be affected by the German offensives were those who had been entrusted by the French government from July 1917 with the reconstruction of five villages in the area in the departments of the Aisne, the Somme and the Oise evacuated by German forces in the spring of 1917. Both land and infrastructure had been left devastated by the departing Germans. As the Germans advanced in late March 1918 to retake the sector, these workers had to be evacuated by train along with inhabitants fleeing the region.[7] Gertrude does not mention this setback, but does record, on 6 April, that the offensive had begun again, with Amiens targeted and "badly knocked about", apart from the cathedral. She noted further on 30 March and 3 April 1918 that Châlons-sur-Marne was again coming under bombardment and that FWVRC colleagues in the maternity hospital there were having a bad time. Acquaintances and colleagues who had been in Paris relayed the dangers of life there, as she reported in a diary entry for 31 March 1918: "Apparently another bad long-range bombardment Good Friday [29 March 1918]. St Gervaise shelled while people there – sixty five killed chiefly women and children and very many wounded."

During the first half of the year, Gertrude was busy with driving patients or the mission's doctor, conveying elderly women to the équipe's evacuation centre at Charmont, visiting in the villages around Bar-le-Duc, distributing seeds, dealing with embroidery orders, continuing with accounts and handling household matters in Bar. There she had responsibility for two houses, one in the lower town, the other in the upper. Time, and energy, had to be spent on maintaining her car. From late May 1918, however, as German operations moved into Champagne, the routine of these activities was starting to be broken.

American troops had already passed through Bar-le-Duc on 20 May on their way to fight alongside Allied troops in Champagne.[8] On 27 May, a German offensive to secure and hold passage of the Marne along the section Château-Thierry–Dormans–Epernay was launched (see Map 1). On 30 May, Gertrude reported the news that Soissons and Rheims had been taken. Her entry for 31 May was even gloomier, as she had heard Epernay, Château-Thierry and Châlons were being evacuated. On 3 June she reported that "[t]he Bosch have Chateau Thierry and are after Dormans". A chance meeting on 11 June in Bar with four British men working with unit SSA14 of the Friends' Ambulance Unit yielded more information on the confrontation at Château-Thierry. As Gertrude recorded in her diary for that day, the men had been driving in the retreat on the town, in the course of which two of their colleagues had been killed by a shell. They gave a poor assessment of the Allied and American performance, describing it as a rout. "Château Thierry was a conglomeration of all troops of all nationalities, running up and down in utter ignorance of where they should be and what they should do."[9]

With the advancing enemy came the refugees. For some it meant a second or third evacuation from their homes. From May through to July they came in large numbers from the areas already re-occupied or from the threatened regions around Epernay and later Verdun. Some ended up near Bar-le-Duc, but many were directed further south, to the departments of the Haute-Marne or the Aube and its capital, Troyes. Evacuations and resettlement were largely handled by the military and prefectural authorities, with assistance from the French Red Cross, but the FWVRC also played a part in the evacuations around Epernay. The mission was starting to take steps to find suitable new accommodation further south for its maternity hospital at Châlons-sur-Marne, the hospital at Sermaize and the convalescence home at Bettancourt.[10] The Sermaize équipe, meeting on 31 May 1918, expressed fears of an enforced evacuation – the implication is of itself. Three weeks later, it discussed schemes and listened to an explanation from Gertrude, who outlined three stages of evacuation via Bar-le-Duc to a town about thirty-five km south of Bar.[11]

Gertrude starts to appear as someone speaking with some authority on evacuation within her locality. On 12 June she met Monsieur Piette, the prefect of the Meuse, in Bar-le-Duc to convey a FWVRC offer of assistance with evacuation. This he willingly accepted, as Gertrude noted in her diary for that day, but told her he would only consider "the possibility of evacuating villages N. of the Aire [tributary of the Aisne], and offered us work among the refugees who might come to us here". There was no question of evacuating Bar, he told her, and thought in any case "there would be such a pause that organization of evacuation would be impossible. All the schools here are ready for refugees, and supplied with everything to put them up for 24 hours." In early July the army general commanding the sector ordered the evacuation of a certain number of communes in the department of the Meuse. The prefect asked the FWVRC to help in seeing to the needs of the people displaced.[12] They, or at least some of them, did indeed come from villages north of the Aire, more precisely from the district immediately to the south and southwest of Verdun, a sector where, it may be presumed, enemy probing beyond the front line was anticipated.

Gertrude's diary shows a gap between the end of June and mid-July 1918. It is likely she was assisting in the evacuation of these communes during those weeks. By the time she resumed it, on 13 July, she was in Poissons, a small town some fifty-five km south from Bar-le-

Duc, in the department of Haute-Marne, with several co-workers, as a new équipe. She had driven there and made much use of her car in visiting the Verdun refugees billeted in the district around Poissons. Again, they were grouped by their home villages in small settlements, each with its 'chef', who served as a point of contact. The FWVRC's tasks led in several directions. One was to assist with provisions, and Gertrude returned to Bar on 14 July to load up with cases of milk, beans, chocolate, sago and soap. Rations were distributed to the refugees by "village".[13] Immediately questions arose, as Gertrude recorded on 15 July 1918, on whether the village pigs would be allowed to eat the food remains or whether these should be kept for the following day, as the village heads preferred. The équipe offered to provide pens to contain the hens and to label the hens – "but whose will be the eggs laid?" (How the pigs and the hens materialised is not clear. Had they made the journey with their owners? Or had they been supplied from official or voluntary sources?)

Following the FWVRC's customary practice, the équipe offered small items of equipment to the refugee households: wire-netting for the hen runs, and 'bâches' (probably glass frames). There was concern over the harvesting of crops in the home villages, and the mission's workers tried, unsuccessfully, to devise a scheme whereby they would undertake this job. In the end, the French army carried out the harvesting, to the anger of some of the refugees. The Poissons équipe made home visits, organised recreational activities for the refugees and distributed toys to the children. She visited the local French military command at Wassy to offer FWVRC assistance with the refugees. There she spoke to the officer in charge of billeting, Captain Tilley, who accepted her offer with alacrity. At Wassy she also looked in on the (American) YMCA, where she was given "cold coffee and lemonade".

The war in mid-July remained grave as the Allied struggle to prevent the Germans from penetrating beyond the Marne culminated in Champagne, in the battle of 15-16 July (sometimes known by the French as the Second Battle of the Marne). The Germans succeeded in crossing the river, but were prevented from advancing further. In Poissons, Gertrude noted on 15 July 1918 that "[t]he guns are terrific, bright, you can hear them here". Late the following day, at 11 pm, the Germans launched a bombing raid over the Poissons area. The Allied resistance at the Marne, principally mounted by French and American troops, proved, nonetheless, to be a turning point. Thereafter the Germans were on the retreat.

For the refugees at Poissons, this easing of danger heralded the return home. On 28 July, Gertrude, still in the Poissons area, saw a telegram sent from Clermont-en-Argonne (in the heart of the territory that had been evacuated) with the message: "Annoncez le retour aux evacués". She was relieved at the news, as she confided in her diary, as the refugees had been getting rather difficult.

The move back to the Verdun area took a full week. The journey was undertaken in five stages, often in heavy rain, with four overnight stops for the refugees and those accompanying them. The FWVRC worked closely with the French army, which supplied some rations for the refugees and fed Gertrude and her co-workers, and which laid on lorries to take the refugees to their destinations once they reached the Verdun sector. For the earlier journeys out of the Poissons area, it is possible that the mission's drivers and vehicles provided the means of transport, travelling in convoys. Gertrude mentions ten male colleagues who may have been involved at one time or another in the driving. She herself was making up to seven return journeys a day between stopping points and was acting as an ambulance service for the sick or injured. Others of the refugees returned to their villages by train, accompanied by FWVRC workers, and were met by army lorries.

There were adventures aplenty, recorded in Gertrude's diary for the days 2-11 August 1918. At Poisson, Captain Tilley took an emotional farewell of the équipe. Food distributions had to be arranged with the army and stores handed out. One lot of refugees "had eaten their evening ration at midday!" The staging arrangements were not always satisfactory: she found one convoy "not pleased, as had poor quarters and very little food". The fifth day was difficult, for "the Major de Cantonnement had absolutely no provisions no bread Nor nothink" at the place where the refugees were staying. She returned to Bar-le-Duc and fetched tinned food and a sack of rice from the Bar équipe's reserves and other provisions from a nearby outpost of the American Red Cross, so "we did eat after all". The following day, the "last day of the pilgrimage" went better. They convoys were expected at their halt and were greeted on arrival by the billeting officer. By that point Gertrude was within reach of another FWVRC équipe and could telephone for petrol.

She and her companion Jane Pontefract (Ponty), who travelled with her, had a series of improvised lodgings on the journey, arranged through local doctors or local residents. In one village, lodging was in an empty house – the lawyer's. "It had so many cupboards and passages that Ponty and I decided to sleep together, which we did. We had to fetch our water from three houses up the street and to provide our own candles." At another village, Gertrude's room at the Château "was taken by the Commandant and the troops who arrived for 'repos' at 5.30. two minutes after I left it!" Midday and evening meals were taken with the army. One such experience was a disagreeable one, since their host for each was a "coarse" lieutenant who addressed the "awful old hag" serving them as "Mon ange", and was continually evoking her tender smile. Others were pleasant occasions in the officers' mess. The French military and gendarmerie were generous in their expressions of admiration for what Gertrude was doing, praising her devotion, but embarrassing her. The small, grey-clad figure, who emerged from her car with an air of competence and authority to address them in fluent French, must indeed have intrigued them.

The journey ended for Gertrude at Jubécourt, where the FWVRC had an équipe. From there she continued ferrying returning refugees to their homes and visited several of the villages from which people had been evacuated, to see them settled in again. Then it was back to Bar-le-Duc, where the prefect was laying plans for future evacuations. He asked Gertrude to undertake the direction of a reception centre at Fains, a village just outside Bar, for refugees expected from the St Mihiel district, where an American attack was expected.

The US First Army, by then 1.5 million men strong, did indeed attack St Mihiel a month later (12-16 September), forcing the Germans from a position they had held since September 1914; and the refugees did arrive at Fains. Gertrude, however, was diverted from this assignment by Sophia Fry, her équipe leader, with a request to go to Moulins in central France. "Mon Dieu. What a mix-up, I don't feel as if I could start anything else" was her reaction in her diary on 18 July 1918. She had intended to go on leave in mid-July. Events on the ground, however, and the request from Monsieur Piette to help with the flow of refugees to and from Poissons, overrode those plans. Instead she found herself involved not just in the Poissons adventure, but also in the further project at Moulins. As a disciplined worker she acquiesced and sent a telegram home to alert her family to the change in plan.

Although it is never spelled out, it may be supposed that the French authorities indirectly instigated the visit to Moulins. Jean Grillon, sub-prefect of Verdun from January 1914, had come into contact with the FWVRC and was clearly impressed by its work. It was he who invited the mission in late 1917 to undertake the eventual rehabilitation of districts west of Verdun. Grillon himself was promoted in June 1918 to the post of prefect of the department of the Allier, in the centre of France, of which Moulins is the capital. The department had its share of refugees, and it may be surmised that Grillon thought of suggesting to the Friends that they extend their relief work to his new patch: there is no other likely link between Bar and Moulins. The aim was to provide housing and occupation to refugees in liaison with the local authorities and with other relief organisations in the area. Gertrude was to go with two other workers to establish the proposed schemes, for others to follow up. She foresaw problems – "various knotty points in connection with existing societies there and much to be fixed up with the Prefet" – as she told Agnes in a letter of 16 August 1918. The rush and postponement of leave were also making her on edge.

Her doubts over the Moulins project were confirmed. The first blow was that Grillon, the patron of the scheme, was posted from Moulins after less than two months (19 June to 13 August 1918) in the job. He was moved as prefect to the nearby department of the Indre. Gertrude met him in Moulins on 22 August, the day after she and her colleague Henry Weston arrived. Grillon was looking "very unhappy", she noted in her diary for 22 August 1918, and alone among the officials and relief workers showed enthusiasm for the FWVRC's presence. Gertrude felt it was "difficult to know whether to stay or go". The contretemps with existing societies were quick to materialise. The American Red Cross (ARC) already had two delegates in Moulins, Mr Clark and Miss Wilson, with whom some understanding over the apportioning of areas and types of activity had to be sorted out. Two long interviews with the ARC workers did produce agreement that the FWVRC should have responsibility for ouvroirs and a definite area, but Gertrude still chafed under what she saw as indecision and Mr Clark's wish to "run this show" himself. She, Mr Clark and a new FWVRC worker managed to visit five villages in the vicinity of Montluçon, some 140 km southwest of Moulins, on 1 September, and discussed schemes for housing and employment for refugees. Gertrude drew up a report on their visit for Mr Clark, but it is not clear what became of it.

Her spirits sank very low over the Moulins project. "How I weary of this show. ARC – ARC and brother Clark – and Nothing on my side but scrap, scrap scrap so as to hold end up", she complained to her diary on 31 August 1918. The hot summer temperatures made things more difficult. She had observed in her diary on 23 August 1918 that Mr Clark was "much too much a blower of his trumpet and a preacher", who had opened his first interview "with a sort of Primitive Methodist discourse and said he was there 'to love the refugees, to love and be loved'." Miss Wilson was better company, though

Gertrude did not like her methods, as she noted on 24 August 1918: "She took me round to several houses where there are refugees and played the Fairy Godmother to a T." They had several dinners together, at which they enjoyed sparkling Chablis and old Bordeaux. Gertrude was shown Miss Wilson's new clothes, bought in Paris, and sat in her hotel room on 27 August 1918, polishing her nails – "[a] very pre-war occupation!" And when the young woman heard on 2 September 1918 "that her adopted brother had been killed – and that the hospital where her fiancé was doctor was blown up – no news since", Gertrude commiserated and admired her pluckiness.

By 8 September, Gertrude was back in Paris, and the Moulins scheme seems to have evaporated; certainly Gertrude was no longer involved in it, beyond completing the accounts. The two weeks spent there were not entirely wasted, however. She managed a brief visit to Vichy to meet her friends Charlotte and Anette Dyckoff whom she had known first in Bar-le-Duc. Both sisters were nursing. Back in Moulins she bought herself a watch for 100 francs plus 10 percent tax. "It was a horrible lot to pay, but I think it's worth it as it has beautiful works and luminous dial and unbreakable glass. I shall give it myself out of the Englishwoman cheque", she reasoned in her diary on 27 August 1918, referring to the money she had earned from an article she had contributed to the June 1918 issue of *The Englishwoman*.[14] By 10 September Gertrude was on her way home, and arrived in London on the 11th. News that the assault on St Mihiel was beginning reached her on the 12th, and she commented in her diary that day that she had chosen "a bad time to take leave". On 14 September she noted that St Mihiel had been taken and felt anxious about events in the region: "Am perturbed at being from Bar just now". Thereafter family and holiday occupied her thoughts.

End of the war
When Gertrude returned to Bar-le-Duc on 1 November 1918, the situation was much changed. After re-taking the St Mihiel salient in mid-September, the American First Army was engaging with the Germans in the territory to the east and north of St Mihiel. German resistance was fierce, but the Americans and the French maintained the pressure there with the intention of preventing the enemy from reinforcing positions in what was the bigger target, the Argonne. The double campaign, St Mihiel and the Argonne, had been entrusted to General Pershing by General Foch, by then the Allied supreme commander.[15]

The Americans were ready to launch their first attack on 26

September. The US First Army was to tackle the central section of the Argonne, while French forces were to lend support on either side. They faced the German Fifth Army commanded by General von Gallwitz. The joint aim was to drive the Germans back over the Meuse and to deny them their main lines of railway communication. This aim was accomplished, but at a slower pace than Pershing, for one, had intended. His troops did indeed recapture the two hilltop sites of Vauquois and Montfaucon and the town of Varennes within the first two days, but thereafter the fighting became protracted and bitter. The terrain was heavily forested, with few roads, cut by ravines and frequently waterlogged from the many springs. In some areas, the ground had already been fought over in earlier skirmishes between French and German troops. Fog and incessant rain further hampered the American attack.

The Germans, who had held the area from 1914, had constructed efficient defences along three lines, of which the second was the most important. Their artillery and machine-gun fire inflicted heavy losses on the Americans, who found they had to take out enemy emplacements one by one in order to progress. German use of gas was a further hazard. Gradually, however, the Americans, through force of numbers and repeated attacks, started to wear down German tenacity and to push the enemy back. By mid-October the German second line of defence had fallen. A new American assault was launched on 1 November. By then, the line of fighting was spreading out from the earlier nineteen-km (twelve-mile) front to encompass the east bank of the Meuse. By that time, too, Germany, and the Allies, were preparing for an armistice, and German withdrawals were aiming at a retreat north. On 7 November, French troops entered Sedan, and on 11 November the armistice was signed.

The bitter fighting inflicted damage on the countryside and villages and towns over which it raged and some places suffered considerable destruction in the final days of the war, as the sub-prefect of Verdun, Monsieur Roimarmier, remarked.[16]

A week after her arrival back at post, one of the FWVRC's doctors asked Gertrude to go to Auzéville, west of Verdun, an area where the mission was already installed. Eight hundred refugees at a camp needed attention. At the prefect's request, she had been about to go to the workhouse at Fains, where relief workers from the Bar-le-Duc and Sermaize équipes had been contending for some time with an influx of refugees fleeing from battlefronts, and "civilian prisoners" – people who had been detained or removed to the rear within the former occupied regions. She dropped that job and straightaway drove to

Auzéville on 8 November with her colleague Jane Pontefract. They found three camps, four km apart,[17] "mud up to knees" and no palliasses, but people ill with influenza.[18] The two women spent three days at the Auzéville camps, distributing milk and medicine. The majority of these refugees were sent on in batches to the centre at Fains. Gertrude and Jane drove the sick and elderly to the station. They also celebrated the armistice at Auzéville, on 10 November, by making fudge, "using up all the sugar".

The next phase of action was shaping up. On 14 November, Gertrude encountered crowds of Americans on the road, "[g]oing up to the Rhine". The following day, back at Bar, Wilfrid Shewell, secretary of the FWVRC's French operation, asked her if she would go to La Besace, north of Buzancy, where the mission had been approached for help. "'Yes' says I – Anyone I'd like – You'll have to ax [sic: ask] Sophia [Fry] says I – And Rachel and Jane were chosen to accompany. Six days after the armistice we go 60 kilometres beyond the lines and over the Argonne battlefield – Not bad", was the diary entry for 15 November 1918. In "[a] whirl – a skirl", she and Rachel Alexander packed up seven bales of clothing the next day, got together food and medical stores and sorted out money affairs. On 17 November, she and Rachel left Bar-le-Duc at the same time as a lorry driven by two male colleagues which was carrying the bales and stores intended for La Besace. The women picked up Jane Pontefract at Auzéville.

A dry hard frost made motoring easier. From Bar to Buzancy the road was crowded with lorries and troops. As the FWVRC workers drove north, conditions worsened, as Gertrude notes in a long entry for 17 November 1918.

> From Buzancy to La B[esace] the roads indescribable. A small tank would have been better suited to the holes and gaps. Awful work getting Huppy over it. After picking Jane up at Auzéville, we started off to cross the Front! Anything more desolate and terrible I cannot imagine, land ploughed with shell holes – riddled with dugouts and trenches, dotted with little white crosses. Roads churned up – being roughly repaired by engineers – sticks fir trees, stones for earth. Piles of shells unexploded, 305 – 75, Taubes guns, aeroplanes. And villages – La Neuville [probably Neuvilly] – in ruins Victoire and Clemence's house entirely destroyed Vauquois entirely non-existent Varennes, a skeleton mass of ruins, La Morthomme one vast upturned field of carnage, guns, clothes, shells – mess tins – kitchens, strewn by the wayside all a drab expanse, no sign of green or of life. After Varennes the streets were named in German and German signs were everywhere.

La Besace was in a truly terrible state: "nought but a mud heap and a refuse heap. The streets are furrowed – thick in mud with overflowing streams – and ruts a foot deep. If it rains they will be quite impassable. The houses are ill kept falling to pieces and dust and disease reign." The people gathered there and at two other nearby hamlets did not appear to have all been residents of these villages. The information relayed to the FWVRC in a handwritten note, unsigned and undated (the note was presumably entrusted to Gertrude as the driver and has survived among her papers), indicated that the Germans had brought many of them forcibly to the area from their own villages nearer to Sedan before the German withdrawal. In total around 2,500 people were in need, of whom an estimated 1,800 of all ages had been gathered by the Germans at La Besace. The French military was represented on the ground by a Lieutenant Reichel. The note made it clear that the refugees were being fed by the American military, but lacked sufficient blankets. Sanitary and health conditions were not good. A French doctor was there with some supporting staff. The state of the roads and the paucity of means of transport made it difficult to render assistance. The plea for help pointed out that before the refugees could be taken back to their places of origin, it would be in the general interest if they could receive help from a body as "active and organised" as the Society of Friends.

Gertrude's diary for 17 November expands on the causes of the situation. The people gathered in La Besace

> were forcibly removed from the [their] houses the day before the Germans meant to leave and were taken in camions to la Besace and other villages. Then the Bosch pillaged their houses and left the place. They removed the inhabitants for this purpose, knowing that the next day they were to leave.

Certainly, as the Germans, faced by defeat, prepared to withdraw from the territories they had occupied, they started to clear populations and to destroy bridges, factories, railway lines and public buildings. Looting may also have been one of their intentions. Travelling from La Besace to Sedan on 20 November, Gertrude observed in her diary that "[a]ll the villages [were] deserted and dismal, doors and windows open, all houses pillaged and refuse everywhere." It seems likely too that the people brought to La Besace were intended to serve as human shields in the face of the American advance. Her diary entry for 17 November explains that American troops,

> not knowing that civilians had been placed in La Besace came and

bombarded the village by avion. The curé of Buzaye [*sic*: the village is Bazeilles, near Sedan] came out of the church where they were all hiding and had the white flag put on the steeple. The Americans on seeing it, desisted otherwise a fleet of 150 avions was to have destroyed the village.

(An American account gives a slightly different angle on what is nonetheless, basically the same story; that as the division entered the village, "any large piece of white rag that could be found was floating above the house tops to mark the location of the village so that it would not be shelled.")[19] Despite these efforts, according to Rachel Alexander,[20] some of those in the village were killed or wounded before the white flag went up, and she noted the presence of large numbers of unexploded shells, cartridges and incendiary bombs about the place. The condition of the population was pitiable. Gertrude recorded further in her diary entry of 17 November that

> [a]n average of 3 [possibly 5] of the refugees die every day. They are some of them lodged in barns – open to the wind and cold, some sleep on benches in the church. The misery is awful. Diphtheria, dysentery and grippe – old people and children are the chief sufferers and young women. They have suffered such privation with the Bosch that they cannot withstand disease, and the horror of the last few days has finished them off.

Both wood and nails were lacking to make coffins. Rachel Alexander noted that some bodies were buried in sacks. At a neighbouring village, Gertrude recounted on 21 November 1918, "they took down the cabinets to make coffins" (the cabinets probably referring to toilet sheds).

The FWVRC workers gave out what medicine they had, but were not able to treat diphtheria. On the evening of her arrival, Gertrude drove the lieutenant, "a kind overworked man" who had no vehicle of his own and no means of communication with the wider world, to another village to get an ambulance for a child suffering from the illness. The following day she drove to Sedan in an unsuccessful search for diphtheria serum. As Rachel Alexander admitted, the FWVRC's stocks of clothing were hardly sufficient, but they were distributed, and condensed milk, invalid food and soap were handed out. The American army was supplying rations, and the American Red Cross had its ambulances on the road, but the real need was for the refugees to be returned to their homes. Transport was the problem and that is where the FWVRC may have proved most useful. Gertrude spent much time on the roads conveying sick and elderly people back to where they had been living – and on 21 November 1918, giving a lift to "a Colonel, a captain and a private". It proved difficult to find any department or corps that would accept responsibility for providing army transport for the group at La Besace. Some of the refugees left on foot, pushing their baggage in barrows to reach a main road. In the end, lorries and carts collected many of them, and American ambulances fetched the remaining sick to hospital. By the time the last of the FWVRC team left La Besace on 29 November, the emergency was largely over, and the village appeared to be trying to resume its life. "Several bales of linen have been hauled up from the wells here", Gertrude noted on 28 November. "Hidden from Brother Bosch."

It had been a testing twelve days for the mission's workers. The three women – Gertrude, Rachel and Jane – were accommodated in a "rather dirty room which had been inhabited by German officers for 4 years".[21] Gertrude noted on 22 November that they had had their room washed out – "feels much better". Meals were taken with the French doctor, Dr Chausse, and Lieutenant Reichel at the 'mess' at a small baker's shop, which had housed the local German command until a week before the FWVRC arrived. Gertrude recorded on 21 November 1918 their enjoyment of their company and that of "the old orderly with his drooping moustache and huge bulgy eyes ... To see him opening a jam tin with a German bayonet – is a sight". But the doctor and his orderly and the lieutenant were getting on each other's nerves. By the time the FWVRC équipe left, they were all impatiently awaiting their relief.

The furthermost point north that Gertrude reached on this 1918 trip was Sedan. With some satisfaction she noted in her diary on 18 November that she had driven in there two days after the Germans had left – "I bet I'm the first woman to drive in there". She found the streets "cut up by trenches, the station shattered – the line blown up in six places – and several walls rased [*sic*: razed] to the ground. But Allied flags waved from the houses, the Zouaves defiled on parade, and Generals and big nobs rolled into the Place by the dozen." Even though she saw "lots of sleek and wellfed Generals dining – in style", she could get no lunch for herself and had to beg a bit of bread and meat from a gendarme. A distressing counterpoint to the generals were the "[s]ad and pathetic groups of prisoners ... British French, Russian, Italians, Belgians, all threadbare and thin and hungry." She spoke to "some British who were standing about. They looked awful, dirty clothes, thin, their bones sticking out, and awfully tired ... they had walked in from Germany and didn't know where to find the camions to get along further. So I found out and put them right."

Another group of victims of the war she made contact with was the Bidet family. Alice Bidet was a sister of Madame Bungener, Gertrude's friend in Bar-le-Duc. The Bidets lived in Sedan and had spent the war years under German occupation. Madame Bungener, once she knew Gertrude was going as far as La Besace, seized the opportunity to ask her to write to her sister and above all to visit her to give her family news. Gertrude did not delay in visiting the Bidets on her first trip to Sedan. They were not in good shape and had difficult experiences to relate, as she recorded in her diary on 18 November.

> Mme looks very thin and frail. They are dears, and were awfully glad to see me. They've been exactly 7 days out of 4 years without German officers in the house. They had to leave their doors open day and night, once they had beastly actresses in their salon. Ugh. The Bosch just walked in and took all their brass and copper and mattresses and linen. And the last few days before the Armistice they had to spend in the cave as the Bosch had a mitrailleuse in a trench just outside the house. The two maids had to work for the Bosch one in a mill and the other on the land. At 2 sous an hour.

Her judgement was that "[t]here's no doubt that the Bosch have been brutal and evil".[22] On a subsequent visit, on 20 November, Gertrude and her travelling companion took their own lunch of "sardines etc" and ate it at the Bidets' house. On the evening of the same day, she visited friends of the family living in the Sedan area. Back in Bar-le-Duc on 30 November she was able to give Madame Bungener news of her family.

Sedan in the days immediately after liberation was predictably in some state of disorder. Gertrude had the leather lining of her car and her road map stolen in the city on 21 November. On the other hand, as she noted in her diary entry for 18 November, in her search for diphtheria serum she received "lots of souvenirs" from a sanitary depot, such as gas masks, a flag and a thermos case. And she herself felt free to take down maps and placards from the wall of the station waiting room – "awfully interesting".[23]

The year ended in a more relaxed way for Gertrude, with a visit to Paris in December that combined work, in the form of attendance at a FWVRC meeting on implementing co-operative practices, with shopping and social pleasures. At the end of October 1918, on her way back from leave, she had met her American cousin, Wilmer Powick in Paris (see section on Gertrude and Wilmer in Paris, 1918). The two met up again on this December visit. She also watched Albert and Elisabeth, the King and Queen of the Belgians, as they passed along the rue de Rivoli on a victory visit to the French capital. The boulevards were "gay and crowded" and people were singing and dancing. In her diary for 6 December, she noted: "Paris is delicious just now."

1919: new initiatives
From late 1918, the centre of FWVRC activities moved north from its old base at Sermaize to Grange-le-Comte in the northern part of the department of the Meuse. In this district, the FWVRC, authorised by the French government to take sole charge of rehabilitation and relief work in the area between Verdun and Clermont-en-Argonne (to the west of Verdun), was at last able to contemplate not just the reconstruction it had wished to do from the outset, but also the introduction of more efficient techniques and a co-ordinated approach among the various departments of its French enterprise. Since the autumn of 1917, an agricultural team had been active within the Verdun-Clermont sector, and it was in this area that the mission found the centre it had been seeking.[24] Grange-le-Comte was a large cattle farm that had remained intact through having served as successive divisional headquarters to French, Italian and US troops. Although isolated, it benefited from being near a railway siding. It provided the unified base for personnel, material and stores that the mission had long wished for, able to accommodate up to 100 workers.[25] Eventually it became the headquarters of the FWVRC effort in France and indeed its sole remaining project until the mission withdrew altogether in 1920. From this centre, following the pattern of Sermaize, a much expanded programme of work was directed into the surrounding district, covering house construction, agricultural rehabilitation, livestock breeding, and replenishment of people's household needs through sales of goods. Some of its initiatives reached almost as far north as Sedan. The American contribution was considerable, from the fresh recruits through to providing Grange-le-Comte with electricity, telephones and baths, and access to larger amounts of equipment and vehicles. Many of the latter were procured from the American army,[26] while large quantities of materials similarly became available when Henry Scattergood negotiated the purchase of supplies of tools and stores from several US army engineers' 'dumps'.[27] (The men distributing these materials were called 'dumplings', Gertrude noted in a letter of 11 April 1919.) Alongside these new supplies, huts from the earlier FWVRC bases were recycled to the Verdun area and hospital equipment was reutilised.

In the enlarged vision of the FWVRC's activities there was still a need for close work with refugees, with the difference that this time

34 *7 place de la Fontaine, Bar-le-Duc, August 2012*

they were being helped to return to their homes or resume lives disrupted by occupation. Gertrude continued to visit in the surrounding villages and drove elderly people back to their homes in areas that had lain behind enemy lines during the fighting. "It's very sad sometimes though as their houses are often quite destroyed and they have such a shock on arriving", she told her mother in a letter of 11 April 1919. In the same letter she described a long trip on 8 April covering 250 km (155 miles) that had taken her and Jane Pontefract through the terrain they had crossed a week after the armistice. They were delivering their old cook back home "with 3 rabbits, 3 hens, and all her possessions". Inadvertently they came right across the Argonne front. It remained largely as they had seen it in November 1918: shell-burnt forest, great shell holes, graves and skeletons. On 15 April, she visited Vauquois, where, as she recorded in her diary, she "went right down from the top, gruesome. All the time afraid of treading on bombs or percussion caps. Nothing at all left of the village."

Gertrude was now head of the Bar-le-Duc équipe. As one of the veterans in the French expedition and by dint of seniority, she had moved into that position. In November and December 1918, she was already signing off the monthly reports sent from Bar.[28] She was now responsible for organising the activities of others. New workers were arriving, jobs had to be sorted out, village itineraries planned and relief workers' meetings organised. Among the most pressing tasks was that of arranging accommodation for her team. The old base at 99 boulevard de la Rochelle was still in use, but in early February she had to set about looking for a new place. This she found at 7 place de la Fontaine, in the upper town. Utilities, an adequate toilet ('cabinet') and a telephone had to be arranged, a maid found and furniture arriving from other FWVRC bases received. On 27 February, Gertrude (and others) moved into the new house. From correspondence, it is clear that yet a third apartment was necessary.

The burden of her new responsibilities was clearly heavy at times, as when pipes froze, the gas failed and the 'cabinets' stopped functioning. To her sister Agnes she explained in a letter of 19 March why she had fallen behind in her correspondence:

> It is hectic the way work just comes rattling in, and I tell you, me dear, it's some job being 'chef' of 20 grown women, all with their own fads and fancies, in a society which boasts that it has no blooming rules. It casses my tête pretty well. And I've *three* houses to look after and four women (1 cook 2 housemaids and a general) and a booby of a man o la la.

The "20 grown women", moreover, had to be trained, and humoured. The reason for the presence of such a number is not clear. Some will have been new relief workers, but others may possibly have been working still at the Foyer des alliés, which appears to have continued functioning until the spring of 1919.[29] The style of work in the équipe had changed. The pressing needs of refugees, of exhausted soldiers and anxious relatives, and the danger and disruption of bombing raids had passed, but there was still plenty of work to supervise: embroidery and sewing commissions were still being handed out, and the shop was still catering to refugees, who stocked up on furniture and materials in preparation for their return home.[30] The accounts continued to require attention. There was a constant coming and going of FWVRC colleagues. The atmosphere, however, had lightened. Soldiers were still around, but in Bar they were as likely to be American as French. Gertrude noted an American band playing in the boulevard de la Rochelle on 17 March 1919 – "very exciting". The locally stationed American military looked for relaxation and entertainment and had noticed the group of women attached to the FWVRC. This brought its perplexities for Gertrude as head of the team (and representative of the Society of Friends). She noted on 4 March that two of her colleagues "had 4 American officers in to play bridge. I went for 5 minutes to chaperone." The following day, on 5 March, "the girls" were going to a dance, "but the transport failed. They were all dressed up too. So Freda and Sterling asked their

35 *The 'shop' at Bar-le-Duc, March 1919. From left to right: two unidentified women, Edith Sheffield, Gertrude, Mary Sterling*[31]

American friends, much to my horror. However we just had to go thro' with it." On 14 March, six of the girls were off to yet another dance. Gertrude may have felt the situation was getting a bit out of hand, for on 18 March a meeting of the équipe was held "re dancing". The gatherings continued, nonetheless, and Gertrude, it must be said, enjoyed dancing herself. When an invitation was conveyed to the équipe from a Colonel Cook and his officers to a dinner and dance as their guests on 3 May, she was very happy to go, as is clear from her diary entry for that day.

Throughout April and May 1919, the Bar-le-Duc équipe was working towards its closure. Its clientele was shrinking as refugees returned to their homes. A growing number of case cards were marked 'Left Bar'.[32] At the end of April, the shop had a final jumble sale, the beds loaned to the covered market for the Verdun refugees in 1916 were retrieved, and 99 boulevard de la Rochelle was emptied of its contents. Some of these went to charitable organisations in the town, others were destined for re-cycling. Gertrude was evidently responsible for the sorting and listing and the inventories. On 19 May, she made farewell calls on the mayor of Bar and on French friends, then left number 99, "all bare and deserted" to go on to Grange-le-Comte.

This prolonged activity came at some cost to Gertrude. On 10 March, while out driving, she sprained her wrist while cranking the car. The wrist was put in a sling for nine days and recovered, aided by a leather strap sent by Nancy. On 16 May, however, after her return from her trip to Luxembourg, she ran the head of a nail into her shin. The injury was seen to and kept under observation, but less than a month later it flared up and she was admitted to the mission's hospital, by then at Brizeaux, on 9 June with a swollen leg. The leg was X-rayed, which revealed nothing wrong with the bone, and the hole was then scraped. She remained in hospital for nearly a fortnight.

One bonus of peace was the re-opening of frontiers that had been closed for four years or that could be negotiated only with official authorisation. FWVRC workers began to catch up with their families. Between February and May 1919, Gertrude met up with first Maurice, then Agnes, who had both come to France on work.

From mid-January to mid-March 1919, Maurice was in Paris, where he had been drafted into the British delegation to the Paris Peace Conference by virtue of his war work in the War Trade Intelligence Department. Gertrude was able to go to Paris on 31 January for the weekend. Brother and sister met twice for lunch and visited the sights of central Paris. In letters to his wife (1, 3 and 4 February 1919), Maurice gave Susan news, and views, on Gertrude. He observed that she "flirted with the elderly waiter" at one restaurant, but got the impression that she had "not tasted an omelette or had really good well cooked food for months." He thought she "looked very tired, and I feel rather anxious about her. But we had a good time." Even though she looked "pretty well", he fancied nonetheless that "her experiences have rather pulled her down." Gertrude for her part told her family in a letter of 17-18 February 1919 that she had had "a ripping time" with Maurice, but lamented that her wardrobe had not been more "splendiferous" for him. "I felt plain Jane." They visited the Latin Quarter in Paris and took tea at Maurice's hotel. If Maurice was concerned about Gertrude's health, she on her side thought he looked "as if he'd do with feeding up and fresh air".

Late in April, Gertrude and Agnes managed a fleeting reunion. By March, Agnes was working at Le Havre as an instructor for the YMCA (which had a large base there). On 27 April, a Sunday, the two sisters met at the station at Epernay, had lunch, then took the train to Rheims for the afternoon. Agnes had departed from Le Havre, travelling via Paris. Gertrude had started off at Bar-le-Duc. They had dinner in Rheims, then took the 7.30 train back to Epernay, where they waited together until midnight for Gertrude's train back to Bar. Agnes had to wait on until three in the morning for her train to Paris. As Gertrude told her diary on 27 April 1919, "[s]he came all the way from Havre to see me It was just heaven to be together for a bit."

In early May, Agnes was moved to Cologne, and so the opportunity arose for the two to meet again. Gertrude combined her leave entitlement with driving a sick woman who had been in hospital in Bar-le-Duc back to her village of Beckerich in Luxembourg (an indication of how far some refugees had been forced from their homes in the German invasion). Gertrude left her car at Strassen and continued the journey by train, first to Cologne, then to Bonn, where Agnes was working. The sisters spent five days together before Gertrude took the train back to Strassen to retrieve the Hupmobile. (For a longer account of this journey, see the section on Luxembourg and Germany, May 1919.)

In early 1919, Gertrude acquired a dog, whom she named Peter, maybe after her little nephew, Maurice's and Susan's son. She had been looking for one since November of the year before, she told her mother in a letter of 18 February 1919, to guard her car, from which many things had been taken lately. He was waiting for her on her return from Paris and Troyes on 6 February, "a dear black and white spaniel". She paid 10 francs for him to a Madame Maréchal. Peter accompanied her on car journeys and to meetings (even if he was not always allowed to join the gathering, to his chagrin) and went visiting with her to her French friends' house, slept beside her on occasion, took advantage of her when she was underneath the car to lick her face, visited her in hospital at Brizeaux and went with her to Mouzon: in short, a true companion. On 8 April, Gertrude noted that Peter was ill; the diagnosis was distemper, and he had to be fed "on hot milk and a little red wine (some style for a Quaker dog!)", she told her mother in a letter of 11 April 1919. He soon recovered and a week later was able to eat all the salmon that was being kept for Sophia Fry.

Gertrude enclosed some snapshots of Peter in her letter to her mother. Although the dog is unidentified, a photograph (see Figure 19) of a fairly large spaniel – possibly a springer spaniel – leaning its paws over the front window of a car marked with the Red Cross emblem is probably of Peter; all the more so that a dog of similar appearance features in the hand-painted decoration of an invitation to breakfast from some of her French friends in April 1919 (See Figure 40).

There were other dogs around. Long before she became Peter's owner, she recorded encounters with Zep, Wilfrid Shewell's dog, whom she watched burrowing into foxholes on 18 March 1917 and went swimming with on 14 May 1917 in a woodland pool, when, as

36 Varennes co-operative store, Meuse

she noted in her diary, the two of them "swam slowly and luxuriously round and round the pool – like Alice and the mouse in the pool of tears". And on 30 March 1919, Peter, Tom and Guerrier roamed over the snowy ground with their owners near Brocourt (west of Verdun) against a "lovely grey" sky.

From the beginning of April 1919, Gertrude had been expecting to move to Mouzon, on the river Meuse about sixteen km southeast of Sedan, in the department of the Ardennes. The town had been occupied by German troops throughout the war and for that reason suffered "less devastation and therefore less misery", as she wrote to her mother on 8 (possibly 10) June 1919 from hospital in Brizeaux. The surrounding farms and the bridge over the Meuse had nonetheless been damaged in 1914 and the town "half destroyed in the 1918 retreat".[33] In an earlier letter of 11 April 1919, also to her mother, she explained that "there is a tremendous amount needed there the people stayed till a few days before the armistice – with the Germans – and then had to flee, so they lost all…"

She finally arrived on 24 May 1919, together with Peter, who barked nearly all day at the rooks and crows in the yard. Her task was to set up a store selling the goods and implements, even small livestock, that people might need to re-establish their households. The Society of Friends' policy, which on their own admission veered more towards commerce than charity,[34] was to offer people the goods they needed for purchase at below-cost prices. The British and American committees of the FWVRC allocated £10,000 towards providing goods for sale to the returning inhabitants of the Verdun area.[35] The shop that Gertrude started up, with the help of two assistants, was probably typical of the mission's initiatives in the region.

In the letter from hospital of 8 (or 10) June to her mother, Gertrude described the very varied goods they were expecting to sell: "grindstones and kegs of nails and coils of rope and tarpaulins" as well as food, "material and furniture and clothing and hardware and bedding and agricultural tools – almost everything in fact, all at ¾ price. And all in one room!" She and her assistants made lists of those in the surrounding villages who wanted to buy chickens, hens, rabbits and goats. "I've had to ask for 1500 hens and 1000 rabbits and 50 goats!! Imagine the fun when they all arrive!" The hens required negotiation with the town hall. The opportunity to register for hens was announced. Sorting and pricing the goods that came in was another duty. Heavier work was involved when 'dump' material had to be collected from the station on 27 May, and she applied for assistance with transport and labour. A lorry was supplied and four German prisoners-of-war were assigned to help with transferring the loads from station to shop. (Earlier in the year, the FWVRC had discussed how they would treat POWs and had clearly decided they would use their labour.)

The POWs were also drafted in to help with repairs and repainting of the premises the FWVRC had been offered for its shop and living accommodation (the only drawback seems to have been that they had to be watched at all times). The building allocated was the former Benedictine monastery that abuts the abbey church in the centre of Mouzon. The historian in Gertrude was fascinated.[36] The monastery now houses a retirement home. When Gertrude set up shop, the building was the town hospice, staffed by nuns. She makes no mention of patients, so perhaps it was largely empty. When the German POWs set about decorating the rooms the équipe had been able to secure for their offices, they discovered that an under-layer of wall paper included several sheets of what looked like old hospital documents. "They have on them the date 1808 and have lists of German names, which are I think, entries of the names of patients admitted to the hospital. Which looks as if Mouzon hospital had served as such during the Napoleonic wars", she told her mother.

In the end, Gertrude spent less than a fortnight in Mouzon. On 30 May she went to Dun-sur-Meuse to visit the équipe there. It was

American Decoration Day, and she saw President Wilson and General Pershing twice as they toured the area. (Wilson was in France at that time, where he was participating in the Paris Peace Conference.) A week later, on 6 June, she left for Grange-le-Comte to attend the wedding of her American assistant, Ruth Clark, to a fellow American worker. After a civil wedding, the two "married themselves" in a Quaker ceremony on top of the hill at Clermont-en-Argonne, as she related in her diary on 7 June 1919. Her leg had by then puffed up, and it was decided she should go to hospital for treatment. She returned to Mouzon on 24 June, but it was to "square up papers and accounts" and to hand over to her successor. The Mouzon shop carried on for a while longer, but was expected to close by the end of August.

The Poland project
Once the Society of Friends had had its offer of help in the anti-typhus campaign accepted by the Polish Minister of Public Health in mid-May 1919 (see Chapter Seven on Poland), it set about choosing a suitable team to form the Polish unit. On the advice of its Polish contacts, it was looking for good organisers.[37]

The first mention Gertrude made of going to Poland was in a letter to her parents dated 13 June 1919. She wrote from hospital in Brizeaux to tell them that she had agreed to the Society's request to her to form part of the unit, adding that she had had to reply by return of post. She told them she had read the report made by the Society's "commission" and hoped her parents would think as she did, that she ought to go. The tone of her letter is constrained, hinting at a measure of doubt, even conflict. Her diary entry for 13 June confirmed her acceptance of the Polish invitation, but with the proviso that "I'm not particularly happy about it now I've done the deed".

When news of the Friends' plans for co-operation with the Serbian Relief Fund reached the FWVRC workers in France in the autumn of 1915, Gertrude, as well as a number of others, was keen to go to Serbia. This time, her response to an assignment in a new country was muted, even wearied. Four years of hard work may have left their mark, physically as well as mentally. Among those around her the news of her departure seems to have sparked mixed reactions. Her fellow-worker Ernest Montford had also been invited to join the Polish unit, and the two were able to discuss the idea. Others, however, challenged her decision to go to Poland and engaged her in "fierce argument" over the "needs of France and Poland", as she made clear in her diary entry for 14 June 1919.

On 1 July 1919, Gertrude left the French expedition. She consigned

*37 Médaille de la reconnaissance française,
awarded to Gertrude, 1919*

Peter to the care of her French co-worker Paule Brunot. In Bar-le-Duc, she visited the prefecture for an exit visa, took farewell of French friends and, on 3 July, left Bar. The prefect, Monsieur Piette, was among those seeing her off, to her great satisfaction. At some point she had received a standard letter (undated) of appreciation and thanks for her work with the Anglo-American Mission in France from the Minister of the Liberated Regions. She was also awarded the Médaille de la reconnaissance française, second class (silver), in recognition of her work for refugee relief, an honour she shared with Rachel Alexander, Sophia Fry and Dr Rosslyn Earp.[38]

By 6 July she was back in London and by the 7th back at home.

Chapter Six

Life in the équipe

When Gertrude arrived in Bar-le-Duc in June 1915, she joined a small team of women, her équipe. For at least two and a half years it had its office and living accommodation in a house at 99 boulevard de la Rochelle, where it had the use of premises lent by the owner of the house.[1] "I am in a room surrounded by cupboards," Gertrude wrote of her arrival in her diary on 10 June 1915, "it is rather too much of a passage to quite suit me. Things are rough and ready – but the sanitary arrangements beat Sermaize hollow". The borrowed furniture in the house was scant and simple and there were no carpets. Gertrude hung her clothes on a few pegs and her towel and ties "on a piece of string tied from the window to a nail in the wall". Her portable bath sat in the middle of the room, she told her mother in a letter of 14 June 1915, and the équipe could heat up water for their baths, to the envy of other teams. She shortly moved to another room at the top of the house, but soon afterwards was sharing it with a newly arrived fellow worker, the space divided by a curtain down the middle. Shared sleeping accommodation became the general experience, rooms were re-organised and sleeping arrangements disrupted, and no one could claim a space for their exclusive use. The fluidity of FWVRC activities meant that visiting fellow-workers had to be provided with lunch or, if staying overnight, with makeshift beds. On one such occasion, as her diary recorded on 4 April 1916, Gertrude "bathed in the little nook or cranny between Miss Day's and my curtains – very like a bathing machine." (The preferable arrangement was a bath in front of the dining room stove.)

The équipe had use of the upper floors and of the entrance hall, with a boot store in a closet at one end of the hall.[2] From these premises it gave out relief goods to the many refugees who visited it. It con-

38 View of 99 boulevard de la Rochelle (house with double entrance), August 2012

tinuously asked the owner of the house for use of the rest of the building. She refused, and Gertrude claimed in her diary on 4 May 1916 that she had been playing "a double game" for which she would "now repent her", since she had to yield up her ground floor to accommodate an officers' mess. The courtyard at the back of the house had a stable, but Gertrude makes no mention of horses, only of noisy dogs that had to be coaxed into the stable, as she recorded on 9 July 1915. Across the street was a *familistère*, a 'co-op' shop.

Lighting in the house was provided by town gas, which was also used for cooking and heating water, though the gas supply could fluctuate or be cut off. When it failed, stoves had to be used for both these purposes. Stoves, fired by wood or oil, also provided heating. Sufficient supplies of wood were essential. In the cold months of early 1917, as Gertrude told her mother on 11 February 1917, "[o]ur precious lives were just saved by the arrival of the wood on Friday. It had been expected from S[ermaize] for the last month and we were shiveringly chopping up old cases when it arrived." At 99 boulevard de la Rochelle, the only stove appears to have been in the dining room, and so a colleague's habit of washing clothes and drying them in front of this stove was not appreciated. In the absence of reliable heat, Gertrude found washing and drying her hair was a problem, and she seems to have washed her hair infrequently enough to record the times she was able to.

A series of *femmes de ménage*, recruited from among the refugees, cleaned, shopped and cooked for the équipe, a washer-woman known as 'C'est ça' did the laundry, and Monsieur Godard, who had fled his home with his two daughters, gave his services as a handyman and carpenter, installed in the woodshed. One of his daughters, Madame Philippot, looked after the équipe for a while. Susanne Day praised her ability to produce a three-course meal every night on "two gas-rings, with a tiny hot-plate in between".[3] The FWVRC workers in Bar became attached to their staff and interested themselves in their often traumatic experiences; though Gertrude felt far from kindly towards one of them, known as Dan Leno, who went "off her head" and issued a summons against her for libel in April 1919. She had to appear in court, but 'Dan Leno' did not attend, so the case was dismissed.

The fuel shortages of the winter of 1916-1917 seem to have been predominantly in coal supplies, though wood was clearly also in short supply. In the interests of conserving coal stocks, a prefectural notice of 1 January 1917 renewed earlier restrictions on the consumption of gas and electricity, bearing on illuminated signs, street lighting and restaurant hours.[4] The public baths closed from 2 January through shortage of coal. From 1916 to 1918, daylight saving was imposed.

The sale of meat, fish and vegetables was controlled through restrictions on the opening hours of markets and shops. Bread and sugar were subject to rationing.[5] Conditions deteriorated as the war progressed, and on 1 January 1918, the *Echo de l'Est* announced the sugar ration would be 500 grams per person per month for January and February. By May, as Gertrude reported in her diary on 2 May 1918, it had shrunk to "[o]ne lump a day ... and 300^{gr} of bread". FWVRC colleagues coming to tea a month later brought their own bread and sugar. Close price controls and warnings against speculation issued from the town authorities in August 1917.

Despite such restrictions, the shopping and cooking skills of their femmes de ménage, aided by sufficient funds, meant the équipe fared reasonably well, and Gertrude was even of the view that she was better off in Bar than her family was at home in Britain. In a letter to her father dated 11 February 1918, she explained that "[h]ere we don't have queues, and we get all we want, *if* we pay for it". When members of the équipe were working to regular hours in Bar, they ate lunch and dinner. When they were out visiting or travelling, roadside picnics, snacks in trains and makeshift meals were common.

Life in the équipe had its mishaps, and twice Gertrude and her fellow-workers put themselves at risk. On 4 June 1918, a fire broke out in their accommodation when the gas meter started to burn. It was brought under control by a man who "leapt thro' the window and hammered in the pipes", as Gertrude related in her diary for that day. At that time, such may have been the standard way to cut off the gas supply in an emergency. Eight months later, on 15 February 1919, Gertrude and Jane Pontefract discovered

> [a]t 1.am ... that the carbide in the wash house had been reached by water flooding from the tank. The air was thick with acetylene Made us think as we had our fire on and 400 litres of essence [petrol] in the wash house. The tin was red hot when I picked it up.

Gertrude's nonchalance, as revealed in her diary entry for that day, is amusing, if only in retrospect.

The FWVRC workers were distinguished by their dress, to which the term 'Quaker grey' could be applied. Gertrude referred in her diary of 9 January 1916 to her "Quaker dress". A sense of pride in her uniform is discernible. She stands composedly, even proudly in her full kit – suit, blouse, tie, hat and gloves, with the Quaker star prominent on the left arm of her jacket and a cockade on her hat – for what might be described as her 'official' photograph. For her, the uniform fulfilled its main function of identification with the FWVRC among the public. At a time when so many others wore a uniform announcing a particular role – soldier of whatever army, gendarme, nurse, Red Cross worker – it was essential that the FWVRC made clear its particular contribution. The star served as the FWVRC's 'logo' and appeared on the équipe's visiting cards. It also gave some authority to the wearer, as Gertrude found when travelling. On 26 February 1916, when she and Rachel Alexander found themselves in the midst of soldiers arriving in Bar, an agitated soldier "accosted us – or rather me – because of my badge" in search of bread for his famished men (see Chapter Four above).

Whatever the deficiencies of this uniform in the eyes of some, such as Gertrude's colleague Susanne Day, who found it unflattering, or her cousin Wilmer (see section on Gertrude and Wilmer in Paris), the Society of Friends required its FWVRC workers to wear it when on duty and when they were travelling. In off-duty hours and at the weekend, they were free to wear their own dress. The men's uniform was a military-style tunic and breeches, worn with shirt and tie and a peaked driver's-style hat. Photographs show male workers so attired even when engaged in house-construction or agricultural work. The women sometimes wore smocks (see Gertrude's attire in Figure 17) and in the summer were clearly allowed to wear hats of their choosing. The Society supplied the cloth and recommended that its recruits

39 Photograph of Gertrude Powicke in her FWVRC uniform

order the uniform, if necessary by post, from one London-based manufacturer (this was a source of further irritation to Susanne Day, who would have preferred to have had her uniform made up by her own tailor). In practice, FWVRC workers did get replacement uniforms made locally or purchased them ready made, provided material and colour were suitable. Uniforms wore out and hats became shabby. New purchases and repairs to garments and boots had to be authorised. Sometimes the occasion made it impossible to look presentable. On 28 November 1918, Gertrude drove into Sedan from La Besace, where she and others were engaged in relief work: "We caused much astonishment I saw, our muddy boots and queer get up", she acknowledged in her diary entry for that day.

From top to bottom, the FWVRC in France had to meet the constant demands of official control. The mission was, after all, operating within the zone of the armies and as such was subject first and foremost to military supervision, but also to civilian oversight. At the highest level, sometimes tortuous negotiations took place to secure the basis of the mission's work. (These have already been discussed in Chapter Two) For workers at équipe level a routine of passes and permits had to be observed at all times.

Ruth Fry detailed the documents required for anyone going to France: a passport, a certificate from the French Red Cross, and a carnet d'étranger for those entering the war zone.[6] The passport was essential for travel between France and Britain.[7] Gertrude's was issued on 21 May 1915 for two years only. Unless viséd (stamped with the appropriate authorisation), it was not valid for the zone of the armies. It bears the stamps of various civil and military authorities, both French and British, endorsements and various handwritten observations. From June to September 1915, it was used to record local travel in the region around Bar-le-Duc. The last entries are for 21 September 1916, when she was returning to Bar from leave. Then the passport was cancelled, presumably because all usable pages had been filled up. This first passport is the only one to have survived, and of later ones there is no trace. The Society of Friends issued Gertrude with a letter of introduction to the French authorities, dated 4 June 1915; if she received a certificate from the French Red Cross, it has not survived. The British Committee of the French Red Cross acted as the sponsoring agent for FWVRC workers and was involved in the issuing of a range of documents authorising them to travel.[8]

Once in Bar-le Duc, Gertrude registered with the local civil authorities on 11 June, using her passport as authentication, and received a *permis de séjour*, a residence permit, the same day, complete with photograph, allowing her to remain in Bar throughout the war. A letter to her mother of 14 June 1915 suggests she may have needed one also for Sermaize. The regular creases in the permis de séjour for Bar suggest it was folded down to fit into a pocket or purse. For a bicycle permit she had to apply to the local military authorities, which she did on 2 July 1915 (see Figure 18). Later on she received a special blue permit for driving. Documents had to be renewed frequently, and a good supply of passport-size photographs was essential.

The third vital document was the red carnet d'étranger, issued by the army authorities. Gertrude's carnet still exists, its cover and pages, fifty-nine in all, very worn. Some of the wording on the front cover, including the date of issue, is hardly legible. The carnet records permission for travel from March 1916 onwards within the area of the army zone, to points outside of the zone, such as Paris, and to Britain. As it renews her permis de séjour on 15 March 1916, it may take its validity from that date. (The permis de séjour issued on 11 June 1915 would have fulfilled the same function of sanctioning local laisser-passer and safe-conduct passes.) Up to April 1919 the army was the authorising body for local travel, however short the distance, prescribing minutely the routes that might be taken. The carnet had pages for single-journey safe-conduct travel out of the zone, which also had to receive an army stamp, as did the safe-conduct pass for Gertrude's trip to Beckerich in May 1919. In the zone of the interior, and from mid-1919, the local police or the local prefect signed the authorisations. The most interesting entry in Gertrude's carnet relates to her journey to La Besace immediately after the armistice. A note, pasted into the carnet, warns that the safe-conduct is issued at the holder's risk, that they should beware of unexploded devices, and that excavations were strictly forbidden without the authorisation of the military authorities and required the presence of the nearest gendarmerie.

Permit checks happened anywhere, even when the mission's workers were out on a walk locally. Losing one's carnet was a serious matter, as without it, a safe-conduct pass would not be issued. Any irregularity in one's documentation also caused problems. In July 1916, one of Gertrude's fellow-workers was found to have resided in Bar for over two months without a permis de séjour, but had one for Troyes. Gertrude recorded on 13 July 1916 that she went grovelling "and craving for mercy to the 'autorité militaire compétente de la zone des armées'" on the part of this colleague. "Terrible uproar and much horror expressed by the authorities. However I helped her to draw up a form of apology etc ... so it may blow over."

Restrictions on movement were matched by the usual restrictions on correspondence. From an early point the military authorities demanded caution in what was said or written, and throughout 1915 and 1916, Gertrude had to exercise restraint in her letters. In a letter of 8 May 1916 to Professor Tout, as battle raged around Verdun, she expressed her exasperation in not being able to recount anything, despite the interest of the situation. From 1917, however, this form of control may have relaxed, as she makes no further mention of it.

Working together
With her over four years' attachment (June 1915-July 1919), Gertrude was among the longest-serving members of the FWVRC's French unit. The minimum stay expected in France was six months, although some people came for shorter lengths of time. Volunteers undertook to accept whatever assignment the London Committee offered them. Inside France that might mean transferring from one équipe to another; as the FWVRC's work extended beyond France, the more experienced workers might be asked to move to a new country and a new unit. Some of the men left the FWVRC to work in the Friends' Ambulance Unit. Gertrude, by contrast, stayed remarkably put. She

was drawn towards work in Serbia for a while and put her name forward at the end of 1915 for a transfer, but was told she should remain in Bar-le-Duc, where her work in running the ouvroir was much appreciated. Thus she got to know a succession of fellow-workers who passed through the Bar équipe. Some she was glad to see the back of, others she became attached to, perhaps too much so for her own peace of mind. Eventually she seems to have become hesitant in forming new close friendships, recognising the pain of losing someone she had come to like.

Nonetheless, some fellow-workers did stay for longer periods of time. The three Alexander sisters, Rachel and Jean Alexander and Emily Dinely, were among Gertrude's most constant colleagues between late 1915 and 1919. Rachel was one of the most creative members of the FWVRC. As seen above, she was credited with reviving the handicraft of fine white embroidery in Bar, and played a leading part in the installation of the soldiers' canteen at Bar-le-Duc station in November 1916. Gertrude hinted at business activities on Rachel's part when she wrote to her mother on 8 April 1917 that in November [1916] "Miss Alexander offered me the management of her toy industry in London to work up". The two of them, together with Jane Pontefract, undertook a relief mission to La Besace, north of the former line of fighting, in the days immediately following the armistice. Clearly they were judged capable of working together in difficult circumstances. Gertrude found Rachel "very exasperating" at times with her "high-pitched giggles", but also acknowledged and welcomed her "kind and cheering ways" and her caring attitude towards her younger colleague. It is appropriate that she and Gertrude were among the four awarded the Médaille de la reconnaissance française in 1918-1919. Her sister Emily Dinely had charge of the Maison des parents at Revigny, another of Rachel's initiatives; and the sisters' brother-in-law Bernard Spring Rice also involved himself in relief work in the region over the winter of 1916-1917.

A different and more challenging character was Susanne Day, a talented, if moody, Irishwoman. In Ireland she had been involved in social and suffrage issues and was a playwright and author. She too arrived in Bar in June 1915. Gertrude's feelings towards her were ambivalent. On the one hand she admired her achievements – two "Irish plays" and a book on the poor law, appreciated her knowledge of French literature and modern writing, was entertained by her descriptions of Parisian variety theatres and her contribution of "wonderful" Irish stories to a conversation about magical creatures, and was instructed in the meaning of Irish words, expressions and customs. Against that, the équipe had to endure "black moods lasting for days on end" (Agnes Powicke, memoir, page 69).

Susanne left the Bar team on 20 February 1917, ahead of the production of her new play *Fox and Geese*, which opened on 26 February 1917 at the Abbey Theatre in Dublin. A couple of days before she left, she read the play to Rachel Alexander and Gertrude. Despite this excitement, Gertrude admitted to her sister Nancy in a letter of 18 February 1917 that she was not sorry Susanne was going. Her colleague's legacy was "a mass of accounts", she complained to her mother in a letter of 11 February 1917. "She's going now to write a book. We are all wondering if she will 'take us off' in it." A book did indeed appear the following year, *Round about Bar-le-Duc*, but although sharp in some of its comments, the author dealt affectionately with her former colleagues.

Many male members of the FWVRC faced the urgent need to clear themselves with the military recruiting authorities once the Military Service Act (MSA) of January 1916 came into force in March of that year. The issue of course was that of conscientious objection. In the early months of 1916, conscription and exemption from the requirements of the MSA were much debated within the FWVRC équipes in France, and meetings were convened at Sermaize. On 6 February, Edmund Harvey spoke at La Source about the passage of the bill in the House of Commons. Gertrude observed in her diary on 6 February 1916 that "[t]here was some discussion as to whether the men out here should apply for exception 'en masse' or separately". They did not know how long they would be allowed to stay in France and some felt they ought to return to Britain. To help those who were planning to seek exemption, mock tribunals were held at Sermaize on 18 March, which Gertrude found "very amusing". In the event, a number of men were granted exemption on condition that they continued to work with the FWVRC.

In Bar-le-Duc, Gertrude was working on a day-to-day basis with other women, and her contacts with these male colleagues were less extended. She received much practical help from them over fitting shelves and cupboards, adjusting smoking stoves, working in the garage on her car, or opening up the soldiers' canteen at Bar station. Many of them were specialists in their earlier fields of work and could talk knowledgeably about subjects new to her. Some of them she liked and was not averse to 'playing' with them, to use her term, in social gatherings and to receiving their attentions, but she was mindful of social conventions and would not risk behaviour that might be construed as compromising, such as taking a late-night walk in the woods or accepting a drive with a group of men. Other male colleagues were just that: people to discuss work with. One such was Ernest Montford, Monty. In July 1915 an unspecified misdemeanour by him and another man which appears to have involved a female colleague led to their returning to Britain. Gertrude wrote guardedly about the incident, and it is hard to know what really happened. Ernest then accepted a post with the British Army Sanitation Corps in Egypt. He rejoined the FWVRC in February 1919, when the two met again. Later that same year they both travelled to Poland with the newly formed Polish unit.

A man, or rather, boy for whom she had a soft spot was the seventeen-year-old Gilbert Lamb from Northern Ireland, a Quaker, whom she wrote of as 'the Lambkin'. He had left his mechanical engineering course at Belfast to volunteer in November 1915 as a chauffeur with the FWVRC. He had four sisters and was clearly at ease among women. Gertrude bandaged his chilblained foot, gave him a lesson in waltzing and measured him and another young man for smoking jackets. She liked Gilbert's thoughtful nature and attachment to his family and his willingness to discuss serious subjects. By April 1916 he had left the FWVRC to return to college. Gertrude regretted his departure, but the two kept in touch. In July 1919, he was among those she wrote to at the start of her journey to Poland.

After her decision to break with Harry Pickles, Gertrude does not appear to have sought any further close relationship with a man. Mild flirting was one thing, but any serious commitment was not pursued. Instead, she became the recipient of other people's confidences. She related romances and engagements sometimes in exasperation or surprise, more often in a wry way, as in her diary on 11 February 1916: "Martha and Mr West have got to sharing a muff – oh me – I hope I won't be 'de trop'". Not all of these affairs endured, but several ended in marriage, including that particular relationship.[9]

The FWVRC was the creation of, and under the management of, its Committee, normally meeting regularly in London. All aspects of the mission's work were carefully, if unobtrusively, guided by the London Committee, from policy-making to recruitment, financial accounting, distribution of tasks and, very importantly, the tone and spirit of the work. Members of the London Committee made pastoral visits and tours of inspection to the various équipes, and Gertrude records some of these visits. A chain of responsibility led upwards from the chefs d'équipe at the base through a supervisor at district level, the country secretary and country organiser of relief work to the secretariat in London, backed by regularly submitted reports and meetings convened at all levels. Within that framework, FWVRC personnel were free to organise their own schedule and follow their own initiative, while submitting to the 'line management' of their local organiser. A chef d'équipe was not necessarily a Friend, but above that level, guidance of the country organisation was in the hands of members of the Society. At the same time, the emphasis was on wide participation in discussion of issues of work and organisation and of strategic problems such as conscription and the deployment of workers. General meetings, held less frequently at the FWVRC's headquarters in Paris and from 1919 at Grange-le-Comte, were attended by delegates sent from the various équipes. In 1918 and 1919, Gertrude represented Bar-le-Duc at several such meetings.

Relations with these 'line managers' were generally cordial but inevitably a little formal, since they implied the right to supervision and sometimes criticism. When Gertrude first arrived, Margery Fry headed relief work in France. She was based in Sermaize much of the time, but also stayed in Bar-le-Duc. Gertrude's work at the ouvroir impressed her, and she was anxious that she should not leave it to move elsewhere in the FWVRC network. In March 1916, she undertook to write to Miss Burstall, headmistress at the MHSG, to seek a year's extension of Gertrude's leave of absence, to allow her to remain with the FWVRC.

A new head for the Bar team, Sophia Fry, was in place by March 1916. Although not mentioned by name, she is almost certainly the 'Directrice' with her 'protecting pince-nez' who kept her team hard at work, as described by Susanne Day.[10] She too seems to have appreciated Gertrude's abilities and in May 1917 also asked her to consider staying on further with the FWVRC. Later that year Sophia was given wider responsibility for the organisation of relief work in France. She hoped Gertrude might act as her secretary, but Gertrude had no wish to undertake the "eternal typing and writing of letters", as she confided to her diary on 7 July 1917. In September 1918, Sophia was nominated head of relief in France.

Other British in Bar-le-Duc

During the war, Bar's population was augmented by several hundred foreigners. Many were refugees, such as a large group of Belgians. A smaller number, probably between thirty and forty at any one time, were relief workers and nurses, of whom the FWVRC équipe and the women arriving through the French Red Cross to staff the soldiers' canteen formed the greater part. This was an English-speaking, female contingent of British, Irish, American and Canadian citizens, most of them known to Gertrude at one time or another.[11] Five to six other such women, all described as nurses, appear on the registration lists, but were working elsewhere in the system. The FWVRC team got to know one of them, an Irishwoman, Mary Guiness, active in and round Bar from 1915 to 1918. When Gertrude met her, she was nursing at one of the military hospitals in the 'Pavillon Irlandais', so named after her, according to Gertrude's diary entry for 13 January 1916.

A more mysterious figure was Miss Lendrum, an elderly Scottish lady resident in Bar-le-Duc. How she came to be there is never explained. She knew the French Protestant community in Bar, and was taken up by the temporary influx of her fellow British in the town during the war years. Gertrude and her fellow-workers visited her for tea and lunch in her flat, where the drawing-room was "stately, a mixture of French and Scotch. The dining-room more the latter, with a large portrait of Gladstone on the wall!" is Gertrude's description on 6 August 1915. They were pressed to sing 'Tipperary' and 'God Save the King'. Miss Lendrum had experienced the German assault on Bar in September 1914. The équipe kept an eye on her during the air-raids, which much upset her, and then, in 1919, they left. There is no further indication of what happened to her.

Contacts with the French

Day in, day out the Bar équipe was dealing with the French. Contacts ranged from the official, whether military or civil, through business and work to clients and fellow relief workers. Gertrude writes almost as fully about her French acquaintances and contacts as she does about her British colleagues, and it may be supposed that she spoke French nearly as often as English.

Out in the field, the mission's workers had to co-operate with the army, who were closely involved with refugees when they were either evacuating them or moving them back home. Gertrude wrote about Captain Tilley, who was in charge of billeting at Poissons, and the hard-pressed Lieutenant Reichler, alone in charge at La Besace. She and her fellow-workers took all these encounters in their stride, whether they were being entertained in the officers' mess or were serving hot drinks to the poilus in the canteen at Bar station. The need to renew permits or seek permission to undertake various activities or make journeys meant constant visits wherever they were to a variety of officials at the local military headquarters, the police station, the prefect's office or the town hall. Sometimes officialdom came to them. On 20 December 1915, a "magnificent commandant", whether from the military, gendarmerie or fire brigade is not clear, called at the ouvroir to check that Gertrude had taken sufficient precautions against fire; he pronounced that she had. The local mayor, particularly at village level, was an essential figure in tracking down the refugees accommodated on his patch. He was likely to be an overworked man, responsible for the administration of bread and sugar rationing. Rachel Alexander found the mayor of Ligny, southeast of Bar, selling sausages over his counter, Gertrude noted on 27 April 1918. On 23 May 1918, Gertrude had to drive the wife of the mayor of Sommelonne, southwest of Bar, in search of him. He was busy ploughing and greeted Gertrude with "Ça va?"

In Bar-le-Duc, Gertrude was in contact with the town architect, Charles Boller, who was much involved in initiatives to help the refugees. Another indefatigable mover in these and other projects was Pol Chevalier, who appealed to the *dames anglaises* to join in the various relief organisations. If Monsieur Chevalier was anxious to draw on this extra resource, Gertrude was as ready to solicit his influence in achieving various plans of her own. The relationship must have been amicable, since Monsieur Chevalier commented gallantly about her absence in early November 1918 that Bar without her was like "les feuilles sans la fleur" – leaves without the flower. "Ahem!" was her response in her diary for 15 November 1918. It would seem likely that it was Chevalier who argued the case with the higher French authorities for the award of the silver Médaille de la reconnaissance française to three members of the Bar-le-Duc équipe in 1918 or 1919, including Gertrude.

The requirements of the ouvroir meant that Gertrude had to make frequent purchases at the town's fabric shops, sometimes at the textile mills, to buy the material and sewing goods needed by her women.[12] She got to know these businesses, their owners and their families. Such people formed part of Bar's middle classes. The FWVRC équipe was in turn taken up by elements in this section of society, especially those of a philanthropic disposition, and a coterie of 'ladies' offered their assistance to the ouvroir in such specialised jobs as cutting out the garments (the sewing was left to the 'women'). Gertrude does not mention these social distinctions and may in fact have judged them as entirely normal and in keeping with her experience of life. As a daughter of the manse, she knew the necessity of working with people from differing backgrounds. Thus the 'ladies' received flowers at Christmas 1915 and visiting cards at new year.

Bar-le-Duc's middle and upper classes did not, of course, form a homogenous group. Town office-holders and other leading members of local society, together with their wives, sat on the committees of the various organisations formed to deal with the problems thrown up by the wartime situation. Members of the FWVRC team in Bar joined in their activities. All seem to have agreed that this small band of foreign women in their midst were in the town on good authority, with serious intentions, and, although a religiously inspired group, were not there to proselytise. Moreover, they were of sufficiently good education and social skills to be acceptable acquaintances. The local Catholic clergy for their part were very wary at the arrival of such English 'heretics'. The curé of Sermaize overcame his fears to welcome the intruders as 'good Samaritans',[13] but other priests were not prepared to compromise. Susanne Day, a member of the (Episcopalian) Church of Ireland, wrote amusingly of such encounters.[14] Within this larger circle, a smaller number became close to the FWVRC workers. Gertrude termed them her 'special ladies'. Several, if not many of them were Protestant. Some of them were already friends of Miss Lendrum and thus had the measure of foreign ways. Their practical support and involvement in the équipe's mission, their warmth and kindness and readiness to open their homes to Gertrude and other members of the Bar team, must have offset the stress and demands of the work and offered the women of the équipe something approaching a familiar social life. Gertrude wrote frequently of her French friends. There were the Dyckoff sisters, Charlotte and Anette. Charlotte was a nurse in charge at one of the hospitals in Bar-le-Duc; Anette worked alongside Gertrude at the station canteen and helped at the ouvroir. The Kleinknecht family also welcomed Gertrude while they were living in Bar. Madame Kleinknecht took Gertrude shopping for material for the ouvroir and often invited her to tea, where she appreciated Madame Kleinknecht's accurate use of French and occupied herself with the family's young daughter Elisabeth.[15]

She became particularly close to Madame Dann-Reuther, the widow of a former Protestant pastor in Bar, and to the Bungener household. When Madame Dann-Reuter was in Bar, she often invited Gertrude to lunch, quiet occasions that Gertrude enjoyed, as she noted on 27 April 1916: "we get on well together – tho' we don't talk much". With the Bungeners, she became almost a member of the family, to the point where Madame Bungener referred to herself in a letter of 31 August 1917 as Gertrude's "vieille maman de France". The Bungeners were Protestants. Monsieur Bungener was manager of the Brasseries de la Meuse, one of the town's breweries, and the family lived close to the brewery. On one occasion, in February 1917, he showed Gertrude over the fermenting room with its huge boilers and let her taste the malt. Both husband and wife were active in the public

40 *Breakfast invitation, 21 April 1919*

life of the town and supported the nascent co-operative movement that was developing in Bar-le-Duc under Emile Bugnon (in which the Society of Friends, through Sophia Fry, also took an interest).[16] Madame Bungener was attached to the Red Cross and involved herself during the war in many of the initiatives to relieve the needs of both soldiers and civilians, including the FWVRC's operations. In one of her more unusual roles, she dressed up as St Nicholas, told stories and distributed presents at the équipe's Christmas parties in 1915.

The Bungeners do not appear to have had any children, but had living with them Monsieur Bungener's brother, referred to as Monsieur Adolf, and his wife Wanda, a young woman of rather delicate health. Wanda had been born in Poland, but her family was settled in the Paris area. Gertrude became very attached to both women. Over time they evolved a set of nicknames based on military terms. Thus Madame Bungener was referred to as the E. M. – 'Etat major' or 'general staff', Wanda was 'mon colonel' and Gertrude was known as the general, or 'petit général'. Both Bungener ladies suffered bouts of ill health, which caused Gertrude concern. In turn, when she was in need of attention, she was looked after in the Bungener household. Madame Bungener was a lady of refined, if old-fashioned, tastes. After a visit to Madame Dann-Reuther on 30 August 1915, she drove Gertrude, who was also there, home "in her quaint old landaulette behind an old coachman and an older horse", as Gertrude noted in her diary. Her affection for Gertrude and constant hospitality must have eased life for the younger woman. The Bungener family was probably the source of a charming water-colour invitation to breakfast dated 21 April 1919. In return, Gertrude was able to bring Madame Bungener news of her sister, who had spent the war years in German-occupied Sedan, when she visited the newly liberated city in November 1918.

Personal matters
Communication between FWVRC workers in France and their families and friends was on the whole reliable, thanks to the Army postal services to which they had access. At the outset, the Society of Friends had secured agreement that its workers might use the Army Post Offices,[17] and Gertrude's postal address for correspondence from Britain was A. P. O. S5, B. E. F. Through this route letters and parcels could reach her via Paris, although subject to weight restrictions and sometimes severe delays. Christmas packets and parcels of clothing thus got through, and she was able to send off parcels of magazines and books from Bar-le-Duc to her friend from university days, George Glover, who was serving at the front in France.

Her letters to her family, as might be imagined, centre often on an 'edited' version of what had been happening to her. She was sometimes careful to play down elements of danger, especially when writing to her mother, and to choose entertaining subjects, such as the Christmas parties. But every so often correspondence had to deal with a more intimate matter and in direct fashion. Such a letter might go to one or other of her sisters. In a letter of 28 January 1916 to Agnes she wrote restrainedly about Harry Pickles' marriage on 20 January 1916, but in April-May of the same year she wrote in some distress to her younger sister Nancy and to her mother about the double blow of hearing of Harry's death on 26 April and of the decision by Nancy's fiancé Leonard Harris to break off their engagement.[18] It was a dark moment for the two sisters, and Gertrude was in as much sorrow for Nancy as she was for herself.

Gertrude used the time in Bar to reflect on her career. In her rather protracted decision to leave her post at the high school and by extension the teaching profession, she used her family and Professor T. F. Tout, a family friend and mentor, as a sounding board. Tout (1855-1929) was head of the history department at Manchester University (where Maurice had been his assistant lecturer from 1906 to 1909) and chair of the board of governors of the Manchester High School for Girls. In 1914 (before the outbreak of war), the MHSG had already granted Gertrude a year's leave of absence to teach English in France and thus probably found it easy enough to release her for work with the FWVRC in May 1915. The school kept her on an allowance from June 1915 and held open her pension fund, into which she and they continued to pay. This arrangement was later confirmed by the school governors. She wrote to Professor Tout on 6 December 1915 to acknowledge "this pleasant surprise", which she judged was due to him.[19] The first year's leave of absence was prolonged in May 1916 for a further year after Margery Fry and Gertrude both requested this from Miss Burstall, headmistress of the MHSG, and the board of governors. Miss Burstall pressed Gertrude strongly to return to the MHSG, but agreed to the extension. Her appeal to Gertrude caused the latter some anxiety, as her diary entry for 26 May 1916 reveals: "I am inclined to think it is merely a panic she has got into. But it is rather terrible to deny one's Head!"

A year later Miss Burstall returned to the subject. Gertrude's reply, as she noted over the period 19-25 March 1917 was to say she would return " – unless they don't want me, but ... I should love to stay on here till the end". She outlined this conflict between her own preferences and her sense of obligation to the school in a letter of 24 March 1917 to Professor Tout, making it clear that she particularly relished the "freedom and responsibility" of the work she was doing in Bar and that it gave her far more satisfaction than teaching had. In short, she would rather abandon teaching and try her hand at something else.[20] Tout had supported her appointment to the MHSG, but was now ready to ease her withdrawal from the school. He discussed this development with Miss Burstall, who responded with a note written in her own hand to Gertrude dated 10 April. The tone initially is one of mild exasperation: "If you are going, go now", but the letter ends with good wishes for her new plans and cordial greetings. Thus released through Miss Burstall's firm touch and Professor Tout's understanding attitude from any duty towards the MHSG, she shortly submitted her resignation to the board of governors. Her relations with her old headmistress appear to have remained cordial and the two met at the school on 9 July 1919, when Miss Burstall was "very affectionate and amusing".

Her ideas on what new lines she might tackle had already been forming. She recognised she enjoyed, and was good at, organisation, and the concept of running some kind of business was developing. She discussed some of these ideas with her family in letters, but her closest advisors were those around her in the FWVRC. As early as 7 September 1915, Margery Fry had said she intended to set up a business with Gertrude when they got back to England. "I said 'what in'. She replied that 'it wouldn't much matter, I'd make anything pay' Whereat much laughter, for 'twas a two-edged remark!". In November 1916, her colleague Rachel Alexander had already offered her the management of her toy industry in London to "work up". In spring 1917, Margery Fry, with whom Gertrude had discussed her plans, returned to the idea of her setting up in business, perhaps combining that with a managerial role in overseeing women, and promised to use her influence in the search for new openings. In the meanwhile, the Society of Friends was urging her not to leave her post with them – new initiatives would have to wait.

Finances were a constant preoccupation. In a letter of 16 December 1915, Gertrude asked Agnes to act as her "executor" in the settling of bills, using her own bank account, to which any sums coming to Gertrude would be sent. It was a matter of making small sums stretch a long way. Gertrude was receiving £40 a year from the MHSG, and family and friends sent her money from time to time. The Society of Friends provided food, accommodation and uniforms to those working with the FWVRC, and in-country travel seems to have incurred no charge. Volunteers, however, received no remuneration as such. Personal expenses had to be met, and there were no privileges once back at home. One of Gertrude's ostensible reasons for returning to teaching was to allow her to earn again and contribute to family finances.

Gertrude was not spendthrift, but she seems to have had difficulty in managing the admittedly small budget at her disposal. Twice she notes in her diary that she found herself left very low after doing accounts. For years she had been accustomed to asking for money from those in her family, such as Maurice, who had a decent salary, or to borrowing from them. Some of her instructions to Agnes involve arrangements for repaying debts to Agnes and others. What was left was to be sent to her. Now and again she asks Agnes to send her a cheque or money order, never for more than £5, which she might arrange to have cashed by one of the mission's organisers. On 15 July 1919, she noted in her diary that she had "polished off" all her debts at home. This state of solvency soon gave way, however, to yet more tortuous arrangements with her father, as she was about to leave for Poland, over repayment of £6 she had borrowed from him so as not to be left without any money at all in her new post.

Apart from personal necessities, some of her money went on small luxuries, such as tea in a patisserie in Bar-le-Duc or a jar of the town's famous currant jelly. Other expenditure was on clothes and shoes. In a letter of 3 November 1918, she warned Agnes to expect a bill from Kendals, the Manchester store, for new shoes and a hat. Gertrude put considerable thought into her wardrobe and often commented, if only to her diary, on what she was wearing. There are references to fittings with local French dressmakers, to purchases of hats and to her own making and mending of clothes. Her sister Betty was a skilful dressmaker, and Gertrude commissioned a number of items from her. All these garments came wending their way out to France in parcels, including, one must suppose, the size 3 pair of court shoes available at Kendals for 12 shillings and the third woollen bodice and woollen knicker-linings she had left at home but needed badly in the cold winter of 1915.

One of the arguments used by Miss Burstall in her attempt to persuade Gertrude to return to Manchester was the effect on her health of the work she was doing. "It would be a terrible calamity for you and your family if you stayed too long in France and ruined your health for ever." Professor Tout also mentioned her health, to which she replied, in a letter of 23 May 1916, that she felt she was generally better in France than she had been at home and doubted she would injure herself. Certainly there were bouts of sickness – gastric problems, nausea brought on by the smells and heat of summer visiting in refugee quarters, colds, chills, flu and coughs, sometimes the result of sitting in damp cellars during enemy bombardments and bad enough to put her in the hospital at Sermaize with tonsillitis and a high temperature in March 1917, chilblains in winter time, headaches, neuralgia and sciatica, insect bites that turned to abscesses – and occasional minor injury, such as the bicycle accident in May 1917, a wrist sprain in March 1919, and hospitalisation in June 1919 when she drove a nail into her leg, which then became infected. Remedies relied on what was available: tea and rum, hot lemonade and cinnamon, licorice, mustard baths and a hotwater bottle for chills and colds, thermogene wool for coughs; bicarbonate of soda, rhubarb and soda, arrowroot, castor oil, chlorodyne and brandy for gastric troubles; poultices and boracic compresses for insect bites and abscesses; eau de cologne; and cod-liver oil and malt, Horlicks and Virol for general health. Sickness justified a fire in one's bedroom. A recipe for treating chilblains is contained in her pocket diary for 1915-1916: alum water, glycerine and iodine in equal parts. Mustard and water are also noted. Among procedures and medication that might still be recognised today are X-rays, curetting (of an infected wound) and aspirin. Silver nitrate was used as an antiseptic in hospital. There were, of course, no antibiotics.

Despite her brother Maurice's doubts, the FWVRC fed its workers well enough. Their frequent moving around meant a number of scratch meals, but they rarely went hungry. Gertrude enjoyed good dinners and noted the best ones, culminating in those to which her cousin Wilmer treated her in Paris and the outing with two American colleagues to the Tour d'Argent in Paris in February 1919.

What did tax her were the long hours of work she, and her fellow-workers, regularly put in, particularly when they were combining local duties at the soldiers' canteen or the covered market with their routine FWVRC work. The year 1916 seems to have been heavy, with the rush of refugees arriving from Verdun. Shifts at the Foyer des alliés might last into the small hours. In a letter of 10 December 1916 to Nancy she admitted to being so busy with work from the moment she got up to the moment she fell asleep at night that she found herself with little time for thought. "Besides we go to bed late so often now – I only get in from the Foyer (twice a week) after midnight – there's precious little room for reflexion."

When both Wilmer and Maurice met her in Paris, Wilmer in October 1918 and Maurice in February 1919, each expressed anxiety about her health in letters to their families. Wilmer noted she had a cough, and Maurice thought she looked tired. The cough may have been aggravated by her smoking. She does not seem to have been a heavy smoker, but cigarettes were an indulgence. Several of those around her, both FWVRC colleagues and French friends, also smoked and gave each other presents of cigarettes. That said, hers was not a restful life and it undoubtedly left its mark. When Miss Burstall met her on 9 July, Gertrude struck her as "pale, a little worn, but brave and hopeful as ever".

In her scant free time Gertrude liked to have a book "on hand", even though it might take her a month or so to get through one. She had her favourites, George Meredith, Rupert Brooke and Rudyard Kipling in particular (Meredith accompanied her to Poland), but seems to have been ready to consume almost whatever was available, in English or French. Her diaries and letters note constantly what she is reading. Before the war, she aimed at a substantial reading programme. A list headed 'Books to read' jotted down in her diary for 1915 went from works on and of French literature to suffrage subjects and then to a choice from the English classic canon. Once in France the range grew more varied, taking in further classics – *Crime and Punishment*, Stendhal's *Amitié amoureuse*, Edmond Rostand's *Cyrano de Bergerac*, the Brontë sisters – along with lighter books such as *The Knave of Diamonds*, a "thrilling badly-written novel" that nonetheless cheered her up, as she noted on 5 October 1915, and *Trents Last Case*. Books arrived from friends and family in Britain, some she borrowed from fellow-workers and French acquaintances, and some were probably just lying around.

Gertrude had learned to play the piano and was able to accompany the songs at the Christmas parties in Bar-le-Duc. She appreciated the skills of good performers, and accepted Madame Kleinknecht's invitation to visit her house to play the piano there. She took a camera to France and photographed her "girls" and fellow FWVRC workers. Snapshots of her dog Peter were enclosed with a letter of 11 April 1919 to her family, and one of these, possibly taken by Gertrude, has survived (see Figure 19).

Private thoughts

Gertrude's faith was deep rooted, nurtured by her upbringing and education and reinforced by the pattern of life in a minister's family. She became a Sunday school teacher after she started at university (she was living at home), sang in the church choir and continued to involve herself in local church matters. Her instinct was to seek out ways of expressing her faith through her personal life and work, rather than follow a theoretical approach. This caused her some doubts with the Christian Union (CU), which she joined at university. She was wary of the CU's emphasis on meetings and public speaking and its drive to be a 'converting' force. Nonetheless, she judged it to be a sufficiently good organisation, as she explained to her friend Connie Lansdell in letters of 28 February and 2 May 1909, to serve on the university branch committee, eventually as under-secretary, to attend CU conferences in 1909 and 1910 and even to give an opening address at the November 1910 gathering. By personal predilection and her upbringing in the Nonconformist tradition, she seems to have generally felt at ease with the Quaker ethos.

Travel abroad dictated an open-mindedness about places and forms of worship. On occasion Gertrude would join the Quaker meeting held on Sunday evening at Sermaize. While she was in Bar-le-Duc, she sometimes went to Sunday morning service at the Protestant church – the *temple* – where she saw the Bungeners and Madame Dann-Reuther. At other times she attended mass or evensong at one or other of the Catholic churches in the town or elsewhere. On Easter Sunday 1916, she went to mass at Notre Dame in Bar. The singing pleased her, "everybody seemed so quiet and eager", and she felt "it was good to be there. It is the first time I have felt like that about a Catholic service – usually I feel rather restless and as if I were at some sort of show." A month later, on 28 May 1916, she attended a service for first communion at the same church, to support several of her ouvroir girls who were receiving it. Generally, however, she liked to spend quarter of an hour in the course of the week meditating in one of the churches: "the kingdom of God is within you". The one nearest to the équipe was St Jean, then still a newish church, which she became very fond of. Some of her pleasure in entering a church was aesthetic. Visits to the Protestant temple were not always comfortable. On 29 October 1916, she noted in her diary, it was "like a vault for creeping dampness and chilliness". The music and fine architecture of other places, such as Notre Dame in Paris, captivated her. Her brother Maurice had taught her to appreciate the history and design of old churches. The villages around Bar and Sermaize all had their parish churches, many of them damaged in the fighting, and Gertrude often gave an appraisal of their architecture and state of repair.

From time to time, she would succumb to 'le cafard' – the 'blues' – when feelings of hopelessness, weariness and home-sickness overwhelmed her. Then the diaries, or a letter home, would provide the essential release for emotion. Sometimes the cause was obvious, such as Harry Pickles' death in April 1916. At other times, a piling-up of work, as in the spring of 1919, led to exasperation, or the news that a colleague was about to go on a posting elsewhere left her with a dissatisfied feeling that she was stuck in her job; or she simply regretted that she was not achieving enough. In a letter of 10 December 1916 to Nancy, she tried to analyse the "queer mixture" of life in Bar, where in one sense one felt "so near the things that matter", yet was living "entirely among people 'who [had] lost all these things'" and who had therefore to be assured of the comparative unimportance of those things. The effect was "that one does feel that they don't matter a bit. And yet it is often the stupid everyday 'ennuis' that catch me up." Again she longed for her family, with whom she could let off steam "and be mad dog a bit, but there's no one here who plays with me!...I wish often for my own precious family to indulge me."

But then, in her diaries, as on 23 June 1916, she reproves herself for such thoughts. "Am getting wickedly depressed this week – I am heartily ashamed of my egoism." She sought a remedy in work, or in a brief spell of reflection. On 27 August 1915, she "went into S. Jean for about ¼ hr to get peaceful – it did me good. I just sat and looked up at the windows and arches and gradually got back some sort of perspective. Sometimes I feel desperate and then the only thing to do is to sit down and think myself right" – or else apply herself to hard work.

Chapter Seven

Poland

In the late morning of 4 August 1919, the main party of the FEWVRC Polish Unit arrived at Warsaw station.[1] It had been travelling for three nights and two days on a route that took it from Paris via Switzerland and Austria to Vienna, then on through Czechoslovakia into Poland. A forward group of three led by Dr E. W. Goodall, head of the new unit, had left on 23 July and was already in Warsaw. Places on the train departing from Paris, described variously as the 'diplomatic' or 'military' train, were hard to secure. Dr Goodall told Ruth Fry in a letter of 20 July 1919 that the French Ministry of War controlled seats on the train, but that he had been promised a carriage for the unit, for twenty persons, for 1 August.[2] Tickets do not seem to have been available until the day of departure, and Gertrude noted on 1 August that she went that day to the ministry to collect them. During the second half of July she had visited diplomatic missions, first in London, then in Paris to secure visas for Czechoslovakia, Poland and Switzerland. The Swiss authorities issued the party with three group transit visas. She also received two inoculations against cholera (she had been inoculated against typhus in February 1919). There were arrangements to be made for sending mail to Warsaw, Polish lessons to embark on, meetings with Polish contacts, discussions of the work ahead with colleagues, and farewell outings with American fellow-workers who were returning home to the United States.

For some of the party, including Gertrude, the journey east from Paris was new territory, as they passed through the Swiss mountains and the peaks and meadows of the Austrian Tyrol. Accommodation and catering on the train were comfortable, even luxurious, she told her family in a letter dated 5 August 1919. Gertrude shared a compartment with Dorothy Good, a young American woman of twenty-

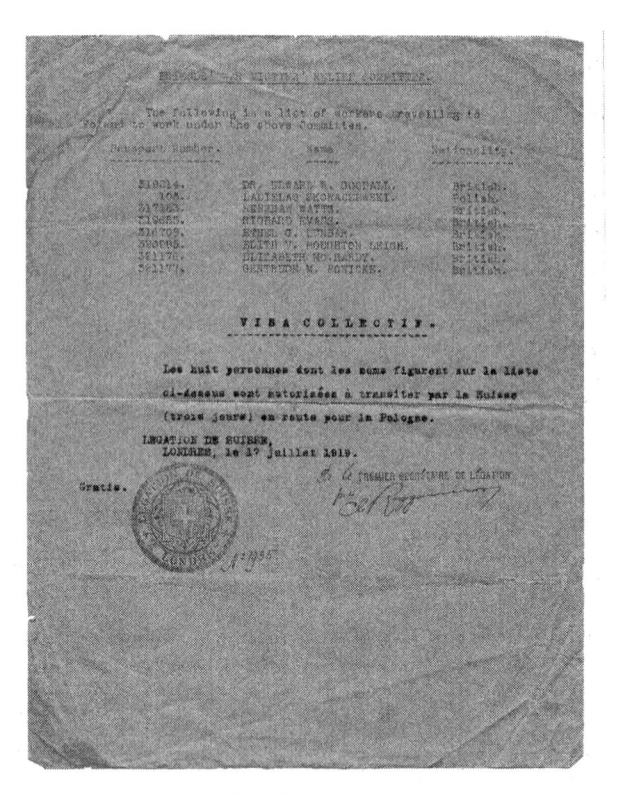

41 *Group transit visa issued by the Swiss Legation, London, on 17 July 1919 for Gertrude and seven of her colleagues*

six (at that point the only American in the unit) and her "protégée and pal", whom she had got to know in France. During the day, the members of the group took in the passing landscape, read, visited each other, made tea with a spirit lamp and played bridge. In Vienna they had an hour's wait, too short a time to visit the city. Gertrude took stock of the people she saw from the train window, their appearance and varied dress.

The party, when it assembled itself on the platform in Warsaw, presented quite a sight as it stood guard over an enormous pile of hand luggage. "It was interesting watching the people go out of the station – they found us even more so, and came and walked right round two or three of us – and brought their friends who did likewise", Gertrude reported to her family in her letter of 5 August. Eventually they moved off in a long crocodile to their hotel, the Angielski – the English Hotel – in central Warsaw.[3] Business started straightaway with a general meeting that same day, at which Gertrude was nominated acting secretary of the unit until the designated secretary, Cuthbert Clayton, arrived (he and two other members of the unit were travelling by ship together with the heavy supplies ordered by the Society of Friends). An executive committee was named, of which Gertrude was also the temporary secretary. For a couple of weeks, she prepared the minutes of both committees in her own hand. A maintenance committee was set up to handle the unit's practical needs. Weekly Polish lessons were arranged.

When it finally came together on 4 August, the Polish unit numbered twenty. Others were expected to join later. In a continuation dated 10 August to the letter she had started on 5 August to her family, Gertrude sketched in the chief characteristics of her fellow-workers for their benefit. Of the three doctors, two, Dr Goodall and Dr Wilson, had had military ranks. Dr Goodall, she understood, was "*the authority on Fevers* – and is, I believe, 'a great find' for the Unit".[4] Although brusque, Gertrude judged he made a good head of unit. The third doctor, Dr Truby King, was already well known by the time he visited Poland for the Society of Friends for his teaching on infant feeding and rearing (see Biographical notes). Gertrude supposed that Nancy had "heard all about him". She described him as "the most absent-minded man I ever met", but still liked him. He does not feature again in her account, so may have visited Poland only in an advisory capacity to the government.

These men had been chosen for their known professional expertise. Other members of the unit were equally experienced in the kind of work the FEWVRC had been undertaking for years. The unit's sanitary inspector was Ernest Montford, who had first joined the FWVRC in 1914. Of the four qualified nurses, Edith Boughton Leigh and Ethel Dunbar had worked in France, Russia or Serbia. Jane Miller was "a crack hand at typhus nursing and delousing" and had been "through the Serbian campaign and in prison with the Scottish Women's Unit". Of the four orderlies, two were already known to Gertrude: Renshaw Watts, an old friend from France, and Richard Reynolds Ball, a Russian speaker, who had served in the French and Russian units. Gertrude described him as an artist, "quite unaware of his own existence I should say", and living "an entirely objective life. He will, he anticipates, be no use at all at the actual job in hand, but he'll be a tremendous help in dealing with the people." Some of the other men she judged to be "mere boys", who should, nonetheless, turn into good workers. "About four of them have been in prison [as conscientious objectors] and seem to be just waking up again to ordinary life." The unit's treasurer, Richard Evans, was "as sombre and serious as he can be, for he was over two years in prison and only came out this spring." (He served three terms of imprisonment and was released in April 1919.)[5] The young woman in charge of equipment (on the maintenance committee) was Kathleen Conry, Irish, aged twenty-eight and familiar with Poland, where she had lived all through the war as a governess in a Polish family. The unit numbered two drivers, of whom Gertrude counted herself as one. The job description she gave her sister Agnes in a letter of 13 July 1919 was to do delousing, drive and investigate openings for relief.

Two Poles had travelled with the unit from Paris: Ladislas Skoraczewski and Jadwiga Białowieska. Their role as interpreters was essential. Jadwiga also gave the unit language lessons. For Gertrude, and probably for many among her fellow-workers, this was a new situation. For the first time in her life, she was not able to communicate directly with most of those around her. She and Dorothy Good, with whom she was sharing a room, worked constantly at their Polish, had equipped themselves with dictionaries (Gertrude's seems to have been a French-Polish one) and practised on the hotel staff. In the shops, French and German could often be deployed, but Polish had to be mastered, even though, she told her family in her letter of 5 August, it "might be compared to a snake in the grass as far as hissings and elusiveness are concerned".

In other crucial respects too the Polish situation was different. Those who had come from France or Britain had left countries in a state of recovery; in Poland, issues of national security, economic rehabilitation and public health were still urgent as the new state fought over its boundaries, tried to reinstate its industry and infrastructure and grappled with a typhus epidemic. Links with the outside world could be unreliable, for supplies as much as for personal communications. Gertrude was optimistic, however, in the same letter:

> The longer I work with the Friends' the more I realize what a unique work it is – and certainly it's [sic] virtues grow with the years and it's [sic] drawbacks don't, tho' they stay. I've never come across any 'body' that seemed to push its way into the heart of things and to lay its finger on real need and the means to allay it with such simplicity. This expedition is going to be a success, I am sure of it, and I can't say how glad I am I've come.

Poland in 1919[6]

The country that the Polish unit had arrived in was not yet a year into its new existence. The reformed, independent republic of Poland was proclaimed on 9 November 1918, bringing to an end well over a century of dismemberment. Three treaties of partition, in 1773, 1793 and 1795, between Prussia, the Austro-Hungarian empire and Russia, had led progressively to the extinction of Polish independence, and during the First World War, Poles were enlisted in all three of the armies fighting on the eastern front. From the onset of war, Germany pushed steadily eastwards across Poland, forcing Russia out until in August 1915, Russia withdrew from Warsaw and left Germany, together with Austria, in eventual control of the whole of Poland, a control largely maintained until November 1918. Great numbers of refugees accompanied the retreating Russian troops, or were forced out by them, and found themselves pushed into the interior of Russia as the Russian imperial authorities tried to disperse them.

Polish organisations in Europe and the United States worked to channel aid to the devastated country and to maintain the Polish cause. They found encouragement in the inclusion of Polish independence in Woodrow Wilson's Fourteen Points (at thirteenth place), which the American president presented on 8 January 1918, and in further Allied statements. On 29 August 1918, the new Bolshevik government in Russia issued a decree repudiating the former imperial secret treaties, which included the partitions of Poland. Austria and Germany, faced by impending defeat, chose to withdraw their troops from the Polish territories they had been occupying, Austria in October 1918, Germany in November. In face of the lack of any outside opposition, the Poles proclaimed their independence and entrusted the country to Marshal Józef Piłsudski as head of state and commander-in-chief. He was joined in January 1919 by the pianist Ignacy Paderewski as prime minister.

The Treaty of Versailles, signed on 28 June 1919, was the culmination of the Paris Peace Conference, which had opened on 18 January 1919. The treaty confirmed Poland's independence, but on the question of the country's borders pronounced only on those with Germany. A Polish request to the peace conference that its pre-partition frontiers, which represented the widest extent of Polish influence in the past, be reinstated, was refused. It took several years and much further fighting for the new state's borders to be settled. Even those along the southwestern frontier with Germany, in Upper Silesia, and the new state of Czechoslovakia, in Cieszyn, provoked armed disputes and had finally to be settled by Allied arbitration. To the southeast of Poland, the region of Eastern Galicia remained a point of conflict. It had formed part of the Austro-Hungarian empire as Austria took the larger share of the southern part of Poland in the partition of 1773. During the First World War the territory was incessantly fought over, and even after the Austrians withdrew, the pattern continued as Poland and Ukraine sought to establish control there. Ukraine's attempt in November 1918 to set up a People's Republic of Western Ukraine, as it termed Eastern Galicia, led Poland to invade the region in the spring of 1919. By the summer it had driven the Ukrainians back over the river Zbrucz (which had formed the eastern boundary of pre-war Austria), had occupied most of Eastern Galicia and formed an administration. The region turned once again into a battleground as Bolshevik, White Russian and Polish troops fought over it from the end of 1919. Only with the Treaty of Riga (18 March 1921) was Poland's sovereignty over Eastern Galicia formally recognised.

That treaty concluded the war of 1920 between Poland and the new Bolshevik government in Russia. Skirmishing and political manoeuvring to determine mastery over the terrain – the Baltic states, Belarussia and Ukraine – that lay between the two had gone on throughout 1919, complicated by the interventions of White Russian armies intent on challenging the Bolsheviks. (The best known White army leader was General Anton Denikin.) In February 1920, Lenin decided to attack Poland. It seems generally agreed that his ultimate aim was to carry Bolshevik doctrines into Germany, which he judged to be in a state of political, social and economic unrest that would make it receptive to a message of revolution. The Red Army pressed on into Polish territory and by mid-August 1920 had reached Warsaw, where it engaged with the Polish forces. In a great reversal of fortunes, the Poles succeeded over ten days of fighting in encircling and routing the Bolshevik troops. Fighting still continued between the two sides until brought to a halt by a ceasefire in mid-October.

Unwelcome doctrines were not the only threat to Western Europe's peace of mind. The spread of typhus was another source of fear. The disease was endemic in Southeast Europe, the Balkans and Russia, and once it took hold in Poland late in 1916, probably entering the country from Galicia, it lasted nearly four years. During 1919 alone, over 230,000 Poles became ill with typhus, of whom nearly 20,000 died.[7] The aim of the Polish authorities was to enforce a sanitary cordon along the eastern border of Poland in order to prevent infection from entering the country from further east and, where the illness had already been brought into Poland, to bring it under control. With an end to the fighting, huge numbers of refugees were returning home to Poland from points east – over 2.5 million refugees and prisoners-of-war crossed into the country in the period 1 November 1918 to 1 January 1920.[8] These numbers threatened the efficacy of the cordon, while the Bolshevik incursions of the spring and summer of 1920

Map 3 *Poland, 1920*

damaged further the measures put in place.

Epidemic typhus is carried by lice, on the body or in clothing, and passed on through bites or exposure to lice droppings. The appalling deprivation in which the Polish refugees lived provided the conditions most likely to encourage the disease: inadequate diet, crowded and insanitary living conditions and a lack of medical attention. Cold weather brought on more cases as people bundled into heavy clothing which was rarely washed or cleaned. Their constant movement as they made their way home or to places of safety carried and spread infection.

The Polish Ministry of Public Health led the campaign to improve the nation's state of health, but in this and in its drive against typhus it accepted a measure of international support. American organisations took the lead in offering assistance. From the spring of 1919, the American Red Cross (ARC) sent personnel, eventually numbering over 150, who distributed clothing and provided medical care and advice on preventive measures.[9] Later that year, Herbert Hoover (see Biographical notes) launched the American-Polish Relief Expedition (APRE) with the backing of both President Wilson and General Pershing, then commander of US Army forces in Europe, in support of the delousing programme. APRE was active for over a year. It used US army volunteers to work in co-ordination with the Polish Ministry of Public Health, especially along the country's eastern border. The necessary equipment had been donated by the US Army or purchased by the Polish government from US Army surplus supplies.[10] (This was not Hoover's first initiative in Poland. As director of the American Relief Administration, which co-ordinated the feeding of children in war-ravaged countries, he organised a supply of food to Poland throughout much of 1919. He visited Poland in August 1919.)

The League of Red Cross Societies also intervened in Poland in support of the anti-typhus campaign; and the Society of Friends sent its unit.

Society of Friends' involvement

As early as 1916, the Society of Friends had corresponded with one of the Polish relief organisations (based in Switzerland) on the needs of Polish refugees in Russia, but it was only after the armistice that it became able to engage in a meaningful way with Polish requirements. The Polish Information Bureau in London served as one point of contact and information, various British officials involved in the rehabilitation of Poland as others. In December 1918, the FWVRC asked Mr R. E. Kimens, Acting British Commissioner in Warsaw, to distribute funds to charities in the city.[11] In April 1919, Colonel S. G. Tallents, chief British delegate to the Allied Commission for the Supply and Relief of Poland, based in Paris (one of the Allied commissions that sprang out of the Paris Peace Conference), relayed an appeal to the FWVRC for help from the Polish Ministry of Public Health. The British government and British Red Cross were prepared to supply drugs and hospital supplies, but medical personnel were also needed. The ARC had already sent workers, but a British contingent was also desired. In response, and in keeping with its accustomed procedure, the Society of Friends sent a delegation to Poland in mid-May 1919 composed of Ruth Fry, J. Thompson Eliott, chair of the London Committee, and Dr Walter Stephens, an American doctor working in France. They were shown typhus hospitals and disinfecting facilities, visited districts in the southwest of the country, and met the Minister of Health and other health officials. The Society's offer of help was accepted by the minister, Dr Janiczewski, in a letter of 14 May 1919 and backed by a memorandum on the unit's conditions and methods of work and the terms of Polish assistance to the project, signed by Dr Rajchman, director of the State Epidemiological Institute. The eventual unit was to work as an integral part of the Ministry of Health's anti-typhus campaign and under its direct control. The delegation made it clear that such control should signify co-ordination rather than dictation and that the Society must be left free.

The area of Poland to which the FEWVRC unit was sent in the days after its arrival was the southwest. Parts of the region had already been visited by the Society of Friends' delegation in May. It was (and still is) a heavily populated and industrialised part of the country. An investigatory trip to three sites undertaken by four members of the unit resulted in the choice of Zawiercie. The other two centres proposed, Będzin and Sosnowiec, were considered too unsettled, and indeed, the surrounding area, known then as Upper Silesia, remained under dispute between Poland and Germany. Fighting broke out in the third week of August 1919 and led to the appearance of 'Silesian' refugees in Zawiercie at the end of the month. Gertrude visited them and found conversation easy, since the refugees were German speaking.

The delay in settling on Zawiercie extended the unit's stay in Warsaw. The time was filled by visits to bathing and disinfecting stations and lectures from Dr Goodall on typhus and the habits of 'The Louse', and in investigating and discussing the needs of the work. The maintenance team stocked up on basic household goods in expectation of rough living quarters. Large quantities of equipment and supplies and cars had been entrusted to a ship going from Britain to Gdansk (Danzig), but it, and the three members of the unit on board, were delayed, first by a strike at Gravesend, then when the vessel, the *Falkefjell*, ran on to a sandbank. The unit was thus left underequipped. Gertrude was able to sort out arrangements for private mail and sent addresses for correspondence to her family: the old A.P.O. address, the FEWVRC address in London, or c/o Captain Crewdson at the Allied Food Mission. Letters would travel by the diplomatic train, which left twice a week. (This service was later curtailed to once a week.) Unit members had to get accustomed to a new currency and new food and styles of eating (Gertrude regretted the large amounts of meat they were offered). Their stay in Warsaw coincided with Herbert Hoover's visit to Poland, and on 13 August Gertrude and Dorothy Good saw the children's procession to greet him and then the man himself, also the prime minister, Paderewski. There was time also for sightseeing in Warsaw and a visit to the theatre and an art gallery.

On 12 August an advance party of four had left for Zawiercie, charged with investigating living and work arrangements. Three days later, on 15 August, the rest of the party joined them. Both groups left Warsaw station for the overnight journey of nearly eight hours laden with both personal luggage and the household equipment. Dr Ryder, the medical officer of health for Zawiercie, was there to meet the main party on the 16th. He had found accommodation for the unit in a former clubhouse known as Resursa (shades of La Source at Sermaize!) built for the employees of one of the town's factories. This "large nicely furnished" place with a garden of grass and trees at the front, "a large and very beautifully decorated dining room, and a huge room upstairs which was meant to be a ball room!", as Gertrude described it all to her family in a letter of 18 August 1919, was very welcome to the unit, which had been expecting to camp out in unfurnished quarters. Instead there were iron bedsteads and straw pillows. There were no bedrooms as such, so the ballroom became the men's dormitory and the women were dispersed around the smaller rooms. The delousing and disinfecting station was elsewhere, on a site shared with the local poorhouse and a small disused hospital that offered space for the unit's stores and car, when they arrived.

In lengthy meetings the unit's executive committee (of which Gertrude was a member) hammered out details of their plan of action with Dr Ryder, and inspected the cleansing station. In the evening of 17 August the unit was introduced to the town leaders at a public meeting. Posters had already announced the unit's arrival, and they soon found crowds of curious children at their heels. Their hosts at the meeting comprised the mayor and his deputy, town councillors and the priest and the rabbi. Eloquent speeches of welcome were made. The following day members of the unit were invited to see the distribution of milk and bread to the schoolchildren, given under Hoover's feeding scheme. "[T]here were 700 of them, all lined up against the walls, with bare-feet, they each had a little mug" was Gertrude's report to her family in the same long letter of 18 August. The milk was, in fact, diluted Nestlé Swiss milk – that is, condensed milk – which the children had to drink on the spot. One of the unit's nurses rebuked the headmaster for diluting it too much, to the man's distress. Gertrude "could have bitten her" – "She surely is a vulgar person."

Zawiercie itself made a poor impression on the foreigners. Ruth Fry described it as "a dreary industrial town of about 37,000 inhabitants", of which textiles had formed the staple production. The cotton factory, however, had closed down through lack of fuel and raw materials, depriving large numbers of people of employment. The town was flanked by two dried-up lakes.[12] In a letter of 22 August 1919 to her family, Gertrude was more forthright:

> Zawiercie is the dirtiest, ugliest and dullest place I've yet seen It reminds me of Stockport slums and hasn't, as far as I can see, a single nice house or road. All the streets are cobbled with stones of all sizes and shapes – terrible to walk over in thin shoes. The gutters are whitewashed, and look so quaint. Most of the houses are of wood, low and often thatched. I've not seen a decent shop yet. But I saw a girl driving geese down the street today. She was keeping them together in a marvellous way. They have long wooden carts, sometimes pulled by oxen – The Jews go about in their black coats and skull caps – they are extremely dirty. Little boys sell cigarettes in the street – 1 mark each!!!

The neglect showed itself with immediate and painful effect on the new arrivals. The party that went to examine the bathing and disinfecting post returned with an abundance of fleas. Gertrude was among them, and soon she was notching up catches of ten, twenty and even thirty at a time, sometimes to a total of sixty. Her fellow-workers were similarly plagued, but she seems to have attracted the greatest numbers. Searching for fleas often required undressing, sometimes up to six times a day. The discomfort kept her awake at night and made it difficult to relax. In a letter of 22 August, she gave up trying to spare her family's sensitivities and wrote bluntly of "louse bug and flea", saying she could not "feel any delicacy on the subject".

The letter ended with a request for Keating's powder or even something stronger.

Among the first tasks were the cleaning and disinfecting of their living and work quarters. Gertrude had been put in charge of distributing ARC clothing and probably for that reason had been asked to sleep at the stores section on the bathing site, in order to keep an eye on the unit's relief goods. (Dorothy Good joined her there.) She included a sketch of the site in a letter to her mother of 18 August 1919, which shows how close they were to the workhouse and all its insect life, harboured in the straw that the inmates had for bedding. Conditions there were worse than anything she had seen in France, even during evacuation work when thousands were sleeping on straw. Both the premises and its occupants were in line for thorough cleansing, and after four fumigations the two women's room seems to have passed muster and the flea problem to have abated. It still remained, however, and a "flea-dance" was instituted which allowed members of the mission "to leap up and down and twist about when too much tried and troubled", as she told her family in a letter of 31 August 1919. She herself covered her bed and pyjamas in Keating's powder.

Some of the unit laid on a tea party and games on the grass on 24 August for their new neighbours in the workhouse. All ages were there, from children to elderly men. Large amounts of food were consumed and the afternoon passed off to general delight.

Nowadays typhus can be treated with appropriate antibiotics. In the absence of adequate treatment, delousing was the only effective way to halt the disease. It was a potentially risky, 'hands-on' task, requiring supervision of the whole process of body-washing, hair-cutting, sterilisation of clothes and disinfection of houses and bedding. Gertrude described the procedure for those needing bathing to her family in a letter of 22 August 1919:

> The first room they go to is a waiting room, the men and women go in alternate batches. The second is where they undress and get their hair treated, then they go into the bathroom. The children are put into the baths and the grown ups go under the hot sprays. You have to be sure they scrub well – they don't do so if they can help it. You go round and flourish the soap – In the meantime their clothes have all gone into the disinfector. Eventually they (the clothes) emerge and are given back to the people who have been waiting in a fourth room. There too they get a final treatment for their hair. Then orf they go.

Clothes were disinfected by being baked (or steam cleansed) at 150 degrees Centigrade for thirty minutes. The delousing regime for

42 Clothing disinfecting, Baranowiczi (now in Belarus)

supervisors was strenuous: an early start for an eight-hour shift, with main meals before and after work.

People seem to have had little choice over being bathed, and reacted some with suspicion, others with apathy. In some places, the FEWVRC workers had noticed, the Polish health officials employed police or militia to enforce disinfecting.[13] The unit was determined to proceed more gently and seems to have succeeded in easing apprehension. Still, as Gertrude conceded to her family in her letter of 22 August, the whole business must have seemed incomprehensible to the children: "They are suddenly surrounded by three or four [workers], who undress them and put them into a thing they've never seen before and scrub them and dress them again and never speak a word they can understand." Those carrying out the cleaning wore bright blue protective clothing, turning them into "blue Goblins". For many of the women workers, the garments were far too big.

House disinfestations required vigorous action, as Ruth Fry observed, quoting one of the workers: the furniture was first moved, and the cleared space then swept and sprayed with carbolic; finally the floor was scrubbed. Beds were pulled to pieces, straw mattresses were burnt and windows were forced open.[14] Understandably, those being put through the cleansing process, whether of their persons or of their

43 One of the FEWVRC unit's nurses, Ethel Dunbar, in disinfecting kit

homes, did not always welcome it, preferring the state they had been in. The delousing programme proceeded nonetheless, and Dr Goodall was able to report on 24 September 1919 that in the month 20 August to 22 September, all the children in the school, to the number of 2,462, had been bathed, their heads cleaned and a bar of soap given to most of them. The team had deloused 1,245 adults, together with their clothing, had disinfected 198 rooms along with the bedding and had inspected just over 3,000 "tenements" or sets of rooms occupied by one family.[15] Some of the equipment the unit employed had been in use earlier by the German occupying forces and was still in good working order.[16] Some was supplied by the Polish authorities and some was acquired by the FEWVRC. The Polish government had bought large amounts of surplus stock from the US Army in France, where the Americans had run a similar delousing programme after the armistice.[17] The necessary hot water was heated by coal, and when supplies of fuel ran out, bathing had to be halted. In Gertrude's sketch map of the Zawiercie site, a smoking engine on wheels appears as the

44 The 'disinfecting engine', Zawiercie delousing post

'Disinfecting engine', possibly intended for cleansing clothes.

The FEWVRC's remit was to work with the Polish anti-typhus campaign, but it hoped from the outset to undertake relief work alongside the disinfection programme. Shortly after the unit's arrival in Zawiercie, the town authorities asked it to help in distributing a large consignment of clothing received from the American Red Cross. Dr Goodall, writing to Ruth Fry on 17 August 1919, anticipated that Gertrude would "soon be at work".[18] She was put in charge of the ARC clothes and a few days later was cleaning and sorting them and handing them out to people as they came out of the bathhouse. The delousing team aimed to give an item of clean underwear to those who had been bathed and sought the London Committee's support in ensuring this, but supplies ran out, partly because some recipients contrived to collect more than one set of clothing by coming twice to be bathed. Gertrude's views to her family in a letter of 31 August 1919 on the ARC garments were disparaging: "such rubbish I never saw – I don't know how people dare send such stuff. But they've proved useful after all, since old rags are better than None, I suppose." (She already knew about the low quality of clothing sent as relief goods from her days in France.)

By the end of August, the unit's own supplies had arrived – or such as had made the journey. A quantity of equipment, stores, food and relief clothing had disappeared en route, estimated at about 8-10 percent of the material sent.[19] Gertrude's understanding was that the stuff had been stolen, probably when the goods were transferred from the ship to the lighters when it ran aground on the sandbank. She expected that this loss of clothing would hinder her work, but nonetheless was making plans, based on her experiences in France, for home visiting (in company with Jadwiga Białowieska), a shop selling clothing and material at half price, and workrooms. The unit's cars had arrived, and she looked forward to making use of them. She was tasked with preparing a report on relief work for the London Committee of the FEWVRC. While the means she proposed may have been drawn from her earlier work, she was aware of the enormity of the problems to which she thought to apply them: the near absolute poverty, the inadequate housing and the lack of employment and of raw materials for industry.

Life in the unit
By the end of August, new workers had joined the unit, bringing it up to its full strength. They included the secretary, Cuthbert Clayton, to whom Gertrude handed over her temporary duties. In the usual way, people chose companions whom they found congenial, particularly for their scant leisure. The pinewoods around Zawiercie provided walks, and also concealed a small restaurant where tea or an omelette in clean surroundings were possible. The "boys" had taken to going there after supper in the evening. There was also the local scene to observe. One thing that struck the members of the unit was the distinction between the rich and poor, with no intermediate class. Dr Goodall, writing to Ruth Fry, had already commented on the way "flaunting wealth" jostled with "repulsive poverty" in Warsaw.[20] Gertrude told her family in an undated letter how they saw "some of the 'uppers' at the club as they stroll in almost every evening to play billiards or bridge and watch the 'Angielski'". The other group that aroused the unit's comment was the Jewish population. The incoming British were not drawn to them, finding them clannish, some speaking only Yiddish, others illiterate, often dirty (and thus high users of the disinfecting baths), and adept at driving a bargain in the market – all the customary unfavourable characteristics attributed to them. Gertrude shared these views, but also found the Jews she met "calm and serene", to the point that she began to think that reports of their oppression were exaggerated. Nevertheless, the Jewish population of Zawiercie formed part of the unit's flock, and she prepared to negotiate with the local rabbi over their welfare.

As with the whole of the FEWVRC relief operation, the Polish unit's work proceeded along structured lines. Among the unit's first actions on arrival was the formation of general, executive and maintenance committees under a head of unit, secretary and treasurer. Membership of the executive committee was on an ex officio basis or by election. This democratic principle was the cause of a challenge to Dr Goodall over his decision to select heads of the delousing and house-disinfecting teams, where some in these teams wanted to elect their own heads. The disagreement blew over, but led Dr Goodall to point out to Ruth Fry that he could not accept the procedure of election as applying to the anti-typhus work to which he had been appointed.[21] Gertrude's diary entry for 25 August 1919 on the issue noted elliptically a "General meeting in Dormitory – Serious – democracy and autocracy Friends v military". Whether for this or for other reasons, both doctors, Goodall and Wilson, decided they would leave the unit after a further month. In fact, the prevalence of typhus in the region was generally diminishing, and the unit was reviewing its work for the winter months.

The Poland unit was conscious that the Society of Friends' offer of help to the Polish government had been accepted on the understanding it would assist in the country's anti-typhus campaign. A change in direction towards relief work, however well thought out, was clearly not something it felt able to make entirely on its own. There was furthermore the question of resources. For such reasons the unit felt it should make contact with the London Committee of the FEWVRC. Gertrude, as the person already heading the relief effort in Zawiercie, was seen as a suitable emissary, and on 2 September the executive committee asked her to go to Paris, then London to convey the unit's concerns and needs, get instructions and urge the dispatch of relief goods. Despite the considerable initiative allowed to country units, the FEWVRC was a centralised organisation in its decision-making and carefully supervised from London, hence the need to refer this particular issue back to the centre; and the unreliable quality of Poland's international communications made it difficult to settle questions by correspondence or telegram. To release a worker for a period of a month may seem extreme, but that is what the unit decided to do. The choice of Gertrude reflects her by then senior status in the unit as someone who could be trusted to put its point of view effectively.

She stayed long enough in Zawiercie to have the town's Charities' Committee confirm the unit's relief scheme and hand the job to her unconditionally, and then she set off on 4 September with Cuthbert Clayton to Warsaw. A seat on the Paris train could not be procured for four days, so she and Cuthbert Clayton took in the entertainments of

Warsaw – the theatre, a concert, an open-air band, the art gallery. Gertrude attended mass at the Russian church. News that Ruth Fry was planning to visit Poland occasioned much debate between Gertrude and Cuthbert Clayton as to whether Gertrude should actually go to London, but on 8 September she left. The journey to Paris was uneventful, with too little time again in Vienna and a beautiful passage through the Tyrol. In Paris there were many colleagues and friends to meet up with, and a long conversation with Ruth Fry and John Hoyland, whom she saw as they were about to take the train in the opposite direction to Warsaw. She hoped she had given them the "right impression". From another FEWVRC worker still in France, Edward West, who had married Eleanor Lindsay, one of the nurses, she learned that they had a nine-week-old baby, Lionel. Accounts and a report on Poland took up more time. She secured a seat for her return journey on the diplomatic train for 2 October. Finally she caught the boat train for Le Havre and crossed on 15 September with the Chinese Consul and "a nice family from Shanghai" (though whether also Chinese is unclear).

The next fortnight was crowded. Straightaway there were meetings with the FEWVRC committees dealing with finance, Russia and Poland, where she had to do a "power of talking". On 18 September she had to address the First General Meeting of the FEWVRC and the Emergency Committee on Poland. Many of the leading Friends involved with the FEWVRC were present, some of whom she knew. The question of the recent disagreement within the Polish unit was brought up, and she tried her best to give only a general outline. At the Polish Committee she was "again" asked to head the unit (there is no record of the first request), but refused. All in all, it was an ordeal she was glad to see over. During her time in London, she stayed at a hostel. She looked for her friend Dolly Lunn, but found she had moved. She was also working on a report for the Save the Children Fund. A development that left her feeling somewhat astonished was the attention she was receiving from the FEWVRC's assistant secretary in London, John Henderson.

Five days with her parents followed at Siddington, in the Cheshire countryside. She was busy with FEWVRC correspondence, but started to work up an idea her father gave her for an article on Zawiercie, to be offered to the *Manchester Guardian*. (She sent the final draft, which has survived, to her father on 7 October from Warsaw, asking him to check it over and telling him that if he thought it not good enough, he should put it aside. There is no sign of its ever having appeared in print.)[22] On 24 September she was summoned back to London, where the London Committee had evidently accepted Gertrude's and the Polish unit's arguments for promoting relief work. She met Ruth Fry, herself back from Poland, where she had had similar discussions with the Polish unit, and set about buying equipment and discussing supplies with the London staff. There was another meeting with the Polish Committee. A rail strike in London and disruption to the bus services made it difficult to get about, but she still managed to see her London cousins. Relations with John Henderson continued to vex her. She noted in her diary on 26 September that a conversation with him gave her "a shock. I am very sorry indeed"; and she felt it was as well that she was leaving on the 29th for Paris. He came to see her off on the boat train. "Am really sorry I can't do as he wants" was her feeling. (There is no further indication of what this was – it may have been no more than permission to write to her.)

Before the journey back to Poland, Gertrude made a rapid visit to old haunts in the Verdun area and to Bar-le-Duc. She saw many friends, but the Bungeners were away from Bar. Then it was back to Paris and a visit to collect the train ticket for Warsaw. She left, as planned, on 2 October. This time she took a carriage tour round some of the Vienna landmarks. Back in Warsaw there was work, presumably report-writing, and reunions with such of her colleagues as were in the capital, but also reflections on how far she was from home.

Gertrude nearly failed to be reunited with the rest of her team in Zawiercie. The night journey on 6 October from Warsaw was crowded and very cold and on arrival at Zawiercie at six the following morning, as she told her family in a letter of 21 October 1919, she had great difficulty in getting out of the train.

> The corridor and doorways were packed two and three deep with soldiers – all sound asleep. I had to walk over them and then they were leaning up against the door and I couldn't possibly open it. So I shook and shook and the seconds went by and the 'ants' [her colleagues] on the platform continued to run, and just as the train was moving on I got out followed by my luggage which described parabolas in the air.

Straightaway she was back at work, with executive committee meetings and a general meeting at which she reported on her trip to London. Ruth Fry and John Hoyland, on their visit to Zawiercie in mid-September, had confirmed the direction the unit's activities should take once the anti-typhus campaign had come to an end: distribution of clothing by gift or sale, child welfare work, food distribution, and provision of occupation and employment.[23] During Gertrude's absence, the relief room had been cleaned and tidied up and the fleas finally subdued. She arranged an office and started on lists of likely recipients of relief together with her colleague Elsie Ferry, who had "come across-country from Serbia" to join the unit in August. She also discussed the relief operation with Dr Ryder. There were certainly many supplicants for clothing. She had already found that her home visits led to her being inundated with requests that she visit other houses. She worked initially from a list the local schoolmaster had given her of the names of the poorest and just had to harden her heart over the rest. A meeting with delegates from the local charities and workmen's guilds (probably the one held on 3 September) resulted in further lists, long and illegible and "in no order at all", as she told her family in a letter of 21 October 1919. She had not enjoyed that meeting, since "none of them wanted the other to have anything!" Two subsequent meetings on 25 and 26 October with delegates from the trades unions had a more productive outcome, since they and Gertrude managed to fix on a form of relief distribution which would satisfy them all and which they accepted unanimously. To assist her, "five Labour Exchange delegates" were to visit for her. "They are nice men," she assured her family in a letter of 29 October 1919, "and we have amusing meetings conducted in German", which the men understood sufficiently well. To her relief, a truckload of bales that had gone missing turned up in the weeks following her return to Zawiercie, so she felt she would have enough for her distributions. But still more clothing and workers were needed, she argued in a report of 5 November 1919, if work in the surrounding villages were to be carried out.[24]

The unit's work was gradually diversifying. The number of delousing cases was falling, and with the agreement of Dr Rajchman, the FEWVRC's link in the Polish Ministry of Public Health, the unit proposed confining itself to typhus contact cases during the winter months, while remaining ready to undertake epidemic work should the need arise. It started to direct its attention to returning soldiers in need of disinfecting. The unit was already training local Poles in the work, and the ministry agreed to pay their wages and supply the necessary equipment.[25] Clothes distribution was proceeding, and plans were made for a child welfare centre. The possibility of developing the unit's work in the war-stricken areas of eastern Poland was under discussion.

The composition of the unit was also changing. The two doctors, Goodall and Wilson, had left by early October, and the unit was without a head. Gertrude, as already seen, declined to assume that position, and a new man, Sydney Wallis, arrived on 28 October 1919 to lead the unit. Ladislas Skoraczewski, who had come out to Poland with the unit as an interpreter, also left, but his place had already been taken by Paul Mikosz. Paul was joined by his brother Stanley. "[T]hey are tailors by trade, Poles by birth, English by upbringing – artistic in temperament" was how Gertrude described them to her family in a letter of 29 October 1919. Paul played the piano and Stanley the violin and both were willing to entertain their fellow-workers. New people took the place of those who had left. One was Lilian Hockey, an expert in child welfare. She had been in Poland for six years and her mastery of Polish made Gertrude "green with envy". Those not so proficient continued with Polish lessons.

A certain amount of 'house-keeping' was put in hand. With the approach of winter, workers who did not have suitable cold-weather clothing had to be kitted out. Gertrude undertook to make the necessary inquiries and also to purchase relief materials and on 22 October set off for Kraków on her first long drive in Poland. She had an urgent reason of her own to get to a large city: to find a dentist. "About eight teeth raging like young lions" was how she described the discomfort she had been enduring for a week to her family. She had noticed twinges in an already filled front tooth soon after her arrival in Warsaw in August. Jadwiga Białowieszka and Renshaw Watts accompanied her, the former to interpret, the latter to receive treatment as well. Kraków lies southeast of Zawiercie. The journey, in the unit's touring car, was appalling, taking over twelve hours. They lost their way, ran out of petrol, had to waste time waiting to refill and, once in Kraków, spent three hours touring the city to find a hotel and some food. The two women had to share a single bed, while Renshaw Watts slept on a bed in the hall. The next morning the dentist, "without ceremony and without gas", extracted Gertrude's front tooth, which had formed an abscess. He proposed an artificial porcelain tooth, to be held in place by gold crowns at the side, thus avoiding having a plate. When she returned the following Monday, by train, for the fitting, she saw, to her dismay, that four of her front teeth were to be cased in gold to provide the support for the porcelain tooth. The resulting glittering smile filled her with shame and distaste, she told her family in her letter of 29 October 1919.

In Kraków, she and Renshaw checked prices for fur gloves and coats, which they judged very expensive. Gertrude already had a sheepskin coat, but the others needed warm garments. The high felt boots the unit wanted could not be found. A good dinner at the Hôtel de Saxe with music and people to watch restored the party's spirits and they filled up with petrol and drove back to Zawiercie without harm the next day through attractive countryside and villages. The sight of a woman driver seems to have caused some stir. On her second visit to Kraków, Gertrude bought coats and made a tour of the city and its treasures. Later, back in Zawiercie, she and Dorothy Good were fitted for winter boots.

Reports, executive meetings, accounts – again – and work on the car were all demands on her time, but there was enough leisure to play bridge in the evening, attend a concert and teach "the boys" to dance, to the accompaniment of the Mikosz brothers. On 11 October, she went to a dance given by the Silesian officers billeted at Resursa, the clubhouse where some of the unit still slept. A special invitation had been extended to the unit, and as Gertrude was one of the few women left that weekend (the others had gone to Kraków), she felt obliged to represent her group. She was chaperoned by three of her male colleagues, none of whom danced and sat like "solid rocks", though much importuned by the young women there. The evening was enjoyable, if strange.

During the early part of November, Richard Reynolds Ball had travelled to Eastern Galicia on five days' leave and reported to the unit on his return on the terrible conditions there. The executive committee, meeting on 7 November, made some immediate decisions: Sydney Wallis, Gertrude and Ball were to leave that same night to view conditions especially in the Lemberg (Lwów; Lviv) district of the former Polish-Ukrainian front.[26] The group was also to visit Wilno in the northeastern part of the country (now Vilnius, Lithuania). Gertrude noted in her diary on 7 November that Ethel Dunbar and Edith Boughton Leigh, two of the nurses, wanted to go straight to Lemberg. Gertrude briefed her colleagues working on relief and packed. The whole unit entertained the party of five that evening and then they boarded the night train to Warsaw.

Eastern Galicia
Despite their speedy departure from Zawiercie, the party bound for Eastern Galicia and their nursing colleagues did not move on again for about a week. In Warsaw, the Eastern Galicia group obtained a letter of introduction from Dr Rajchman to the officer for health for Galicia, and liaised with Colonel A. J. Chesler, the American Red Cross Commissioner to Poland, from whom they heard about conditions in the region. Chesler offered them accommodation on the ARC special rail coach that was to take one of his officers, Major Gruver, to the

*45 Opera programme for performance of The Tales of Hoffmann,
12 November 1919, Warsaw*

area on business. From Ladislas Skoraczewski, who was in Warsaw, they learned much about the political history of Eastern Galicia and Ukraine. They shopped for warm clothing and they went to the opera. Gertrude managed three visits, once to *The Tales of Hoffmann*. She also visited the art gallery. The two nurses had applied to the ARC to work in one of their hospitals further north and were eventually both accepted. They left Warsaw a few days later.

Finally, on 13 November, Gertrude, Sydney Wallis and Reynolds Ball left Warsaw on a night train. Their route lay through Polish-held territory, much of it recaptured from the Ukrainians during the summer of 1919. Travel was by rail or car. Lwów was their first stop.[27] From there they went to Brzezany, where they received authorisation to visit places in the war zone and a promise of cars for subsequent stages of their journey. The next city they visited was Tarnopol, where they stayed for a couple of days. From Tarnopol they took the train south to Borszczów and from there travelled by car to Kamieniec Podolski, on the Polish-Ukrainian border and the furthermost point in their tour. They then retraced their route back to Borszczów and from there by train to Tarnopol again, from where they toured some of the surrounding villages. On 1 December they left Tarnopol for

Lwów, spent the 2nd in Lwów, and returned overnight to Warsaw on 3 December.

Their purpose throughout was to meet local officials both military and civilian who were in charge of health matters, especially antityphus measures, and to inspect the hospital and disinfecting facilities available. They looked in particular for buildings that the unit might conceivably use for its work and noted the state of the local infrastructure and transport links. They even envisaged the possibilities for future rehabilitation of housing and agriculture. Everywhere, as Sydney Wallis's report makes clear, they met instances of appalling hospital conditions, low standards of hygiene and prevention, lack of coal, shortages of funds and supplies, and overwhelmed officials. The emphasis on treating military cases of typhus meant that civilians were poorly served. The area had been fought over incessantly since the outbreak of the First World War. The uncertain political conditions and continuing fighting in the region forced influxes of Ukrainians, mostly disbanded soldiers escaping Russian White army troops, into what by that time was Poland. The JUR, the Polish agency for resettling refugees, prisoners and workmen, was active in this border region. However, when Gertrude and Reynolds Ball visited Podwoloczyska, east of Tarnopol, they found that no provision was being made for the hundreds of refugees and prisoners-of-war who were streaming in from Ukraine and who ended up at the railway station. They secured the use of rooms at the station and left 1,000 Polish marks (equal to about fifty shillings in sterling currency of the time), with a promise to send further funds through the local military to provide heating, food and clean straw and to pay for the services of local women to look after the refugees, until the JUR was able to take over care of these people. The majority of officials they met were Polish, but they encountered a few Westerners. The ARC had a base in Lwów, and in Tarnopol they met Colonel Register, a member of the American-Polish Relief Expedition, who was advising one of the JUR refugee camps. (He contracted typhus in the weeks following their visit and died in December 1919.)

The FEWVRC party had agreed to keep separate accounts of the journey, to write separate reports on their return and then to compile a joint report. Gertrude's handwritten notes have survived in addition to her personal diary and letters. Ball lost his principal notebook on the return journey, but from papers and a second notebook, the third member of the group, Wallis, was able to extract a certain amount of information. The final, typed report on the journey is based on Wallis's notes, augmented by those left by Gertrude and Reynolds

Ball.[28] His report concluded that the FEWVRC unit should offer its services in Tarnopol.

Gertrude's impassioned account in a long letter of 1 December 1919 to her family must take the place of her formal report. (Extracts from this letter are in the section covering the Visit to Eastern Galicia.) Her other three letters from the trip, dated 14, 17 and 23 November 1919, give the flavour of their journey. Until Borszczów, south of Tarnopol, they benefited from the American coach, which was attached to an ordinary train. Thus they slept in first-class compartments with "fat woolly blankets" and had a stove in the corridor on which they cooked their meals. Supplies were largely coffee, dried goods, tinned meat and fish, "hard-tack" (i.e. ship's biscuits) and equally hard bread until they were able to buy fresh food along the way. Gertrude, their American travelling companion, Major Gruver, and the Polish staff were all content with the coffee, sardines and bully beef, but the two FEWVRC men were vegetarians. Gertrude foresaw a difficult time for them and rejoiced when she got hold of ten eggs. Perhaps inevitably, she found herself cast in the role of cook and domestic carer for the three men and complained to her family that

> I'm blest if I can get everything hot at the same time – for the Major likes coffee for breakfast, Brother Ball likes tea – and porridge. All the men want hot water for shaving and the Pole lies in wait for all the hot water he can get to wash up with.

Her compartment seems to have acted as 'home' for Wallis and Ball and to have been constantly filled with belongings, papers, people and smoke. The enforced proximity started to grate. Sydney Wallis, "slow and stolid", annoyed her by throwing nut shells on the floor of her compartment. He brought her collars to wash and trousers to mend. Gertrude surmised that "his wife doesn't train him to do his own little odd jobs". Reynolds Ball, on the other hand, though he had no notion of how to sew or wash, made an attempt to do so, and Gertrude would find him "with his tongue hanging out of his mouth" as he struggled. She had always admired him for his goodness and lack of worldly concern. He had arrived at the train in Warsaw with his belongings thrown into his sleeping bag, "looking rather like Santa Claus". Major Gruver, a former war correspondent and doctor, was welcoming to them. He entertained them unwittingly by working himself up over a point and discoursing on it "as if he were a Roman Senator" and by unavailing attempts to discipline the Poles.

The excited departure from Warsaw gave way to irritation and weariness as progress slowed and sometimes halted. Their carriage was frequently unhooked from the engine hauling it, which was then diverted to other tasks and returned to them hours later. When the engine was detached, there was no heating in the coach apart from the stove and that smoked. An oil lamp and candles provided lighting. The bitter cold left them chilled: "It's all a picnic and very jolly, except now and again when an interval of black despair suddenly reigns", was Gertrude's comment. She had not brought enough clothes with her, and there were no means of washing them. To temper the cold she put her "doormat" around her shoulders, bought in lieu of a real fur collar. When she and her fellow-workers had to leave the special coach and use Polish trains, both travel and accommodation became much rougher.

Their visits away from the special coach were welcome. From 15 to 19 November, though still sleeping in the train, they visited Lwów, where a hot bath at the ARC centre was much appreciated. Gertrude and Reynolds Ball walked out of the city:

> The light was wonderful, and turned all the houses and churches pink and yellow. We climbed right up till we got a view right across Lwów – which lay in the hollow – with little hills all round running down almost into the heart of the town. The roofs were all white with snow and the ledges on the domes and spires were outlined with it. I never had such a complete view of a town, or saw anything quite so finished and beautiful. Little spiral columns of smoke were rising here and there – and the cathedral with its rather grotesque tower stood out almost golden in the light.

Beyond Tarnopol and down to the Polish border the countryside was often beautiful, with old watermills and villages that were more attractive than those around Zawiercie. Homesteads were built within a stockade, with whitewashed or colour-washed buildings and maize stacks filled with corn cobs. The houses contained fine oak chests, spinning wheels and looms. In one village they were invited into a house where a wedding was under way, to watch a dance and listen to the music. When they left, their host told them: "Allright, I spik English". Gertrude was very struck by Kamieniec Podolski, on the Polish-Ukrainian border, approached by ramparts and towers "built by the Turkish prisoners in the thirteenth century. These ramparts go right round the town. Then when you get inside you see deep ravines and the river winding beneath the viaducts."

An unexpected contact was the driver of one of their cars. As a Silesian, he had fought with the Germans, had been taken prisoner and spent time in British camps in northern France. But their most

46 Menu for dinner offered on 24 November 1919 by the French military medical unit, Borszczów (now in Ukraine)

extraordinary encounter was on 24 November with a detachment of French officers stationed at Borszczów as part of the French military mission to Poland.[29] The Polish military doctor for the area invited the British travellers to his "popotte" – mess – which consisted of eight or nine French officers, "all of them about as French as they could be and making valiant efforts to make their good spirits and wit and humour flourish in this barren wilderness." The Frenchmen described themselves as the health unit attached to a tactical group. The visitors were served "a most wonderful meal" of about six courses, to which Wallis and Reynolds Ball, as vegetarians, could not do justice, to their hosts' dismay. Gertrude named one of the officers as Gaston Roux, an illustrator, who designed menu cards for the occasion, signing them 'GB'.[30] Each guest kept one as a souvenir of 'France in Poland'. The names inscribed on the reverse do not include that of Charles de Gaulle, who was in Poland at that time, but was not attached to the Borszczów medical unit.

Chapter Eight

The final weeks

The two FEWVRC expeditions that had set out in the second week of November both ended disastrously. From Białystok came news that Ethel Dunbar and Edith Boughton Leigh had both contracted typhus in the early part of December through nursing Russian prisoners-of-war. They were cared for by American Red Cross personnel and their colleague Elizabeth McHardy.[1] Both survived and left the Poland unit in mid-January 1920. Of the East Galician investigatory team, Gertrude and Reynolds Ball became unwell shortly after their return to Warsaw on 3 December 1919. Confined to bed in the Angielski hotel, they were both first diagnosed with influenza (typhus can go unrecognised initially or be attributed to other causes).[2] Over the weekend 6-7 December, as they showed no improvement and their temperatures remained high, Cuthbert Clayton and Ernest Montford of the Poland unit, who were both in Warsaw, asked for a further examination and contacted the ARC to request a night nurse. She and Ernest Montford sat up the night of the 7th with the two patients. The following day, Gertrude and Reynolds Ball were transferred to private rooms at the St Stanisław hospital in Warsaw on the recommendation of Dr Rajchman. There the suspicion of typhus was confirmed on the 8th. Cuthbert Clayton returned to Zawiercie to summon the unit's newly arrived doctor, Dr Margaret Merrick, to Warsaw. Gertrude's friend and colleague, Dorothy Good, accompanied Dr Merrick, and the two women arrived on 12 December. Dr Merrick expressed satisfaction with the state of the hospital and the care the patients were receiving. She tended both Gertrude and Reynolds Ball, and Cuthbert Clayton and Ernest Montford continued to visit them both.

Typhus can now be treated with antibiotics to reduce the fever. A century ago, it had to run its course to climax in a 'crisis', after which spontaneous recovery could be hoped for. This did not happen for either patient. Reynolds Ball appears to have been more severely affected and became delirious – an aspect of the disease. Gertrude too had only intermittent periods of lucidity, Dorothy Good told Nancy Powicke in a letter of 25 March 1920. Pneumonia and pleurisy, common complications of typhus, set in with each after the crisis. Reynolds was the first to die, having lapsed into unconsciousness, on 17 December, with Cuthbert Clayton at his side. Gertrude died on 20 December, the day after her thirty-second birthday, also unconscious. Dorothy, who had been sharing bedside duties with Dr Merrick, was with her.

Both Gertrude and Reynolds must have returned to Warsaw already carrying typhus. The illness has an incubation period of five to fourteen days. Gertrude noted in her diary for 29 November 1919 that she felt as if she had been bitten "ever since Kamieniec", which they visited on 25 November, and added: "Am not a bit brave re this typhus question." In truth, they could have been infected on one of a number of occasions. The hospitals they visited were rife with the disease, and on 27 November, Ukrainian prisoners-of-war suffering from typhus were brought into the railway coach in which the party was travelling.[3] Dorothy Good, in her letter to Nancy of 25 March 1920, was of the view that, although Gertrude may have been alarmed in the early days of her illness, she later did not realise how ill she was and indeed smiled when told she had passed successfully through her crisis, and said: "Oh, I *am* glad. I thot [sic] it would be much worse".

Gertrude was buried on 23 December in the Evangelical-Reformed cemetery in Warsaw. (This forms one of the five cemeteries – Catholic, Jewish, Muslim, Lutheran and Evangelical-Reformed – lying to the west of the city's central area.) The day before, Cuthbert Clayton and the Reverend Carl Carpenter, chaplain at the Anglican church in Warsaw, had reported her death to the pastor of the Evangelical-Reformed church, the Reverend Stefan Skierski, who entered it in the church's civil register. All three signed the certificate. Two hand-written copies of the entry, dated 23 March 1925, have survived, along with two typed English translations.[4] The Reverend Carpenter conducted the burial service in a snowy cemetery. Twelve members of the Poland unit were present, people from the ARC, two representatives of the Polish Ministry of Public Health and other friends, as Dorothy Good reported to Gertrude's mother. Reynolds Ball was buried earlier in the Powązowski Catholic cemetery in a plot purchased by the FEWVRC. As Cuthbert Clayton explained to Ball's mother in a letter of 21 December 1919, Reynolds, brought up as an

Anglican, had turned towards Catholicism and had described himself as "thinking as a Catholic" when he entered hospital. The priest who visited him at his request assured Clayton that Reynolds had died "a member of the Catholic Church".[5]

The poor state of communications between Poland and Britain made it difficult to get even urgent news through. It was only on 22 December 1919 that her family had the first news of her illness in a telegram sent by John Henderson in the London office. He himself had only just received two telegrams from Cuthbert Clayton sent earlier in the month, reporting the situation. He wrote daily thereafter to the family and on 25 December sent both a telegram and a letter to tell them of her death. (It is a harsh irony that he had the task of relaying this news, given his earlier tentative approaches towards Gertrude.) The Christmas delay meant that the family did not learn what had happened until 27 December, a week later (Agnes Powicke's memoir, page 238). The scant information that Henderson was able to give them was filled out by Dorothy Good in her letters detailing the course of Gertrude's last days and her funeral. Dorothy took charge of her friend's clothes and personal belongings and arranged for them to be returned to England by members of the Poland unit travelling back to Britain. Ernest Montford took several small items such as her watch, passport and a brooch with him on his trip home in January 1920, but it seems that these got lost en route – there is no indication of how. In June 1920, Dorothy entrusted Gertrude's clothes to Richard Evans.

The family continued to correspond with the London office of the FEWVRC on various matters, in particular about £100 that had been collected through Gertrude's efforts for the work in Poland, and about her dog Peter, left in France with Paule Brunot. During her illness, Gertrude had become agitated over Peter, imagining that he had been killed, but Dorothy Good was able to reassure her he was well. Sarah Connah, one of Gertrude's colleagues from the French days, wrote to her family to offer him a permanent home with the Friends' mission in northeast France. The family preferred to bring him back to Heaton Moor, where they were living, despite the six months' quarantine, and he joined them in June 1921. Again, things ended sadly, for in January 1923 a car caught, and broke, his jaw and he was put down, to the family's sorrow.

The first inscription on Gertrude's grave was a plaque giving her name and age. Her friends tended the grave, but in order to have the family's views on a permanent headstone, Sydney Wallis wrote to her parents on 7 April 1920. They evidently decided they wished to have one erected and chose a design of a Maltese cross filled with a leaf motif and the Manchester University motto 'Arduus ad solem' carved along the central arm. A sketch and proposed lettering have survived, but with no indication of who prepared them. The work was carried out in Warsaw. The stone had not yet been installed when another member of the FEWVRC unit wrote to Nancy Powicke on 22 July 1920, but photographs taken in the snow, possibly in the winter of 1921, show the cross in place. The inscription below the cross reads:

> TO THE DEAR MEMORY OF
> GERTRUDE MARY POWICKE ROBIN
> FRIENDS WAR VICTIMS RELIEF
> COMMITTEE FRANCE 1915-1919
> POLAND 1919 THIRD DAUGHTER
> OF FREDERICK JAMES AND
> MARTHA POWICKE OF STOCKPORT
> ENGLAND BORN AT HATHERLOW
> NEAR STOCKPORT 19TH DEC 1887
> DIED OF TYPHUS AT WARSAW 20TH OF DECEMBER 1919

In August 1927, Gertrude's three sisters made the journey to Warsaw to visit the grave. Thereafter, a Polish acquaintance of Maurice's visited the grave twice in June 1939, doubtless at Maurice's request, and reported that it was in good order. Years of fighting and turmoil followed. The cross on Gertrude's grave, and some neighbouring tombstones, bear the marks of bullet holes, but the cemetery does not seem to have been unduly damaged. In response to family inquiries in 1957, the Friends Service Council in London asked one of the Polish Friends living in Warsaw, Amelia Kurlandzka, to find out if the grave was still intact. She reported that both cross and inscription were in need of repair.[6] The next visit and the first family visit since 1927 was when the author and her husband were able to go in 2003 – a moment of great emotion. The high grave mound had sunk down, but the cross was still standing, though the inscription was almost illegible in places. A photograph taken in 2013 showed that in the interval, the grave had been much tidied up, the grave space enclosed in a rail and two new headstones inserted in the space.[7] In late 2014, the cross and inscription were restored.

On her home ground, Gertrude's death and how it came about were widely known and regretted. As if, perhaps, to express a sense of the distance between them and a grave most of them would never see, those who had known her or knew her family recorded her name on a

*47 Gertrude's grave, Evangelical-Reformed cemetery,
Warsaw, June 2013*

number of memorials: brass plaques in Hatherlow and Heaton Moor Congregational churches; a brass tablet in the Manchester University Women's Union;[8] and eventually on the family gravestone in Hatherlow churchyard. The Manchester University war memorial records her name – the only woman in the list – and she is commemorated on Stockton and Heaton Moor war memorials. She was, of course, not involved in the fighting, but clearly became associated with the general feeling of loss and sacrifice among her immediate community. As early as 1915, she had been seen as part of the cohort that had departed to the war when the Bredbury and Romiley Soldiers and Sailors Recognition Club sent her a writing pocket-book like those dispatched to soldiers. It is easier to explain her inclusion in the Roll of Honour of the Five Sisters window at York Minster, unveiled on 24 June 1925 by the then Duchess of York (later Queen Elizabeth) as a memorial to women who gave their lives in the First World War.[9] A fine photograph of her in formal pose (see Figure 39) is held by the

Imperial War Museum in London among the collection made after the war by the Museum's Women's Work Sub-Committee.

Her work and death stirred contributions to several funds and organisations, and donations were made for a new orphanage in Zawiercie and to the St Stanisław hospital where she died. Further small memorial tablets were proposed for these two institutions, but it is impossible to know if these plaques were ever made and if they survive.

There were obituaries too, the first of which was written by Gertrude's old mentor, Professor Tout, for the *Manchester Guardian* of 29 December 1919. It was reproduced or paraphrased in other newspapers and journals, including in the *Revue de la Meuse* of 29 February 1920, where it was augmented by local recollections. Her old school carried a note in the Miltonian News Sheet for February 1920. Her friend Dolly Lunn, with whom Gertrude had shared the unsatisfactory lodgings in Manchester and in whose London flat overlooking Hampstead heath the two talked and smoked in early August 1916 and watched the aeroplanes rising up above Hendon fort, wrote an appreciation in the Manchester University journal *The Serpent* the same month. Miss Burstall at the Manchester High School for Girls took Gertrude's death as the theme for her Founder's Day address to the MHSG on 16 January 1920, speaking of her as the school's "first martyr" to stand alongside the martyrs from the boys' schools, and an example of love and service.[10] Many letters arrived for the family, from Polish and French officials expressing condolences, to reminiscences and expressions of loss from fellow-workers. One vivid recollection was of "the little grey figure ... dancing in almost elf-like fashion, ... cigarette held high, and her beloved dog leaping and catching at her skirts ... to a tune in a clear soft whistle."[11] Another friend, writing to Nancy on 22 July 1920, related how she had heard of a French woman's distress over news of Gertrude's death. The woman had a group photograph that included Gertrude. When she was told Gertrude had died, she "simply cried and cried".

Perhaps the simplest and most unaffected message came from Wilmer Powick. Writing to Gertrude's father on 18 January 1920, he judged that "[i]t was perhaps characteristic of Gertrude's sterling qualities, that I could acquire so much admiration and affection for her, on such short acquaintance", and ended:

> There is nothing else that I can say, that would do any good, I know. So I am just sending these few lines as a mark of my very real sympathy, and an ever-so-little tribute to the memory of my Cousin Gertrude. How I wish we had more girls like her!

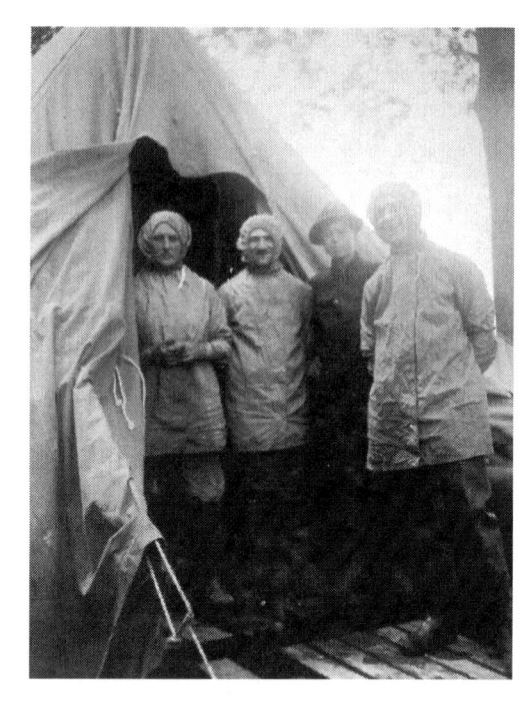

48 Bathing tent at Nadworna (now in Ukraine)

The Poland unit from 1920
The loss of their two colleagues, together with the illness of the two nurses at Białystok, had a devastating effect on the Poland unit. Those who had known Gertrude well, such as Dorothy Good and Ernest Montford, expressed their grief in letters to her family. Dorothy told Gertrude's mother that she had lost all heart for the work. Throughout the winter of 1919-1920, the group at Zawiercie was in a low state. Their distress was compounded by the death of another of their number, Samuel Cole, on 14 January 1920, from pneumonia, in Vienna. Dr Merrick reported to Ruth Fry on 15 January 1920 on an outbreak of influenza that had left every man in the unit ill.[12] Gradually, however, the unit gathered its energies together. The arrival of long-delayed relief supplies that had been transported via Gdansk meant that plans to distribute clothing and to set up a shop to sell clothes to the very poor could be implemented. Dorothy took forward the scheme for a shop that Gertrude had been devising along the lines of those organised in France. Working with Herbert Hoover's ARA, the unit distributed food. A workroom for women needing employment was organised.

Between 4 and 23 January 1920, Cuthbert Clayton, as secretary of the Poland unit, made a solo visit to Eastern Galicia to bring up to date the information gathered by his three colleagues the preceding November. Specifically he was to find out whether the sums of money promised in support of refugee care at Podwoloczyska had reached their destination. He also hoped to visit a particular orphanage. Of the promised funds there was no trace, and he had no time to go to the orphanage, but his report, dated 31 January 1920, confirmed the need for continuing anti-typhus work in the region and again suggested Tarnopol as a likely centre for the unit's activities. In February, a second FEWVRC party visited the orphanage and the area around Nadworna, southwest of Tarnopol. They met with Dr Trenkner, the chief health commissioner for Galicia, who argued for Nadworna as a more suitable place for the Poland unit to base itself. A third FEWVRC investigation in May 1920, made with Dr Trenkner, confirmed Nadworna as a new centre, and the delousing carried on there.

The Poland unit expanded in terms of both numbers and bases. By the end of May 1920, it counted seventy-seven people and was looking for further recruits.[13] That number had risen to eighty by the end of the summer of 1920, most of them British, spread then among four sites: Warsaw, Zawiercie, Werbkowice (east of Zamość) and Nadworna.[14] The increasing incursions of Russian Bolshevik troops into eastern Poland throughout the summer of 1920 caused severe disruption to the unit's activities and a temporary withdrawal to Warsaw until the Russians were routed. Thereafter the work turned in part towards agricultural rehabilitation, housing reconstruction and employment schemes carried out in a number of outposts. The 1920 war between Russia and Poland resulted in the settling of Poland's eastern border in 1921, but also led to renewed flows of refugees and exchanges of prisoners-of-war, who continued to carry typhus with them. The Poland unit found itself again dealing with epidemic conditions. A number of foreign relief workers contracted typhus, among them two in the FEWVRC unit.[15] One of these two, Florence Witherington, died of the disease in early 1922.

The Friends' mission to Poland came to an end in 1924. Before its departure, it put in place an orphanage and an agricultural training scheme, which remained supported by British Friends until just before the Second World War. Two representatives of the Society of Friends remained in Poland to work with these projects.[16] One of them was Jadwiga Białowieska. She stayed on to run the orphanage into the 1930s, but her story also became clouded with tragedy. At one time, it was thought she had been "shot as a reprisal" by the occupying German forces in the early summer of 1940, but this report was later corrected: Jadwiga was still alive, it was stated, but several male members of her family were among a number of people shot at Christmas 1939 as a reprisal for the death of a German soldier found dead in their neighbourhood.[17] It was a common scale of revenge.

Afterword

Gertrude's life and death can be read in a number of ways. Some may see it as a Christian life well led. Some may see in it a continuation of the sacrifices that so many had made in the course of the First World War – those who placed her name on war memorials must have had some such thought. A few called her a saint and a martyr, epithets that she would almost certainly have rejected. Her friends mourned the loss of a spirited character and courageous colleague.

Speculation on what she might have done if she had lived cannot go beyond a few possibilities. It is likely that she would have stayed in Poland with the Friends' relief mission until it closed in 1924. Thereafter she would have looked for employment, since she seemed no longer to expect or even seek marriage and was instead exploring new fields of work away from the teaching profession she had first started in. The feeling among those around her was that occupations for women were extending in many new directions: administration, management, business, local government, journalism, medicine, social work, university work. The emergence of large international organisations in the postwar years concerned with humanitarian issues might have led to a continuation of her work in an international setting. With her good education, varied experience and receptive mind she would have been well placed to take advantage of the new institutions of the twentieth century.

For her family there was and remains a sense of pride that she was willing to throw herself into what was demanding and ultimately deadly work. Perhaps her greatest gift is to remind us that even in the worst of situations there is so often a way forward.

Additional material

Sermaize

While Bar-le-Duc was spared harm in the fighting of 6-12 September 1914, Sermaize-les-Bains, lying due west of Bar in the department of the Marne, suffered enormous destruction. Out of 700 houses, 600 were destroyed, and eleven civilians died during the week. Eight hostages were seized and harshly dealt with. *The Friend* for 22 January 1915 reported that the inhabitants were reduced to living in cellars half full of water. Others took shelter in the town theatre. The town hall, the gendarmerie, the church, which dated from the twelfth to thirteenth century, and the presbytery were heavily damaged, the town centre devastated and the local sugar refinery put out of action. Sermaize was used as a battleground. In a diary entry for 22 August 1915, Gertrude described walking from the FWVRC centre down through the town to the railway station:

> [T]he road leads through what was the intermediate ground between the opposing armies. On our left [west side] were the trenches occupied by the French – and this was borne witness to by a large grave where lie 38 French soldiers and 2 Germans – : on our right [east side] were the hillside where the Germans were entrenched and if we had been there while the fight was on we could have walked along the road, underneath the shells, which would have passed overhead.

Only the fountain in the central square was still flowing.

Sermaize gradually pulled itself together and started rebuilding. The municipality moved to a temporary wooden hut, from which it operated from 1915 to 1927, until the mairie could be rebuilt, in 1926. The railway line (Sermaize lay on the Paris-Nancy route) and the station continued to operate. On 30 December 1915, Gertrude noted, the Hôtel des Voyageurs was open for coffee. She went that same

49 Sermaize as it was when the FWVRC started work there, early 1915

evening to look at the church and the curé's house and found the church still "worth seeing". Church and presbytery were rebuilt, the church at the instigation of the town's priest, Father René Bollot.[1]

A thermal establishment known as La Source had developed from the mid-nineteenth century in woods just outside the town – hence 'les Bains'.[2] The resort escaped being much damaged during the fighting of September 1914 and was thus able to offer some kind of shelter to those who had become homeless. For a while, some 300-400 refugees were crammed into the resort hotel, where, as Hilda Cashmore noted, they lived one family to a room. Various small businesses and shops, moreover, were run in this restricted accommodation.[3] Conditions were unwholesome, there was no proper drainage, and the fear of typhoid fever was present. Improvements in sanitation and rubbish disposal were an early task for the Sermaize équipe's sanitary officer, Ernest Montford.[4] For a while, the FWVRC, which arrived in January 1915, shared the accommodation with the refugees. Eventually the latter were moved out into wooden houses put up by FWVRC construction teams, the elderly who had no support were taken in by an order of nuns, and by early 1915, the FWVRC was allowed to take over the resort buildings as a regional headquarters for their activities. Wooden huts provided sleeping quarters, first for the male relief workers, then for the women. From La Source, as it was generally referred to, FWVRC workers radiated out into the surrounding countryside. From October 1917, they were joined by a number of American colleagues. Very importantly, the centre housed the garage and the mission's fleet of motor vehicles, which provided these workers with a vital means of transport.

The FWVRC never considered the Sermaize centre as ideal. Ruth Fry was explicit about its shortcomings:

> At the beginning, money was scarce and very little was available for such accommodation [for workers]. This, added to the fact that in early days no one imagined that the war would be long continued, disinclined everyone to make elaborate arrangements, with the result that Sermaize was never shipshape, never properly adapted for the large amount of work carried out.[5]

Its value, in her eyes, was more of a spiritual order, contributing as it did to the development for the first time of

> the very unusual community life, which became such a feature of the Mission. It was a real experiment in socialism, and in inter-denominationalism, the most varied characters living together, united in their aim of helping their fellows.

The mission's projects

Despite the drawbacks, a number of projects covering all areas of the mission's activities were run at and from La Source until the centre was closed down in April 1919.

Two teams of house-builders were active in the town and surrounding villages. By the end of 1916, according to *The Friend* for 1 December 1916, they were credited with having put up 500 houses in the area. Their most interesting work was the creation of Sermaize 'garden city', first mooted in the autumn of 1915 and opened in July 1916. Gertrude records visiting it in early December 1916. The intention was to provide accommodation for those prevented by lack of land from taking advantage of the wooden portable houses and who had been living in the thermal resort at La Source. The scheme consisted of twenty-four houses of varying sizes built in brick in timber framing and roofed, originally with tarred felt, but eventually with red tiles. The houses were laid out on each side of a short street that curved at one end in a small circle around a roofed well. Each house had a garden. A drainage system was laid down and fences erected. At least one small shop was provided. The accommodation created housed seventy-six people.[6] Labour from French workmen and even soldiers helped in its construction.

50 Cité des Amis, Sermaize, completed July 1916

After the end of the war, the houses at Sermaize, to this day recorded on the town's cadastral register as the Cité des Amis, passed into the municipal housing stock and were let to tenants of modest condition against very low rents. The deputy mayor of Sermaize in 2012, Monsieur Alain Pauphilet, recalled with feeling his visits as a child to his grandmother who lived in the Cité for many years until her death in 1986.[7] Conditions were simple, with no piped water. As living and housing standards improved, particularly from the 1980s, the Cité was progressively abandoned. The site became subject to flooding after the sugar refinery had dammed a stream to create a reservoir for washing sugar beet. Nonetheless, the stump of the well and two houses remain, one of which was inhabited until the death of the last tenant in February 2012. They were still standing in the summer of 2014.[8]

The mission worked with local farmers out of Sermaize, providing labour, storing and loaning out equipment and tools, distributing seeds, selling potatoes and growing hay and forage for horses, but La Source was never judged a wholly satisfactory site. Over the winter of 1915 it was, indeed, obliged to close for agricultural work. The buildings were used to raise cabbage seedlings and breed small livestock – rabbits and chicks – for distribution to outlying villages. Between 1915 and 1917, Gertrude recorded visits to the incubation station, the arrival of breeding rabbits and her colleagues' distribution of seeds.

In terms of relief work, Sermaize was again both the launching point for trips of investigation into surrounding villages and a distri-

51 *One of the two remaining houses, Cité des Amis, August 2012 (seen at the end of the street in the photograph of 1916)*

bution point for furniture, bedding, clothes and boots (the last two categories of goods were handed out from what had been the spa casino at La Source). This type of relief continued until early 1917. A cause of concern was the dearth of suitable work for the teenage boys and girls who had been thrown out of work by the destruction of the sugar refinery. Embroidery was set up as an occupation for the refugee women around Sermaize

After the FWVRC's maternity hospital at Châlons-sur-Marne, the two Sermaize hospitals represented the mission's biggest contribution to the provision of medical and nursing care. The first hospital, La Source, opened in early 1915 at Dr Hilda Clark's instigation, a cottage-type hospital with two wards and a veranda. It was housed in wooden huts erected beside the La Source hotel and had a dispensary and eventually an out-patient department. The hospital gave emergency treatment to refugees in the neighbourhood and was able to perform operations. It also housed boys requiring prolonged convalescence and cared for its own relief workers. Gertrude spent a week there in March 1917 with tonsillitis and a high temperature.

A second hospital, the Château hospital, was installed in a large mansion, the Château Bischoff or Bischof, again lent by its owner. It was already functioning as a temporary dressing station at the time of the September 1914 fighting in Sermaize, and treated the German officer commanding the enemy attack on the town. He suffered a head wound from which he died at the château on 11 September. This earlier activity may explain Ruth Fry's reference[9] to a "revitalised" hospital formed by late 1917 by Dr James Babbit, a member of the American Quaker relief contingent, and open from December 1917 for patients needing surgery. Deficiencies in nursing staff, utilities and equipment were remedied by June 1918. A dispensary was opened and X-ray equipment was introduced. Capacity was continually increased to the point where, at the armistice, there were one hundred beds and seventy-five patients. A total of around 1,200 operations were performed, with a low rate of surgical deaths.[10] The hospital drew its patients from the surrounding district, which suffered from a general lack of hospital accommodation for civilians, rendered worse by the closure of the town hospital in Bar through the bombing raids of early October 1917.

The château's owner reclaimed possession of the building in 1918, and the hospital had to close in mid-January 1919. Most of the huts and wards were dismantled to be transferred, together with equipment, to the mission's new zone of activity in the Verdun area. The Sermaize équipe itself was run down. Gertrude wrote on 2 March 1919 of the sad sight of "empty and deserted" huts and of the empty garage. By mid-April the équipe had been disbanded.

Sermaize acted as an administrative and social point for the surrounding équipes, who gathered there, especially at weekends. Gertrude was a frequent visitor, sometimes arriving on Saturday evening and returning early on Monday morning to Bar. She delighted in sleeping out of doors in the meadow in summer months. Walks, picnics, swimming and bicycle rides were organised in the surrounding forest. Hilda Clark recalled a French army band practising in the woods near La Source in May 1916 and a celebrated pianist released from his regiment to play on the équipe's piano.[11] A musical evening on 1 July 1916 marked a young worker's coming of age. Discussions and debates on political issues such as Christian socialism and women's suffrage were common. On Sunday evenings a Quaker-style meeting might be held, at which one of the senior Friends such as Margery Fry might speak.

Other visitors came from outside. On 18 September 1915, the curé of Sermaize, Monsieur Bollot, was a guest at La Source for Saturday evening dinner and gave a vivid account of the town, its history, the bombardment, and life before and after the fighting of a year before. It was he, apparently, who first addressed an urgent appeal in January

1915 to the FWVRC to help the people of Sermaize. Conviviality of a less welcome kind surfaced in the form of a café organised in one of the rooms occupied by the refugee families in the former hotel. It was closed after the équipe complained to the local sub-prefect.[12] A week before the curé came to dine, "two cheery men" who must have remembered the ill-fated café, "turned up and asked for 'cafés noirs' – then mounted up above to hear the music!", as related by Gertrude in her diary entry for 11 September 1915. Ejected once, they persisted in returning, to be thrown out a second time.

The town has always been small. Its present population of somewhat over 2,000 has remained fairly constant over the past century. In the second half of the nineteenth century, the town supported a foundry producing iron and cast iron artefacts and bronze statues, which won some renown. Sugar-refining production, another industry, has dwindled. The resort at La Source has not survived. The buildings have been demolished and the site has been developed as a night-club.

On 2 July 1922, Sermaize was awarded the Croix de guerre.

Verdun

Verdun is among the most resonant of the names that have come down from the western campaigns of the First World War. For the French it carries the burden of significance and emotion that the Somme, Ypres and Gallipoli bear for the British and Australians and that Vimy has for the Canadians: places of profound memories, and for those who participated in them, barely communicable experiences.

The battle
The citadel of Verdun lies on the Meuse, at a point where the main east-west route from Metz to Paris crosses the river as it flows north. The ground is high everywhere, but rises further to the northeast and northwest behind the city. Following the Franco-Prussian War of 1870-1871, the existing line of Vauban forts along the eastern French frontier was strengthened by a further system of "entrenched camps", which left the citadel of Verdun protected by a ring of forts.[1] The German invasion of August 1914 failed to overrun Verdun, and it remained in French hands.

The German decision to attack Verdun, developed from late 1915, has been attributed to various motives: the desire to mount a punitive expedition against the enemy, to administer a finishing blow to France in order to bring it to negotiate a surrender, to force it into a costly engagement of men and armaments that would bleed it dry, or, with a longer-term objective, to strike indirectly at Britain through weakening France.[2] The relatively undefended state of Verdun in late 1915, its position as a salient overlooked on three sides, and its poor communications, compared to Germany's access to fourteen railway lines, all undoubtedly entered into German calculations. The attack was entrusted to the German Fifth Army under the command of Crown Prince Wilhelm.

Despite intense pressure from the Germans, the citadel of Verdun did not fall to them. During the fiercest phase of the fighting, from its opening on 21 February 1916 to July, they captured two of the protecting forts, Douaumont and Vaux. Through March and early April, they attacked first on the east bank of the Meuse, then over both banks. The battle ground on, spreading over the surrounding hills. German failure to capture a third fort during June and July then checked their advance and marked the end of the German offensive, although not of the fighting. Command of the defence of Verdun was entrusted to General Philippe Pétain in the first days of the campaign, and it was he who set the organisational framework of the conflict in use of both manpower and transport. However, Pétain's insistence that effort and resources should be concentrated on Verdun at the expense of other campaigns such as the Somme irritated Joffre, the French commander-in-chief, and General Robert Nivelle was appointed in place of Pétain. Nivelle promoted a policy of attack, which allowed him to recapture the two forts during the autumn. A three-day French movement against the Germans on the east bank of the Meuse brought the battle to an end on 18 December. For the Germans, the impetus to take Verdun was extinguished at the end of 1916. Their troops, nonetheless, were not fully dislodged from the area for another two years. In August and November 1917, the French took various German positions on the west bank, and on 16 September 1918, US army forces cleared the remaining enemy back to the initial line of attack of 21 February 1916.

The cost in lives was immense. Estimates of the number of French and German casualties, taken together, range between 708,000 and 717,000, divided very roughly between the two sides. Enormous quantities of ammunition were use in the battle area, the soil was churned up and polluted and trees were blasted away, to the point where cultivation was abandoned after the war and large tracts placed under forestation. Nine villages in the front zone were obliterated and not rebuilt; they were deemed to have 'died for France'. The enemy never reached the actual town of Verdun, but inflicted large-scale destruction on it through severe and continuous bombardment. The civilian population was evacuated, the municipal council left for Paris and the town was given over to the military.

The French soldiers who were poured into the 'mill on the Meuse' (the phrase comes from Crown Prince Wilhelm), whether arriving or leaving, all travelled through the Bar-le-Duc region. Two means were open for transporting both them and the vast amounts of munitions, equipment and provisions the battle demanded: the road from Bar-le-Duc to Verdun, and the local narrow-gauge railway system. From these two initially unpromising supply routes the French army organised an efficient system for delivering troops and materiel. The road in particular, or rather, the memory of the road as it functioned in 1916, has earned its own name, the Voie Sacrée, the 'sacred way', in recognition of the journey of so many soldiers to and from the horrors of the Verdun battlefield. The name was apparently little used by the troops travelling on it, but has acquired a place in popular memory to equal that of Verdun.[3]

From the early months of the war both the road and the local rail network passed under military control. Pétain issued strict instructions on use of the road. It was to be reserved for motorised traffic alone, passing continuously throughout twenty-four hours. Convoys had to drive in strict formation. The flow was not to be impeded, and there was to be no stopping at all. The volume of traffic was immense, particularly during the earlier stages of the battle, to allow the daily delivery of great quantities of stores and munitions and of thousands of men. The journey from Bar could take eight hours, and drivers on this route worked long shifts, often without respite.[4] The constant relay of troops was a consequence of the French high command's decision to relieve the soldiers fighting at Verdun quickly. Pétain's aim was for them to have an eight-day stint of combat followed by eight days' rest. This continual rotation of the fighting force was known as the 'noria' (literally, an endless chain of buckets on a wheel). Troops passed up the road to Verdun by day and night, some on foot, some by lorry. They were conveyed to the area below Verdun, from where they were taken on to their positions. The lorries delivering them would then wait for the troops being relieved. These manoeuvres were often carried out by night. The convoys were lit by acetylene headlights for part of the route; thereafter they travelled in blackout. Such scenes

52 The voies sacrées *leading to Verdun: road and rail*

appealed to the sense of drama among artists; the best known illustration of the endless convoys is probably that by the artist Georges Scott, first published in the French pictorial *L'Illustration* on 11 March 1916.[5]

To back up the road traffic, the one-metre-gauge railway system that had been serving the department since 1883 was diverted to military use from 1 December 1914. The rail network of Le Meusien or Le Varinot, as it was known, spread across the central part of the department. Running day and night, it was reserved for the transport of provisions, fodder and munitions, and for evacuating the wounded. By April 1916, thirty-five trains were circulating in each direction every twenty-four hours. Some were adapted as hospital trains for stretcher and sitting cases. Two to three such trains ran each day, capable of clearing 500 injured and distributing them to local hospitals. Of the 128 locomotives, one has survived, La Suzanne. Both this engine, now restored, and a reconstructed ambulance wagon are on view at the open-air museum in Bar-le-Duc dedicated to the railway.[6]

Bar-le-Duc – the rear base

As seen in Chapter Four Bar itself was in a perpetual state of commotion, especially in the early months of 1916, as lorries pounded through at all hours and trains conveyed soldiers to their units or on leave. The boulevard de la Rochelle was particularly busy, since at its

53 La Suzanne, a survivor of the rail network, August 2012

lower end the road takes a left-hand turn to line up again into the route to Verdun (see Figure 15). The press of traffic bound to or from the Voie Sacrée thus all passed below the équipe's windows. On 16 February 1916, Gertrude reported: "All day the Boulevard one stream of camions, filled with men or horses drawing guns and kitchens. This evening, looking down, I saw a long line of red twinkling lights, as they passed along towards the town." On 22 February, the main route through Bar was closed off to allow the passage of express cars. On the railway troop trains caused long delays to other traffic. At other times, the streets were filled with marching soldiers. The lines of lorries never diminished. On 13 July 1916, Gertrude recorded an evening view from the upper town of the road leading up to Verdun "with the lights of the camions twinkling on it".

The Bar équipe was well aware of the course of the action around Verdun and heard some of the stories of imminent disaster in circulation. Gertrude met survivors of the fighting – on 29 May 1916, a man who looked like "a walking corpse" after three months in the combat zone, as her diary entry related, and the soldiers encountered on a train on 20 March 1916, again recorded in her diary, who were returning to Verdun: they "had been wounded in the battle for Vaux no time

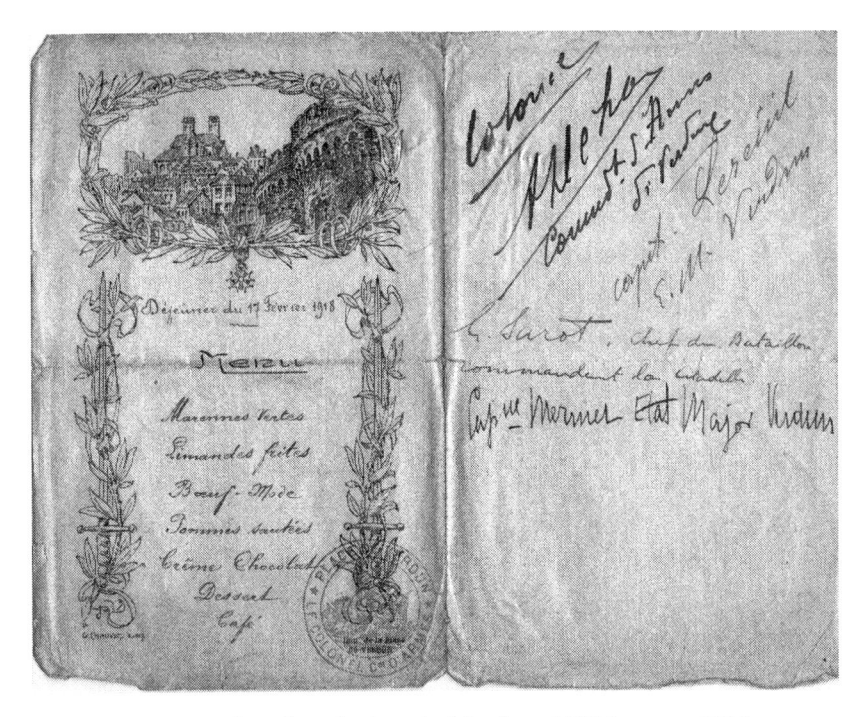

54 Menu for a lunch given in Verdun, 17 February 1918

allowed for convalescence as all men are needed".

From the autumn of 1916, once the French sensed that the town of Verdun was unlikely to fall to the Germans, restricted visits to the citadel became possible. When Gertrude was entertained to dinner at the Les Ambassadeurs restaurant in Paris in late October 1918 by her cousin Wilmer Powick, she told him that "the last such dinner she had had, had been in the underground passages of Verdun." Among her papers is a menu for a lunch given on 17 February 1918 in the 'Place de Verdun', the fortified area of Verdun. The menu is handwritten on a specially designed sheet and bears the stamp of the colonel commanding. On the facing page are his signature and those of three of his subordinates. The menu is accompanied by a receipt for the Verdun medal issued on 20 November 1916, endorsed by the colonel. How did she come to be a guest? She makes no other mention of such an outing.

Gertrude and Wilmer in Paris, 1918

Gertrude was not the only Powick(e) stationed in France during the First World War. Her second cousin Wilmer Powick (see Biographical notes) had enlisted and served there from 1917 to 1919 as a first lieutenant, subsequently captain in the US Army. Her family had alerted her by letter that he was in Paris, and after a first, unsuccessful attempt to meet, they finally met up at the end of October 1918 (as noted in Chapter Five). In letters to their respective families they give pen portraits of each other that at the same time say something about their expectations and how each of them, Gertrude in particular, saw themselves.

Of her cousin she wrote in her letter of 3 November 1918: "He's almost middle height, my colour hair, grey eyes with a twinkle. And he seems as if he wouldn't mind anything." She judged him "less stodgey than his photo, and letters" and went on to say that

> he seemed determined to give me a spree – we went to the most expensive places for meals and drove round in a taxi and went to a cinema. On Tuesday [her diary gives Wednesday, 30 October 1918] he fetched me at the Britannique. I was dressed "quietly" in grey, and looked plain but good. We promptly drove in a taxi to the Hôtel Mirabeau, rue de la Paix where we had tea. During tea we discussed Paris and the war, and took each other in. After tea he asked me if I'd ever tasted an Ice Cream Soda. "No" says I – "Well then, lets have one" says he so we just managed to go on foot to the end of the rue de la Paix to the Maison Ixe noted for such, and there we planted ourselves in a very sumptuous room and ate ice cream sodas with a straw or spoon, and saw life. Ma foi I should think we did. We spent the time discussing everybody in the room. And then we unfolded to each other the intricacies of our family trees and I drew a plan of us – and he did likewise...
>
> Then we walked to the Place de la Concorde and looked at the Bosch guns and tanks etc. and I split my new glove trying to turn a handle. Then at 7.30 we went to Les Ambassadeurs, and had dinner. It's a topping place, wonderfully decorated in gold and white and the joint rolls up to your elbow and you look haughtily down on it and say what you think of it. Six waiters hover round and again you see Life. We were a long time over it nearly two hours, as we had to wait a goodish time between the courses and were expected to eat lovingly, and be entirely 'gourmet'. Afterwards we walked along the river quais and then went and sat in the Tuileries and twas then that I heard all about Victoria May [Smith, his fiancée]. He called for me again the next evening at 6.30 – (I was again looking plain and good and this time sniffled rather too much) We went to an Italian restaurant Poccattis and had dinner – quite different from the night before but

just as jolly – small and snug and select! Then we went to a cinema as it was too late for a theatre and saw some quite good things. The armistice with Turkey was announced in the middle by the manager – there was a great scene, everybody stood up and clapped and shouted and then we sang the Marseillaise. And so to bed and we parted, I for my part much pleased with my new cousin "and quite prepared to like him".

In a letter likewise dated 3 November 1918 to his family, Wilmer gives his account of the evening:

Knowing cousin Gertrude would be in town when Wednesday came I was in a position to go to meet her at her hotel in the middle of the afternoon, and to act the part of a gallant chevalier. As she was stopping at a second-rate place we immediately went out, took a taxi and went out for afternoon tea to one of the best hotels, there in a rather large deserted tea room we sipped our tea and compared notes and exchanged experiences. It was not as gay a place as I had expected to find. I had been there once before when the tea room was thronged with all sorts of interesting people, but that was on Christmas eve. Last Wednesday it was more like a cemetery. I knew another place where we could get ice cream sodas, and as she had never tasted one we went there. There we found things more lively. We each learned something about our foreign relations.

We had next to think about dinner. After we had talked for a long time however, it was still too early. So we spent our time of waiting by going down to La Place de la Concorde to see the trophies, innumerable cannon drawn up in rows, in varying states of disrepair. Some had their barrels broken off completely. Some had their breeches jammed. Some were still whole. There were big ones and little ones, machine guns and trench mortars, aeroplanes and tanks galore.

Gertrude evidently has a mechanical turn of mind for she could not resist the temptation of trying to work the levers and tore her glove in the attempt.

Incidentally I may say there was no fine lady about her dress. She was got up in about the same careless fashion as one would expect of a woman chauffeur. Her costume was not a 'uniform' unless perhaps a small embroidered design on one sleeve would make it such. And the costume was certainly too good for the rough work in the mud, and among automobiles to which she was returning. Yet it would scarcely be considered an ordinary city costume, with its lack of pressing, and obvious oldness. I should imagine that it might be a 'dress up' costume for the front – something that one could put on after finishing a week's dirty work for the purpose of recalling the fact that one once lived in a place where people dress for dinner. However for all that, I could very well imagine her in an evening gown playing the part of a fine lady, and being quite at home in that part.

As to general disposition etc. she reminded me a lot of Mary [his sister], or, still more, of what I would expect May to be after spending

3½ years at the front. She was Mary minus a certain amount of deference to public opinion and plus a little self reliance, perhaps.

However having finished our inspection of the trophies we wended our way to Ambassadeurs, probably the best restaurant in PARIS. We had an excellent dinner of her choosing – for she understands and speaks French perfectly and is familiar with French menus. I was pleased to see that she picked out neither the cheapest nor the most expensive dishes, but was guided by taste. i.e. she was neither penurious nor luxurious. Really we had a magnificent dinner at, of course, a magnificent price – but not more than one would expect at such a place. Incidentally she remarked that the last such dinner she had had, had been in the underground passages of Verdun while the place was being bombarded.

I take it that she has few enough diversions in her rough life. She says it is not unusual to work 15 hours a day and that it sometimes happens that one works right though to the next day. At the end of the days work one is generally so tired that she goes straight to bed, only to take up the grind anew in the following day. Yet she likes the work and excitement. During the time I was with her the only wish that I heard her express on any subject was that she could have electric head lights in her car. How she has ever managed to go through 3 years of that life and still like it I don't know, for she is no higher than you, mother, and looks awfully frail. I say she likes it. I don't mean that exactly. But she likes the feeling that she is doing "her bit", and so enters into it with zest. She wouldn't for the world be anywhere else at present.

The following evening we dined together again, somewhat less pretentiously, however, and after dinner went to a movies [sic]. That night she was troubled a little with a hacking cough, and in view of the prevalence of grippe [influenza] and its seriousness I was a little worried at the prospect of her returning to her rough life the next morning. However she has gone. I only hope she doesn't develop grippe. But I suppose in 3½ yrs she has coughed more than once.

In Wilmer's reaction there is a sense of surprise, even mild shock in the face of a somewhat unusual way of life, one that he did not expect a lady and his cousin to be leading. At the same time he was impressed by her good command of French and her ability to pick her way round a menu. They met again in early December 1918 in Paris, where Gertrude had gone on FWVRC business. She joined him and his landlord, Monsieur Descaves, the literary editor of one of the Paris journals, his friend Captain Klein and three other men for dinner on 3 December. "She made a great hit," he wrote in a letter dated 7 December 1918, "both because of her good French and because of what she was able to talk about. The conversation was chiefly on books and as she was at home on the subject, it pleased M Descaves greatly." The following evening, Gertrude, Wilmer and Captain Klein met for dinner and a theatre visit to see a play in English directed by

Lena Ashwell.[1] On 6 December, she and Wilmer had a quiet dinner together, at which, Gertrude noted in her diary, "he let me pay my share". Perhaps Wilmer was getting the measure of his cousin. "I like Gertrude very much" was his conclusion.

Luxembourg and Germany, May 1919

As seen in Chapter Five, in May 1919, Gertrude combined leave with work by driving a sick woman, Mme Dauphis, from hospital in Bar-le-Duc to the lady's home in Beckerich in Luxembourg. She left the car at Strassen, outside the city of Luxembourg, and travelled by train to Trier, just inside Germany. From there she went on to join her sister Agnes for five days in Bonn, where Agnes's work with the YMCA had taken her.

Gertrude set out on 8 May from Bar in the Hupmobile, equipped with the necessary travel authorisations and taking as a travelling companion, in addition to Mme Dauphis, a French colleague, Paule Brunot. They drove through Longuyon, Longwy and Arlon (in Belgium), showing their papers twice on crossing frontiers, and completed the journey in just under five and a half hours. After delivering their patient, the two stayed the night in Beckerich, "a most wonderfully clean little village" where they "drank [?home] milk and ate fresh eggs ad lib", as she told her family in a letter of 10 May 1919. The clean state of Luxembourg and the chance to eat rich food at leisure clearly made an impression. The two young women visited the ramparts of the city of Luxembourg the next day, she noted in her diary for 9 May 1919, "shop-gawped and sat in the ravine … and … had tea and ices, just like before the war". They then took the car to Strassen, where it was to be left, and Gertrude then set off on her own by train. She spent the night of 9 May in Germany, in Trier, where the YMCA billeted her in "a swagger hotel with a balcony looking down the boulevard. I went to see the old Roman gateway with a YMCA girl in the evening", as she told her family in the 10 May letter. On the 10th, she took the train to Cologne, where she learned, through the YMCA headquarters, that Agnes was in Bonn. She made her way there by train and found her sister in the YMCA book room. Agnes' memoir (page 144) picks up the thread. "Agnes was busy with some clerical work when she looked up and saw Gertrude standing there, a questioning yet exultant look in her eyes. It was a moment that lives in the memory." (In places the memoir is written in the third person, but the at times vivid wording can have come only from Agnes herself.)

Gertrude found the situation in Germany wholly unexpected, as she told her family on 10 May: "I can't believe it everything seems so queer and like nothing I've ever seen or done before". "It's queer to think that I've landed in Germany on the day when the Peace terms are published – people look quite calm I notice." A draft peace treaty had indeed been put to Germany on 7 May 1919, and the terms offered were presumably being publicised at the moment of her arrival. Under the terms of the armistice of 11 November 1918, Allied troops had occupied the left or west bank of the Rhine and had placed garrisons and secured bridgeheads at the three principal crossings of the river: Mainz, Coblentz and Cologne. The British occupying forces, with Cologne as 'their' bridgehead, were constituted on 2 April 1919 as the British Army of the Rhine, and by the end of May had risen to 220,000 men. Gertrude thus found herself in a new environment, where the Allies were no longer belligerents but occupiers. She was accustomed to dealing with French and later American soldiers, but this was the first time she had any close contact with the military of her own country.

At that point, wherever the British army went, the YMCA followed.[1] In Cologne it operated from headquarters in a commandeered music hall and restaurant known as 'Cologne Central'. All YMCA centres had lending libraries, and it was in the Bonn centre that Agnes was working as part of the educational section. Women YMCA workers had been admitted into the occupation zone since March 1919.

In a letter of 15 May 1919 to her family, Gertrude described their time together. Her first night in Bonn was spent at a hotel, where the town mayor had found her "a billet", but for the rest of her stay she slept on "a sort of spring mattress on the floor" in Agnes' room, which was large. While Agnes was at work, Gertrude went sight-seeing, shopped or read. She took tea at Agnes' "Mess, next door but one to her billet", then the two sisters spent the evening together. One day they went to Cologne for dinner at the Central YMCA. "[I]t was most amusing, they were such a motley crew and were dressed in every imaginable style, evening dress among others!" Gertrude found plenty to see in Bonn: the river, the university, parks, the "marvellous shops". She also arranged with the Bonn harbour master and the British officer in charge that she and Agnes should come down the Rhine on a British army boat from Coblentz, at the confluence of the Rhine and the Moselle (and one of the bridgehead cities), to Bonn. They spent a day at Coblentz (having presumably reached there by train) and then returned by boat. On board they sat among the officers and were entertained by the "Lieut and his pal" with afternoon tea and toast while a band played. "It was a novel sensation for me to be with English officers, my first experience of the British Army abroad and they certainly impressed me favourably."

From Bonn the sisters went into Cologne by train for dinner. On the journey back a group of 'Tommies' got into the train. Gertrude later described the encounter as "very amusing", but Agnes gave an expanded account in her memoir (pages 148-49) that suggested impressions this time of the British military were far less favourable. Agnes judged the men were "more or less tipsy". One of them almost sat on top of Gertrude. His companion then enraged her by begging the two women, "in a maudlin voice", to "'say something to us in English, we do so want to hear an English girl speak again."' Gertrude's prickly streak came to the fore. She asked icily for a little more room and only slowly unbent. The men nearly all got out halfway through the journey, and by the end of it the sisters were "shaking with laughter".

The trip on the Rhine led on to other things, and Gertrude found herself with an invitation to an officers' dance the following evening, her last in Bonn. The party was held in a former munitions factory, and she made sure she had every dance. Supper was good too, she told her family in the letter of 15 May. Shortly after eight that same morning (15 May) she was in the train to Coblentz. Agnes saw her off at Bonn station. It was not a comfortable journey. She felt sick the whole way, "probably because I danced too much last night". From Coblentz, she travelled by a "military train" direct to Luxembourg.

From Luxembourg she took the train on 16 May to Strassen to pick up her car. The journey started well, but ended in disaster, since first of all the steering gave way when she got to Lorraine, and then, close to Bar-le-Duc, the front tyre blew out. The car swept into a tree, the back axle broke and she was thrown out. She completed the journey in another car, and the following day the Hupmobile was towed into Bar.

Visit to Eastern Galicia, November-December 1919

Extracts from Gertrude's letter of 1 December 1919 to her family

It's just over a week since I began this letter – and since then so much has happened that I scarcely know how to write it all. We're back at Tarnapol again and it's quite likely that we shall take up work here – as there certainly is plenty of need on all sides. We're in the train (not the special one!) waiting to go off to Lemberg, and then on to Warsaw, but it doesn't look as if we should ever start. Coal is terribly short round here. The machines for disinfecting all the Ukrainian prisoners, and refugees who are pouring over the frontier, isn't [sic] able to work for lack of coal. It's a very grave thing, as they are all of them in need of disinfection and many of them have typhus already. It means that they will spread typhus everywhere they go. Tarnapol is one of the biggest centres for receiving these refugees. I think it's one of the saddest sights I've ever seen – for they have come in in hundreds and sometimes in thousands – and there is no wood or coal to heat the barracks where they are put. There's no soap to wash them, or their clothes or the room they are in and they're in a filthy condition, there's no clothing for them, and most of them have no underclothing at all, they are all huddled together for warmth, and lie on a sort of wooden bed built in along the two opposite sides of the rooms and there are no blankets at all.

But the worst is that the typhus cases have had to remain with the others, as till yesterday there was no hospital for them, and altho' there was some sorting done, many stayed in with the rest. One man died while we were there yesterday – he was huddled up with the rest and nobody knew he was ill. The tragic part of the whole thing is that transport is so bad that you can't hope to get things along for weeks – and by that time the stream of refugees may have finished. They have most of them come in to be out of the way of Deniken's army – as the Ukrainian army is entirely broken up, and he is over-running Ukraine.

There is a Society here to deal with these refugees, but they just haven't got linen and soap and food for invalids, they are now trying to tackle the problem, but I don't know how they'll manage ... We want unlimited stores of under-clothing and bed linen and soap – for the centre here is just typical of others and all the hospitals I've seen have none of these things. I'm glad we're going back for I've reached the point when I feel as if I couldn't bear to see any more misery. It's a different thing when you can relieve it – but to go round day after day and see what would seem unbelievable horrors, and needs which cry out at you, and be able to do nothing at all – it's ghastly. We were taken by car to Kamenice-Podolski, one of the former Ukrainian capitals.. taken by the Poles about ten days ago – we went round one of the military hospitals there, (and it was the best) ... there were 400 men there with typhus only and other infectious diseases, and I shan't easily forget the state in which they were. The whole building reeked, and the atmosphere in the wards was so poisonous, I don't know why they didn't all die. There they had no clothing or linen at all, and the men just lay in the clothes they'd come in with. We saw the Civil Hospital there – that was better but there was the same lack ... and in all the other smaller hospitals the patients have had only one blanket, no sheets, no clothing, there's been no soap – and of course no comfort in any shape or form.

...

All the area round Tarnapol eastwards is destroyed, most of the towns have been pillaged and burnt three times in 1915 by the Russians in 1917 by the Germans and Austrians and this year in May by the Ukrainians. Some have been looted as many as four times. What strikes me most now is that all the Bathing and Delousing stations and all the Disinfecting Machines were destroyed this May by the Ukrainians, and they say that there was a very fine 'line' of Disinfecting Stations all along the frontier, made by the Austrians – As a result there's no means of keeping this flood of Ukrainians and of civilian refugees from bringing in typhus.

We're in a First Class carriage Reserved for the "American Mission" as they always insist on calling us. There are no cushions and just hard boards – the upholstery at the back has gone – and two of the windows are out. We've so far had a slice of dry bread each since 7 this morning.. and it's now getting late. You see I'm already repining for our special car.

...

At Borszczów we packed up our belonging, said goodbye to the Major who was going right back to Warsaw after he's delivered the sweaters – and walked up to the village, which is about a kilometre from the station. There we went to HQ. and were received with much ceremony by the Chief of Staff. He had had the wire from the Central HQ. and had a car at our disposal what! [sic] Moreover he at once sent us round with a 'gendarme' to find rooms. The gendarme's moustache bristled like horns and we at once found what we wanted. But it's best not to say too much of those rooms ... Most of the trains are just as bad.. We came back from Borszczów by train, left at 4 pm and arrived at Tarnapol 10.30 next morning. We started out in style with engaged seats in a so-called First ... but after three hours we had to change into a train which had only thirds ... just wooden narrow benches.. and then we had just arranged ourselves so that three people could stretch out and try to sleep, (which is no small problem) when we arrived at some God-forsaken spot and had to turn out again. We were even less lucky this time, as we got a Third with all its windows out, and in this weather ... taint no little old joke.

...

While we were at Borszczów, we went to several places in the cars. The day of our arrival the Dr took us to see two typhus hospitals in the neighbourhood, one at ?Iwanczow and the other at Korolówka. They are both quite small, and rather miserable, especially Iwankow, as there they haven't more than a blanket each and you can see the patients shivering and the big cold room for they've no coal for the fires – And on top of that if there wasn't a stupid orderly washing the floor in one of the rooms – regularly swabbing the decks, with all the children in bed rolled up into little balls with cold. Korolówka was a bit better as they've a young man in charge who is keen and who fights against the drawbacks as hard as he can – But there they're handicapped because they've no disinfectant to use for the clothes and bedding. A patient who comes in with spotted fever sometimes develops recurrent typhus on top of that because he's been bitten by a louse in the blanket and the louse had been on the last patient who had recurrent typhus It's a cheerful thought.

...

The next day we went in a Lancia touring car to Kamieniec Podolski. It was cold and frosty and the road goes for miles and miles over brown steppes, only there's a curve about them which makes them very lovely. We came to the river Zbrucz, the old Polish frontier and crossed over to what was Russia. There has been a lot of heavy fighting just there.. the bridge over the Zbrucz has been blown to atoms. We had to go round and then over a little wooden bridge. All along there were these wooden bridges, but on the frontier the completeness of the destruction strikes you at once. The woods all round had been reduced to a series of small walking-sticks..

Kamieniec is about 40 versts on the [former] Russian side ... There's as motley a crowd there as you may ever hope to see, all armed to the teeth – many giving you the distinct impression of being great persons in disguise, as they stroll along. And Jews by the hundred.

The fiercest looking are the Ukrainian officers ... You felt distinctly that the taking of the town had been quite a recent affair and that it was seething with excitement.

I should say it was dirty – just as dirty as it could be, and as for the hospitals, I've told you of them, and in addition 1000 cases of typhus lying uncared for in their homes. During the past weeks they had train-loads of Ukrainian soldiers brought in, most of them ill, and some of them without any clothes at all. A lot die on the way too, and are found on arriving at K. I guess it's about the most gruesome town there is just now – in all Europe perhaps. Fortunately there is bound to be an end to the influx of Ukrainians before Deniken and then the hospital will gradually empty. This is the worst time now – just as it is in the Tarnapol area.

The day before yesterday, we (BB and I and the Army Doctor of the Division there) went by car to Podwoloczyska, another frontier town – but further North than Kamieniec – the first station the trains stop at coming in from Ukrania. We crossed into Russia and went to the border station there, to get news of all these refugees and prisoners. I've told you all about them. Anyway we heard that some had to wait 36 hours at the station, without food or warmth, and that many had typhus, so BB and I did the deed. We signed away £250, with a promise of another £250 ... to provide these people with food and a warm waiting room and a room for the sick. . It was certainly not in order to do so, but we knew that if we waited for permission to come thro' the right channels the need would have passed, and the people would have continued to want and starve, so we just let ourselves in.. We found a lady in the town who had been running a canteen for soldiers who was willing to take up the matter and to administer the fund and we found an American chaplain to the Polish army and a Polish Dr who formed a sort of committee. Then we told them what exactly we wanted done – and then we went – by dint of numbers, and a sufficiently authoritative air – forced the Station master to give us one enormous waiting room for the mass and three little rooms for the sick. And so we left – hoping for the best and sure that altho' perhaps the fund won't be administered on exactly the lines we should like, yet the people will be looked after. The lady is going to hire a woman to be in charge, and to get ladies of the town to help. Arrived at Tarnapol we promptly borrowed the £250 from the Chief of Staff and then all was over. Wallis was much amused, as it was the very first time we had been out by ourselves. He had not come because he had a cold, and lo! we ran the Mission into £500 – Anyway we all felt better for it, as we couldn't forget the state of things there, and we've all had more than enough of going round inspecting and doing nothing.

Biographical notes

Alexander, Rachel
Rachel Alexander (1875-1964) was one of seven daughters of W. C. Alexander and Rachel Agnes Lucas. Alexander was a banker, art collector and patron of Whistler, who painted two of the daughters. The family was of Quaker origins on both sides and had a well-developed sense of social concern, particularly for the inhabitants in the poorer parts of the Kensington area of London where they lived. Rachel set up new organisations and involved herself in better provision in health, welfare and housing in her neighbourhood. During the First World War she and her sister Jean (1877-1972) together with their widowed sister Emily Dinely (1871-1962) joined the Friends' relief mission and worked in and around Bar-le-Duc, Rachel for three and a half years. She also received the French Médaille de la reconnaissance française alongside Gertrude in 1919. After the war, Rachel and Jean made the family home, Aubrey House in Kensington, the base for continuing initiatives in social welfare work. Sophia Fry (q.v.) joined Rachel in these, and during the Second World War the two ran a hostel for refugees. One of the Alexander sisters' brothers-in-law, Bernard Spring Rice (1869-1953), who married Cicely Alexander, also visited France with the Friends during the First World War.

Brockway, Fenner
Archibald Fenner Brockway (1888-1988) was born in Calcutta into a missionary family. He became a journalist and entered political life as a member of the Independent Labour Party (ILP) and editor, in 1912, of the ILP's newspaper. His stance as an opponent of military conscription led to four periods of imprisonment during the First World War. On release from prison he became involved in British support for the Indian independence movement. He also resumed his connection with the ILP and in the general election of 1929, was returned as

Labour member of parliament for East Leyton, a London constituency. Increasing disagreements between the Labour party and the ILP led to disaffiliation from Labour, and Brockway lost his seat. He maintained his interest in anti-colonial issues. In 1950, he re-entered parliament as Labour MP for Eton and Slough, but remained always on the left of the Labour party. The Campaign for Nuclear Disarmament and the Movement for Colonial Freedom occupied his energies in the 1950s. He accepted a peerage in the House of Lords in 1964.

Chevalier, Pol
Pol Chevalier (1861-1935), born at Revigny in the department of the Meuse, was a lawyer by training and profession. He entered local politics as a republican and in 1904 was elected mayor of Bar-le-Duc, a position he held until 1912. During the First World War he devoted himself to the wartime needs of the town, and was re-elected mayor in 1919. In 1920 he announced his candidature for the French Senate, to which he was elected to represent the Meuse. Among his other enthusiasms he was a supporter of the political emancipation of women. In 1935, shortly before his death, he published an account of Bar during the war years: *A Bar-le-Duc pendant la guerre*.

Clark, Hilda
Hilda Clark (1881-1955) was a Quaker and member of the Clark shoe-making family. After education at home and at Quaker schools, she trained as a doctor at Birmingham, where her aunt Dr Annie Clark practised, and London in the first decade of the twentieth century. Her first appointment was in 1909 at Birmingham Maternity Hospital, but she soon developed an interest in public health, in particular in the treatment of tuberculosis, for which she advocated tuberculin vaccine as an alternative to sanatorium care. In 1911 she was appointed tuberculosis officer in Portsmouth. Together with T. E. Harvey (q.v.) she urged the formation of a Friends' relief organisation to offer its services to the French government in the autumn of 1914. She helped to set up the Friends' maternity hospital at Châlons-sur-Marne and the first hospital at Sermaize, and involved herself actively in the treatment of tuberculosis, especially among refugee children. In 1919, she went to Austria to administer famine relief for the Quakers. In the inter-war period, Hilda Clark's interest turned towards the promotion of activities and organisations furthering peace and to the care of refugees in Greece and later from Austria and Germany. She was a public speaker and a suffragist, with vivid experiences in 1910 of

being pelted with refuse after a suffrage meeting.

Day, Susanne
Susanne Rouvier Day (1876-1964) was born in Cork in Ireland. She had many political and artistic interests. She was a supporter of the non-militant suffrage movement, co-founder of the Munster Women's Franchise League in 1911 and a member of the Irishwomen's Suffrage Federation. In 1911, she was elected a poor law guardian for Cork, one of the first women to be appointed to such office, and took poor law reform as one of her causes in the years before and during the First World War. She also served on committees connected with public social and welfare issues. In 1914, she presented herself as a candidate in Cork municipal elections but was not successful. She was well read in contemporary literature. In addition to her political writing, which took the form of books, pamphlets, newspaper article and reviews, she was the co-author of two plays and sole writer of several more, all of which were produced in her lifetime. From June 1915 to February 1917, she was in Bar-le-Duc as a relief worker in the FWVRC mission and recorded her impressions and reactions in a book, *Round about Bar-le-Duc*, published in 1918. She continued to write and in the 1930s returned to France. She died in London.

Fry, Margery
Sara Margery Fry (1874-1958) was an elder sister of Ruth Fry. Like her, she was educated at home until she went at the age of seventeen to school in Brighton and eventually to Somerville college at Oxford, where she studied mathematics from 1894 to 1897. Her first post was as librarian at Somerville, from 1899 to 1904. In that year she was appointed warden of a hall of residence for women students at the University of Birmingham, a position she held for ten years. In 1914, she too joined the Friends' War Victims' Relief Committee, assuming responsibility for the Committee's relief work in France. After the end of the war she was able to develop her interest in various problems of social reform when in 1918 she became secretary of the Penal Reform League, later merged into the Howard League for Penal Reform. This remained a lifelong commitment. In 1921, she became one of the first women magistrates and in 1922 the first education adviser to Holloway women's prison. At the same time, she maintained her links with university education when in 1919 she joined the University Grants Committee. A further university appointment came in 1926, when she accepted the position of principal of Somerville college,

which she held until 1931. Throughout the 1920s and 1930s, she became much involved in the campaign to end capital punishment and in questions of international penal reform. She extended her scope into broadcasting and television and continued to write on the issues that engaged her. Throughout her life she remained alive to the concerns of the young, as Gertrude found when she discussed her plans for a career change with her in France.

Fry, Ruth

Anna Ruth Fry (1878-1962) was born into a large Quaker family. Margery Fry and Roger Fry were among her siblings. She was educated at home. Throughout her life she was a dedicated peace activist, working first for the Boer Home Industries Commission following the Boer War (1899-1902) and then moving in 1914 to become honorary general secretary of the Friends' War Victims' Relief Committee, a post she held until 1924. Her work there as administrator, negotiator, supervisor and publicist for the FWVRC involved much travel, sometimes in harsh conditions, and included three visits to Russia during the years of famine. After the FWVRC was wound up, she continued to support peace activities largely through her writing and involvement in the pacifist journal *Reconciliation* from 1935 and the War Resisters' International, of which she was treasurer from 1936 to 1937.

Fry, Sophia

Sophia Matilda Fry (1865-1945) was no relation of Ruth and Margery Fry. She was born into a Quaker family and spent the first three and a half decades of her life at home, although involved in local school boards. In 1904, she became secretary to the Friends' Home Mission. From 1915 to 1920 she was active in the Friends' relief mission to France. She then joined forces with Rachel Alexander (q.v.) to run an adult school for women in one of the hostels established by the latter. Later the two women managed a farm in Buckinghamshire to provide country visits for those in need, and during the Second World War accommodated refugees.

Harvey, Edmund

Thomas Edmund Harvey (1875-1955) was born in Leeds into a Quaker family. He was educated at Bootham school in York and studied later at the universities of Oxford and Berlin and at the Sorbonne in Paris. He graduated with an MA from Oxford in 1900. After four years as an assistant at the British Museum, he turned to social work and the examination of social problems. He was attached to Toynbee

Hall settlement in the London East End, serving as warden from 1906 to 1911, became an elected member in London local government and served on committees dealing with employment. In 1910, he stood for election as Liberal member of parliament for West Leeds and served as MP from 1910 to 1918. He and like-minded MPs worked to ensure that the Military Service Act of 1916 on conscription contained a clause accommodating conscientious objectors. Throughout the First World War he was often in France representing the Friends' War Victims' Relief Committee to the French authorities. He did not present himself as a candidate in the 1918 general election, but entered parliament again in 1923 as the Liberal MP for Dewsbury, only to lose in the 1924 general election. His last stint in parliament was as the Independent Progressive MP for the Combined English Universities seat from 1937 to 1945. He was the author of a number of books.

Hoover, Herbert

Herbert Clark Hoover (1874-1964), thirty-first president of the United States, was born in Iowa to a family of Quaker ancestry. He was orphaned at an early age and raised in his uncle's home. In 1891, he entered Leland Stanford Junior University and graduated in 1895 as a mining engineer. He pursued this career in various parts of the world, including Australia and China. At the outbreak of the First World War he was in Europe and involved himself initially in getting stranded Americans home to the US. He then set up the Committee for Relief in Belgium, which directed food into the country, by then under German occupation. (America's initial position as a neutral country made this possible.) After the US entered the war in 1917, President Woodrow Wilson appointed Hoover US Food Administrator to oversee domestic food rationing. In 1918, Hoover assumed a leading position in Allied initiatives to provide food, clothing and medical supplies to postwar Europe. He headed the American Relief Administration, which was especially concerned with the needs of children (Gertrude mentioned its operation in Poland and recorded seeing him on his visit to Poland in August 1919). In Poland he was the impetus for the American-Polish Relief Expedition's efforts to curb typhus. After the end of the war, Hoover entered government as secretary of commerce. In 1928 he won the presidential elections for the Republicans and served as president from 1928 to 1932, but lost to Franklin Roosevelt in the 1932 elections. After the Second World War, Hoover worked with presidents Truman and Eisenhower on postwar recovery in Europe and American government reorganisation. He was a prolific writer.

King, Truby

Frederic Truby King (1858-1938), more commonly known as Truby King, was born in New Zealand. Throughout his life he was troubled by tuberculosis. In 1880, he left New Zealand to study medicine at Edinburgh. He graduated in 1886 and went on to a further two years' study in public health. On a visit to Paris, on his way to Scotland, he witnessed one of Charcot's demonstrations of hysteria, out of which grew an interest in mental health. On return to New Zealand in 1887, he became medical superintendent first in Wellington, then in Dunedin, where he took charge of a large mental hospital and effected many reforms. His best known work, which followed next, was in child nutrition. Together with his wife he developed methods of feeding and rearing children along regular lines, which were credited with reducing child mortality. He promoted his teaching through books on mothercare and the training of infant welfare nurses. He was invited to Britain to advise on training in child care and after the First World War visited Europe for the Friends' War Victims' Relief Committee. In that capacity he joined the FWVRC Poland unit in 1919. Child welfare and mental health continued to dominate his medical work for the remainder of his professional life. He was recognised as being impetuous and absent-minded, as Gertrude observed.

Lee, Henry Austin

Sir Henry Austin Lee (1847-1918) spent his career in the British Foreign Office and Diplomatic Service, specialising in commerce, trade and transport. His exact position in the Paris embassy during the First World War is not clear, but he evidently had good contacts with the French government on which to draw on behalf of the Society of Friends. In July 1915, he toured FWVRC centres accompanied by Edmund Harvey, John Bellows and Ruth Fry, when he was described, inaccurately, as the 'sub' British ambassador.

Lucas, E. V.

Edward Verrall Lucas (1868-1938) was a writer in many genres: journalism, essays, literary and art criticism, biography, travel-writing, and plays. He enjoyed considerable popularity in his day. His wife was also a writer. Lucas was born to Quaker parents, and he himself undertook writing commissions from the Society of Friends and edited one of their magazines. Gertrude met the Lucases in France in July 1915, but recorded her disappointment in him, finding him "well-fed, prosperous and worldly-looking – Could anything be further from one's idea of a man who writes as he does!"

Powick, Wilmer

Wilmer Chrisman Powick (1886-around 1963) was second cousin to Gertrude and her siblings. (His family retained the original spelling of Powick, without a final 'e'.) His grandfather emigrated from England to the United States in around 1868 and settled in Wilmington in the state of Delaware. His father, William, eventually trained as a minister in the Methodist Episcopal church and received his licence to preach in 1878. He settled in Pennsylvania. Wilmer was a scientist and graduated in 1907 with a BSc degree from Penn State University. His working life, from 1907 to 1953, was spent in the US Department of Agriculture as a biochemical research scientist, with an interest in animal industry and foodstuffs. During the First World War he enlisted and served first from 1916 to 1917 as a private in the National Guard, then from 1917 to 1919 as a first lieutenant, subsequently captain in the US Army in France. In that capacity he met Gertrude in Paris

Pye, Edith

Edith Mary Pye (1876-1965) was born in London and qualified as a nurse and a midwife in 1906. By the following year, she was superintendent of district nurses in London. In 1908, she became a member of the Society of Friends. Her professional knowledge and her friendship with Hilda Clark (q.v.) led her to join the Friends' relief expedition to France in 1914. The two set up a maternity hospital for the care of refugee women at Châlons-sur-Marne, which Edith Pye managed until 1919. The French government awarded her the rank of Chevalier of the Legion of Honour in recognition of her work. She then joined Hilda Clark in Austria from 1921 to 1922 to organise food distributions among famished children. From 1928 to 1949, she was president of what became the Royal College of Midwives and encouraged the development of pain alleviation in childbirth. In the 1920s and 1930s she was much involved in the Women's International League for Peace and Freedom. She upheld her commitment to Quaker relief and rescue efforts towards German, Jewish and Spanish refugees in the years preceding the Second World War and urged famine relief and the partial lifting of the economic blockade against Europe during the war years.

Streatfeild, Granville

Granville Edward Stewart Streatfeild (1869-1947) was an architect based in London and Kent. He worked at one point for Sir Reginald Blomfield. His work focused largely on houses and church building and restoration. In addition to assisting the Society of Friends with architectural designs, he advised the FWVRC on how to organise its building work, recommending that it form a central office responsible for construction at each centre, regularise output and the distribution of labour, and order materials. He is mentioned in February 1915 as a member of the committee for the Châlons maternity hospital.

Notes

Chapter 1
1. Stockport Metropolitan Borough Council, 'Hatherlow conservation area character appraisal', October 2006 (updated 2012). On Powicke House, see pages 15 and 46. Online: www.stockport.gov.uk/2013/2978/8803/9020/12299/hatherlowapp1, accessed 19 May 2014.
2. Alan Tunnicliffe, *Powicks Past and Present*, Christchurch, New Zealand: Alan Tunnicliffe, 1989, page 158.
3. Woodbrooke was founded in 1903 under the impetus of John Wilhelm Rowntree (1868-1905), prominent in the British Quaker movement in the late 19th century, as a permanent centre for religious and social study. His fellow Quaker George Cadbury (1839-1922) offered his former home as premises for the centre. Among the literature on the history of the college is Robert Davis (ed.), *Woodbrooke, 1903-1953: A Brief History of a Quaker Experiment in Religious Education*, London: The Bannisdale Press, 1953.
4. Alan Tunnicliffe, *Powicks Past and Present*, page 158.
5. If the milk was not fortified with vitamins or minerals, Gertrude may possibly have suffered from a deficiency of Vitamin D, or she may have had an intolerance to cow's milk. I am indebted to Ingrid Kolb-Hindarmanto for her suggestions as to the possible cause of the bow legs.
6. Lynda Edwards, 'Milton Mount College, Gravesend, to be demolished', *Kent Archaeological Review*, 26, Autumn 1971. Online: KAR Articles, http://cka.moon-demon.co.uk/KAR026/KAR026_Milton.htm, accessed 19 May 2014.
7. This success was recorded in the school's News Sheet for September 1906. My thanks to Margaret Clark, archivist of the Miltonian Guild, for sending me this information.
8. The connection continued until 1931, when Gertrude's niece, Janet, the author's mother, completed her schooling. Maurice, who was Janet's father, had been a governor from 1920 to 1928. I am grateful to Dr Christine Joy, archivist at MHSG, for her help in establishing these various family connections. For further information on the school's history, see the MHSG website: http://www.mhsgarchive.org accessed 4 May 2014.
9. Jane Bedford, 'Margaret Ashton: Manchester's "First Lady"', *Manchester Region History Review*, 12, 1998, page 7.
10. Janet Howarth, 'Fawcett, Dame Millicent Garrett (1847-1929)', *Oxford Dictionary of National Biography*, OUP, 2004.
11. Howarth, 'Fawcett, Dame Millicent Garrett'.
12. Bedford, 'Margaret Ashton', pages 7-8, 3.
13. Gertrude M. Powicke, 'Women's suffrage and the social problem', *Miltonian News Sheet*, October 1909, pages 17-18; courtesy of Margaret Clark.
14. This was the informal, but expressive, name given to the Prisoners (Temporary Discharge for Ill-health) Act of 1913, which allowed for the temporary and conditional release of a prisoner whose health had seriously deteriorated through that prisoner's own conduct. The prisoner was required to return to prison at the end of a stated period to resume the sentence. The act was used against women imprisoned for offences committed while campaigning for the vote, who then went on hunger strike and were forcibly fed.
15. Bedford, 'Margaret Ashton', page 8.
16. Much of the factual information on Harry Pickles's life is taken from a short cloth-bound In Memoriam booklet, undated and with no named compiler, prepared after his death.

17. The card was designed by Sapper A. St L. Wadmore and the accompanying verses composed by Driver E. S. Knell. The card was printed by Raphael Tuck and Sons, Ltd.
18. Reference by courtesy of the University Librarian and Director, The John Rylands Library, The University of Manchester. See Special Collections, Papers of Thomas Frederick Tout, file TFT/1/963, item 1. I am indebted to Dr Anne-Marie Hughes for drawing my attention to these papers.
19. The Pelman Institute was founded in 1898 by W.J. Ennever, who developed this particular form of memory training. For a detailed account of the programme and its history, see Barry Ennever, 'The Pelman School of Memory, The Pelman Institute and Pelmanism'. Online: http://www.ennever.com/histories/history386p.php, accessed 20 May 2014.
20. Joseph Cockshoot and Co. was a long-established Manchester business that had started off in 1844 as carriage-builders. The company opened a motor garage in 1902 on Deansgate and added car-body production to its lines in 1903. In 1906, it acquired premises on the corner of Great Ducie Street and New Bridge Street. Its records are held at the Museum of Science and Industry, Manchester, Collections Department, Joseph Cookshoot and Co., company records. Online: http://www.mosi.org.uk/media/33871030/josephcockshootandco.pdf, accessed 20 May 2014.
21. The Scottish Women's Hospitals were one of the most remarkable creations in Britain's response to the needs of the First World War. They emerged from the Scottish Federation of Women's Suffrage Societies and were sponsored by the NUWSS. Despite their name, they took women from the whole of Britain and the dominions, recruiting them as volunteers into medical, nursing and administrative positions. Hospital units were active in Serbia, Macedonia, Romania, Corsica, Malta, France and elsewhere. Literature on the Scottish Women's Hospitals includes Eileen Crofton, *The Women of Royaumont*, East Linton, East Lothian, Scotland: Tuckwell, 1997; Leah Leneman, *In the Service of Life*, Edinburgh: Mercat, 1994; and Anne Powell, *Women in the War Zone*, Stroud, UK: The History Press, 2009.

Chapter 2

1. See Dandelion, *An Introduction to Quakerism*, Cambridge: Cambridge University Press, 2007, page 162.
2. That is, responsible to the Society of Friends in Britain.
3. Thirty-three is the number given by Ruth Fry in *A Quaker Adventure: The Story of Nine Years' Relief and Reconstruction*, London: Nisbet and Co. Ltd., 1926, page 6, and by *The Friend*, 54/46, 13 November 1914. T. E. Harvey, however, writing in March 1915, mentions an original figure of thirty-two. See War Victims' Relief Committee of the Society of Friends, 'Behind the battle lines in France: the report of a month's work by a group of members of the mission sent by the above', with an introduction dated March 1915 by T. Edmund Harvey MP, page 3.
4. Henry van Etten, *Chronique de la vie Quaker française*, 2nd edition, Paris: Société Religieuse des Amis (Quakers), 1947, pages 203-204. He suggests that Christine Majolier, a French Quaker married to Robert Alsop, a British Friend, was active in soliciting the support of Friends in England over the war. See also John Punshon, *Portrait in Grey*, 2nd edition, London: Quaker Books, 2006, page 209, for a brief account of this earlier initiative.
5. Ruth Fry, *A Quaker Adventure*, page xv, suggests that the symbol was invented by Joseph Beck, brother of Ernest Beck, secretary to the 1870-71 FWVRC, following the precedent of the Red Cross (established in 1863). Another account is that the star was taken from the marking used by a British newspaper, the *Daily News*, to identify the relief goods it was shipping out in support of the FWVRC's work during the Franco-Prussian War. With the newspaper's agreement, the FWVRC adopted the star as its symbol. See Punshon, *Portrait in Grey*, pages 209-10; and Jack Sutters, 'The red and black star', American Friends Service Committee, https://afsc.org/story/red-and-black-star, accessed 21 May 2014.
6. Fry, *A Quaker Adventure*, page xxi.
7. This government matching of funds was still continuing to benefit the Society of Friends in late 1919.
8. Fry, *A Quaker Adventure*, page xxii.
9. Fry, *A Quaker Adventure*, page xxiv.
10. Fry, *A Quaker Adventure*, page xxviii.
11. Fry, *A Quaker Adventure*, page 1.
12. Fry, *A Quaker Adventure*, page 122.
13. See Annette Becker, *Les Cicatrices rouges 14-18 France et Belgique occupées*, Paris: Fayard, 2010, and Philippe Nivet, *La France occupée 1914-1918*, Paris: Armand Colin, 2011, for detailed accounts of the experiences of these regions; and Helen McPhail, *The Long Silence*, London: I. B. Tauris, 1999, for an examination of life in Lille under German occupation.

14. See Bernard Crochet and Gérard Piouffre, *La 1ere Guerre Mondiale*, Paris: Nov'Édit, 2008; John Keegan, *The First World War*, London: Hutchinson, 1998; and Ian Sumner, *The First Battle of the Marne*, Oxford: Osprey Publishing, 2010, for useful information.
15. FEWVRC/1/2/3, Documentation of initial services, 1914, letter of 25 October 1914 from the Minister of War.
16. 'Behind the battle lines in France', page 3.
17. Writing of Joffre, commander-in-chief of the French forces from before the outbreak of war until December 1916, Keegan (*The First World War*, page 346) comments of his powers within the zone that they "had constitutional force. Even parliamentary deputies lacked the right to enter the Zone without his permission..."
18. FEWVRC/1/2/6, T. E. Harvey, correspondence and reports.
19. FEWVRC/1/3/3/1, Contact French authorities 1915-1920, 5 February 1915. In July 1915, Sir Henry Austin Lee made a visit of inspection to Sermaize and Bar-le-Duc, accompanied by Edmund Harvey, Ruth Fry and John Bellows. The purpose of his tour is nowhere spelled out, but one might speculate that the embassy wanted to assure itself that its efforts in assisting the Society of Friends were proving worthwhile. Sir Henry visited Gertrude's workroom in Bar-le-Duc on 19 July 1915 and asked her a lot about it, as she recorded in her diary on 17 and 19 July 1915. He was presented as the 'sub' British ambassador, but needless to say, the women took him to be the ambassador himself and were "much bucked". Gertrude described him as "an impressive-looking man, very English, full of ceremony, an eagle eye, with a kind expression all the same."
20. Fry, *A Quaker Adventure*, page xxiii.
21. See Philippe Nivet, *Les Refugiés français de la Grande Guerre (1914-1920): Les 'Boches du Nord'*, Hautes Études Militaires, no. 27. Paris: Economica, 2004, pages 113-114, 125.
22. 'Behind the battle lines in France', page 3.
23. Map based on Carte-guide Campbell no. 7-Vosges, published by Blondel la Rougery, Paris, showing the front at 10 May 1917, FEWVRC/3/1/2. With thanks to the Religious Society of Friends in Britain.
24. As reported in *The Friend*, 57/15, 13 April 1917.
25. See Annette Becker, *Les Cicatrices rouges*, pages 74-81; Philippe Nivet, *La France occupée*, chapter 13; Philippe Nivet, *Les Refugiés français*, pages 47-64.
26. This address continued to house a Quaker centre until 1928, according to Henry van Etten, *Chronique de la vie Quaker française*, page 266.
27. Parvin M. Russell, 'Among refugees in the war zone', Chapter 6 in Edward Thomas, *Quaker Adventures: Experiences of Twenty-three Adventurers in International Understanding*. New York; Chicago: Fleming H. Revell Company, 1928, page 57.
28. Quoted in Fry, *A Quaker Adventure*, pages 87-89.
29. 'Behind the battle lines in France', page 10. Quoted with permission of the Religious Society of Friends in Britain.
30. Refugees were officially classified as *sinistrés*, those who had returned to their destroyed villages, *émigrés*, who had fled from their homes now under enemy occupation, and the repatriated, *rapatriés*. Eventually, the first two groups were subsumed under the term 'refugees'.
31. 'Behind the battle lines in France', page 4.
32. FEWVRC/1/2/4, Correspondence with Hilda Cashmore.
33. *The Friend*, 57/12, 23 March 1917.
34. *The Friend*, 55/7, 12 February 1915, and 'Behind the battle lines in France', page 18.
35. FEWVRC/1/2/6, T. E. Harvey, correspondence and reports.
36. Walter G. Bowerman, 'Quaker relief in wartime France', Chapter 4 in Edward Thomas, *Quaker Adventures: Experiences of Twenty-three Adventurers in International Understanding*. New York; Chicago: Fleming H. Revell Company, 1928, pages 42-43.
37. Edward G. Lengel, *To Conquer Hell: The Battle of Meuse-Argonne, 1918*. London: Aurum Press Ltd., 2008, pages 43-44.
38. Society of Friends' War Victims' Relief Committee, 'Report on Three Months' Work at Châlons-sur-Marne from Dec.1914 to Feb. 1915,' signed by Hilda Clark. Quoted with permission of the Religious Society of Friends in Britain. The women were exchanged for a party of German maids who had been interned in France.
39. Philippe Nivet discusses this reluctance in chapter 2 of *Les Refugiés français*.
40. Reference by courtesy of the University Librarian and Director, The John Rylands Library, The University of Manchester. See file TFT/1/963, item 4.
41. FEWVRC/1/2/3, Contact French authorities 1915-1920, letter of 16 October 1914.
42. Clark, 'Report on Three Months' Work at Châlons-sur-Marne, 1915', page 3.
43. Fry, *A Quaker Adventure*, page 66.
44. Authorisation was secured from the relevant authorities for Barrie to visit the Lucases at Bettancourt

on 4 November 1915. Although there is no further mention, he presumably did make this visit. See FEWVRC/1/3/1/7, George Innes correspondence, 23 October 1915; and FEWVRC/1/3/3/2, Contact French authorities, 28 October 1915.
45. Edith Pye gives the number as eleven. Edith M. Pye, (ed.), *War and its Aftermath: Letters from Hilda Clark, M. B., B. S. from France, Austria and the Near East 1914-1924*, [London: Friends Book House, 1957], page 16.
46. *The Friend*, 54/52, 25 December 1914.

Chapter 3

1. Gertrude writes of passing Epernay, which is in Champagne, but must mean Etaples.
2. This, and much other valuable information on the arrivals and departures of FWVRC and other relief workers in Bar-le-Duc is contained in the lists of foreigners registered by the police in Bar during the war years. Despite minor errors in names – Gertrude is listed as 'Marie Powicke' – the record seems fairly comprehensive. See Archives départementales de la Meuse (ADM), E dépôt 460/1431, Statistique des étrangers, 1911-1921.
3. *The Friend*, 55/31, 30 July 1915.
4. *The Friend*, 55/49, 3 December 1915.
5. Susanne Day, *Round about Bar-le-Duc*, London: Skeffington & Son, Ltd., 1918, facsimile reprint by Nabu Public Domain Reprints, 2012, page 30.
6. Voluntary Aid Detachments (VADs) were organised from 1909 onwards under a scheme of voluntary aid to provide supplementary assistance to the military medical services in the event of war. Training in first aid and nursing was given by the Red Cross. During the First World War, the British Red Cross and the Order of St John of Jerusalem jointly administered the scheme. Personnel were commonly known as VADs. They worked in auxiliary hospitals and convalescent homes in Britain and abroad in a range of duties that went beyond nursing and first aid.
7. Day, *Round about Bar-le-Duc*, pages 138-40.
8. Pol Chevalier, *A Bar-le-Duc pendant la guerre*, Bar-le-Duc: Contant-Laguerre, 1935, pages 23 and 31.
9. Chevalier, *A Bar-le-Duc pendant la guerre*, pages 61 and 168.
10. Her sister Agnes writes about this blouse, which appears to have been passed down within the family; Agnes Powicke, memoir, page 47.
11. Quoted by courtesy of the University Librarian and Director, The John Rylands Library, The University of Manchester. See Special Collections, TFT/1/963, item 8.
12. Confiture de Bar is prepared from red and white currants from which the seeds have been extracted by hand with the aid of a goose quill. The fruit, kept intact, is then cooked in syrup. The process is laborious and the product consequently expensive.
13. Gertrude Powicke, 'C'est la Guerre!', *The Englishwoman*, 38, April-June 1918, no. 114, June 1918, page 150.
14. See FEWVRC/2/1/1, Bar-le-Duc, for Gertrude's description of the parties and the accounts therefore, January 1919.
15. FEWVRC/2/1/1, Reports on relief work at Bar-le-Duc, July-December 1917.
16. The 75mm field gun was one of the mainstays of the French artillery, prized for its accuracy, rapid rate of fire, efficient recoil mechanism and maximum range of 11 km. One of these guns, together with its attachment, is held at the Imperial War Museum in London, donated by the French government after the First World War.
17. Among cars, she mentioned the following: Austin, Batz, Barick, Bayard, Belsize, Dodge, Flanders, Ford, Garner, Hodgkiss, Hupmobile, Itala, Napier, Overland, Renault and Sunbeam; and among motor cycles the BSA and 'HD', presumably Harley Davidson.
18. Fry, *A Quaker Adventure*, page xxiv.
19. I am indebted to Brian Spear for sharing his expertise with me. The Hupmobile was manufactured by the Hupp Motor Car Company of Detroit between 1908 and 1940. The company was named after its originator, Robert Hupp. During the first two decades of the 20th century, two models, the 20 and the 32, were offered in various styles, many of them exported overseas. A range of models from the second line of cars was produced during the First World War. A brief account of the Hupmobile is provided at the Hupmobile Club webpage. Online: http://clubs.hemmings.com/hupmobile/hupp-history.html, accessed 22 May 2014.
20. The article, unsigned, appeared in the *Daily Chronicle* of 25 September 1915, under the title 'With the "Friends" in France. The experiences of a lady visitor'. The writer detailed the "good work" that was being done by the Society of Friends, but expressed reservations over the presence of so many young men within its ranks in France, young men who should have been "in the firing line".

Chapter 4

1. Gertrude's note of a conversation with Miss Lendrum, a long-term foreign resident of Bar, 6 August 1915.
2. In a modern, abridged edition published in 2011, Michelin has presented the essential information contained in its original series of illustrated Guides to the Battlefields, the first of which were launched as early as 1917. The new edition reproduces in facsimile some of the pages and photographs of the first edition. See Michelin, *Les champs de bataille: Verdun, Argonne, Saint-Mihiel*, 92100 Boulogne-Billancourt: Michelin, 2011, pages 36, 210-19.
3. Pol Chevalier, *A Bar-le-Duc pendant la guerre*, pages 47-48.
4. See Chevalier, *A Bar-le-Duc pendant la guerre*, chapter 1; Jean Collot, 'Bar-le-Duc en août 1914', *Bulletin des Sociétés d'Histoire et d'Archéologie de la Meuse*, no.2, 1965, spéciale 14-18, pages 35-45; and Emile Bugnon, *La Coopérative Meusienne*, Bar-le-Duc: Imprimerie du Barrois, 1959, page 14. In preparing his account of Bar-le-Duc's experiences of coping with the demands of war, Chevalier solicited the reminiscences of his fellow-citizens. His work is also an exercise in accounting, since he details the financial costs of the various initiatives, which depended on continuing official and voluntary funding, and is careful to give thanks all round. The result is a lively, if idiosyncratic insight into the workings of Bar's war effort.
5. Chevalier, *A Bar-le-Duc pendant la guerre*, page 58.
6. Chevalier, *A Bar-le-Duc pendant la guerre*, page 26.
7. Chevalier, *A Bar-le-Duc pendant la guerre*, pages 56, 54.
8. *The Friend*, 58/42, 18 October 1918.
9. Chevalier, *A Bar-le-Duc pendant la guerre*, page 77.
10. I am indebted to Jean-Michel Althuser for this information.
11. Susanne Day, *Round About Bar-le-Duc*, page 184.
12. Day, *Round About Bar-le-Duc*, page 187.
13. See Chevalier, *A Bar-le-Duc pendant la guerre*, page 58. Philippe Nivet also comments on this reluctance; *Les Réfugiés français*, page 88.
14. Chevalier, *A Bar-le-Duc pendant la guerre*, page 114.
15. This song, with its theme of Madelon, the serving girl in a country inn who cheered up her soldier-clients and received their confidences without promising herself to any one of them, enjoyed great popularity among the French troops. The words were written in 1913 by Louis Bousquet (1870-1941) to an already known march composed by Camille Robert. It took off in 1916, when the singer and comedian Bach (the stage name of Charles-Joseph Pasquier, 1882-1953) introduced it to his soldier audiences. With its regular beat it clearly lent itself to being sung on the march. For the text of the song, see the website maintained by Paul Dubé and Jacques Marchioro, Du temps des cerises aux feuilles mortes, 2001-2012. Online: http://dutempsdescerisesauxfeuillesmortes.net/paroles/quand_madelon.htm, accessed 22 May 2014. For a rendering of the song, see http://www.youtube.com/watch?v=Im4tViuVoJM, accessed 22 May 2014.
16. The *bleu d'horizon* uniform was generally introduced into the French army from early spring 1915. See Ian Sumner, *French Poilu 1914-18*, Oxford: Osprey Publishing, 2009, page 18.
17. The hospital, staffed by British and French, was offered to the French government by the British Union of Trained Nurses. The hospital was administered by the British Committee of the French Red Cross and from July 1917 was taken over by that committee. See Malcolm Brown, *Verdun 1916*, Stroud, UK: Tempus Publishing Ltd., 2000, pages 97-102; and Laurence Binyon, *For Dauntless France: An Account of Britain's Aid to the Frnch Wounded and Victims of the War*, London: Hodder and Stoughton, 1918, pages 150-153, 331.
18. Report dated 16 June 1916 on the functioning of this infirmary. ADM, E depot 460/1204 W/3, item 23.
19. Bulletin of the Société de Secours, reproduced in *Echo de l'Est*, 30-31 July 1917.
20. Chevalier, *A Bar-le-Duc pendant la guerre*, page 243.
21. Literally, 'drip from a monkey's nose'. A term used to denote something worthless or of poor quality.
22. Day, *Round about Bar-le-Duc*, page 231.
23. Chevalier, *A Bar-le-Duc pendant la guerre*, page 242.
24. The Foyer des alliés was not the only British-run canteen in the region. At Revigny, a *cantine anglaise* operated in the station waiting room, equally directed towards soldiers passing through the station. It was privately financed and managed and used volunteers from Britain. See Lyn Macdonald, *The Roses of No Man's Land*, London: Penguin Books, 2013, pages 137-140, and plate opposite page 177. Gertrude makes no mention of this canteen.
25. Médiathèque Jeukens, Ms 821/2; Chevalier, *A Bar-le-Duc pendant la guerre*, page 241.
26. The names of these women are listed in the registration files and statistics for foreigners coming to Bar-

le-Duc during this period, where they give their affiliation as the Foyer des alliés or the Red Cross. See ADM, Statistique des étrangers, 1911-1921.
27. Susanne Day insists that the canteen "was not run by or connected in any way" to the Society of Friends and that she and two other members of the Bar équipe worked there as "supernumeraries" in the evening when other work was done. The fourth member of the équipe was "one of the fairy godmothers whose magic wand had waved it into being", which could be taken as an indirect acknowledgement of Rachel Alexander's role in setting up the canteen (*Round about Bar-le-Duc*, page 242). The author's own interpretation is that the Society agreed to provide on-the-spot management in Bar for an initiative of the British Committee of the French Red Cross. Pol Chevalier points to this committee's support for the canteen, both financially and in easing travel arrangements for the flow of volunteers (whom it may even have recruited). The Society of Friends was well aware of the existence of the foyer, but sought to avoid being linked with its activities, possibly for fear that members and supporters of the Society might object, firstly, to the fact it was ministering directly to combatants and secondly, that the mission's workers were being distracted from the FWVRC's openly stated aims of relief to non-combatants.
28. Day, *Round about Bar-le-Duc*, pages 244-45.
29. Chevalier, *A Bar-le-Duc pendant la guerre*, chapter 6.
30. Chevalier, *A Bar-le-Duc pendant la guerre*, page 111; author's translation.
31. Chevalier, *A Bar-le-Duc pendant la guerre*, page 120. Mrs Griggs appeared in Bar-le-Duc in the autumn of 1916. She had contacts in the Union des femmes de France. It is not clear if she was travelling in a personal capacity or on behalf of an organisation, but she was prepared to support some of the local war work efforts. On 23 October 1916, she visited the FWVRC workroom and questioned Gertrude on its activities, but in the end did not offer any assistance.
32. Chevalier, *A Bar-le-Duc pendant la guerre*, page 92.
33. Chevalier, *A Bar-le-Duc pendant la guerre*, page 96.
34. Chevalier, *A Bar-le-Duc pendant la guerre*, page 103.
35. Chevalier, *A Bar-le-Duc pendant la guerre*, page 98.
36. See Ruth Fry, *A Quaker Adventure*, page 68.
37. FEWVRC/2/5/2, Building, misc.
38. FEWVRC/2/6/1, Building, misc.
39. This is Chevalier's estimate. Georges Dumesnil, quoting statistics published in the local press in 1919, gives 246, of which 145 were military deaths and injuries. See Dumesnil, *Bar-le-Duc: ses rues, places, ponts et cours d'eau*, Bar: Imprimerie du Barrois, 1987, page 277, for these figures and for his estimate of the number of bombs.
40. See Ari Unikoski, 'The War in the Air – Bombers: Germany, Zeppelins', firstworldwar.com: a multimedia history of world war one, 22 August 2009. Online: http://www.firstworldwar.com/airwar/bombers_zeppelins.htm, accessed 23 May 2014.
41. Chevalier, *A Bar-le-Duc pendant la guerre*, page 179.
42. *Echo de l'Est* was published at Bar-le-Duc from 1830 to 1939.
43. Chevalier, *A Bar-le-Duc pendant la guerre*, page 198.
44. Chevalier, *A Bar-le-Duc pendant la guerre*, page 187.
45. Chevalier, *A Bar-le-Duc pendant la guerre*, page 187.
46. FEWVRC/2/1/1, Bar-le-Duc.
47. There was a strange link here with Britain. Two airships passed over Bar-le-Duc on the night in question, but did not attack the town. They formed part of a German raid of eleven Zeppelins directed against industrial targets in England on the night of 19-20 October 1917. These managed to offload their bombs over their destination, but were eventually driven back towards the European mainland when they encountered very heavy winds. Not all of them arrived back safely to Germany. Of the two that passed over Bar, one was subsequently shot down and the other was captured intact by the French. For a detailed account of the raid, see Captain Joseph Morris, *The German Air Raids on Great Britain 1914-1918*, first published 1925, republished, Stroud, UK: Nonsuch Publishing, 2007, pages 124-30. Gertrude may have been a day out in her dating of this event. She was very satisfied to hear that the two Zeppelins had been brought down: "Tant mieux Que le diable les emporte!", which may be translated as "So much the better, may the devil take them!"
48. Chevalier, *A Bar-le-Duc pendant la guerre*, page 196.

Chapter 5
1. Keegan, *The First World War*, page 356.
2. Pol Chevalier, *A Bar-le-Duc pendant la guerre*, page 273.
3. *Echo de l'Est*, 7 August 1917.

4. Chevalier, *A Bar-le-Duc pendant la guerre*, page 273; author's translation.
5. See Howard L. Carey, 'With the wounded and the peasants', Chapter 5 in Edward Thomas, *Quaker Adventure: Experiences of Twenty-three Adventurers in International Understanding*, New York; Chicago: Fleming H. Revell Company, 1928, pages 47-48.
6. See *The Friend*, 57/37, 14 September 1917.
7. *The Friend*, 58/14 and 58/15, 5 and 12 April 1918.
8. Despite Pershing's insistence on the independence of the American Expeditionary Force, he agreed to lend troops in support of the Allied counterattacks in the Somme and Champagne in the spring and summer of 1918.
9. The Germans did indeed occupy Château-Thierry from 1 June to 21 July 1918, Dormans was held briefly, but Epernay, through which lay the way to Rheims, was not taken. Soissons was within the territory invaded in the German push. Rheims was occupied by the Germans for ten days in September 1914, was retaken by the French but subjected thereafter to almost continuous bombardment throughout the war. On 25 March 1918, the final inhabitants were evacuated, but the city did not fall again into enemy hands.
10. In the event, only the maternity hospital was obliged to implement such plans. With Châlons facing heavy German bombardment, the local French military command on 11 July ordered the evacuation of the hospital, and it moved down to Méry-sur-Seine in the Aube.
11. FEWVRC/1/1/1-1/1/7, Sermaize, minutes of meetings of 31 May and 21 June 1918.
12. A handwritten letter from Monsieur Piette, dated 12 (or possibly 17) August gives these details as an explanation for Gertrude's failure to take up the passport she had obtained in July to return to England.
13. Though the diary is not clear on this point, the refugees were presumably mainly fed by the French authorities, and the FWVRC's provisions were supplementary.
14. Gertrude M. Powicke, 'C'est la guerre!', 1918.
15. See Edward G. Lengel, *To Conquer Hell: The Battle of Meuse-Argonne 1918*. Lengel's account of the campaign is lively and detailed. A shorter account of the Argonne campaign, with useful maps, is to be found in the *Illustrated Michelin Guide to the Battle-fields* (1914-1918), *The Americans in the Great War*, vol. 3, Meuse-Argonne Battle (Montfaucon, Romagne, St. Menehould), Clermont-Ferrand: Michelin & Cie; London: Michelin Tyre Co Ltd; Milltown NJ: Michelin Tire Co., 1919, facsimile reproduction, Easingwold, York, UK: G. H. Smith & Son, 1994; see particularly pages 11-28.
16. FEWVRC/2/6/1-4, file 4.
17. The refugees were housed in army barracks sited at some distance from each other in the fields.
18. By that time, the great epidemic had struck Western Europe and was affecting people at all levels, including FWVRC workers in France, five of whose number died of the illness over the autumn and winter of 1918-19. Keegan (*The First World War*, pages 437-38) claims that the first outbreak of influenza on the western front occurred among German troops in June 1918.
19. See Edward Lengel, *To Conquer Hell*, page 402, where he quotes Henry W. Smith's recollection, recorded in Smith's *A Story of the 305th Machine Gun Battalion, 77th Division A.E.F.*, New York: Modern Composing Room, 1941, pages 76-77.
20. Rachel F. Alexander, 'Before the armistice', *Reconstruction*, 1/10, January 1919, pages 165-66. Her account corroborates and amplifies Gertrude's diary entries. *Reconstruction* was published monthly in Paris "for the Relief Missions of the Society of Friends in France, Russia, Holland and elsewhere".
21. Alexander, 'Before the armistice', page 166.
22. This kind of constant, low-level control and harassment on the part of the Germans was the experience of many living through the years of occupation in Belgium and northern and northeastern France.
23. The waiting room wall might just be the provenance of a closely printed poster, produced in the northern German town of Lübeck but undated and bearing no attribution, which has survived among Gertrude's papers. It is indeed very interesting. Under the heading 'Hunger', it lambasts the German government for reducing the people to a state of hunger and want through war, a lust for power and profiteering. It foresees no victory through force of arms and calls on the people to make their voices heard. Its concluding call, 'Long live the international solidarity of the proletariat', suggests the poster's origins in the stirrings of mutiny and revolt among the ranks of the German navy and army and within the civilian population in the autumn of 1918, inspired by the success of the 1917 Bolshevik revolution in Russia. How the poster may have got to Sedan can only be speculated at, and, as Gertrude and her sister Agnes stayed together in Bonn, Koblenz and Cologne in Germany in May 1919, Gertrude may have picked it up there.
24. Birrell et al., 'Beginnings at Verdun', *Reconstruction*, 1/10, January 1919, pages 153-57.
25. Fry, *A Quaker Adventure*, pages 92-93.
26. Fry, *A Quaker Adventure*, page 94.
27. *The Friend*, 59/9, 28 February 1919
28. FEWVRC/2/1/1, Monthly reports, Bar équipe.

29. The aliens' register for Bar-le-Duc gives the total number of British remaining in the town at 31 March 1919 as two men and twenty women; of Americans as ten women. ADM, Statistique des étrangers, 1911-1921.
30. FEWVRC/2/1/1, report of January 1919 by G. M. Powicke on Bar-le-Duc relief work.
31. This photograph was taken by Olive Edis (1876-1955), who in 1919 was commissioned by the Imperial War Museum to provide a pictorial record for the museum's archives of the war work undertaken by the British women's services in France and Belgium. She made a four-week tour in March 1919. See IWM, First World War Official Collection, image Q 8073. Gertrude recorded a visit by a group on 19 March 1919 "to take our portraits".
32. FEWVRC/2/1/1, note on visits of enquiry in Bar, February-April 1919.
33. A collection of photographs of Mouzon taken between 1910 and 1914 by Pierre Poncelet, a former notary and justice of the peace in the town, shows some of the damage. See Les Amis du Patrimoine de Mouzon, *Mouzon il y a 100 ans*, Sedan: Imprimerie Soupalt et Cie, 2009, pages 101, 103-106.
34. *The Friend*, 59/15, 11 April 1919.
35. Fry, *A Quaker Adventure*, page 94.
36. The whole ensemble is magnificent, from the twin-towered church, parts of which date to the 13th and 15th centuries, to the former monastery, constructed in the 17th century. See Les Amis du Patrimoine de Mouzon, *The Abbey church Notre-Dame de Mouzon, Ardennes - France*, Sedan: Imprimerie Soupault et Cie., 2008.
37. Dr L. Rajchman, director of the Polish State Epidemiological Institute, urged this choice in the memorandum he signed with the Society of Friends on 15 May 1919.
38. The medal has remained in Gertrude's family. The order itself was instituted on 13 July 1917. It was reserved for civilians, both French and non-French, and was awarded by the president of the republic acting on the advice of the Ministry of Justice for prolonged acts of assistance in the public sphere to those affected by war. The recommendation for Gertrude and her colleagues was made in a document, undated and unsigned, that was clearly intended for upward transmission. The author is inclined to attribute the initiative to Pol Chevalier. The same document also put forward the Society of Friends for a gold medal (awarded in October 1919), the Foyer des alliés for a silver medal and its manager Bertha Johnson for a bronze medal. Médiathèque Jeukens, Bar-le-Duc, Ms 821/2. My warm thanks to Daniel Labarthe for bringing this document to my attention. For a brief history of the order, which was abolished in 1958, see the website for France Phaleristique. Online: http://www.france-phaleristique.com/medaille_reconnaissance_française.htm, accessed 8 April 2014.

Chapter 6

1. The house itself, built of dressed stone, displays the generally similar style of two generous storeys topped by a smaller floor under a tiled roof characteristic of the town's older houses. Whether decorated with carved bands between the floors or left plain, these houses convey a sense of dignity and proportion.
2. Susanne Day, *Round about Bar-le-Duc*, page 214.
3. Day, *Round about Bar-le-Duc*, page 218.
4. *Echo de l'Est*, 16 January 1917.
5. *Echo de l'Est*, 17 April 1917.
6. Fry, *A Quaker Adventure*, page xxiii.
7. British passports were gradually phased in during 1915 for all travellers. See Twigge, Hampshire, and Macklin, *British Intelligence: Secrets, Spies and Sources*, London: The National Archives, 2008, page 23.
8. I am indebted to Chris Ball, who kindly allowed me to see the various forms of authorisation issued to her grandparents, Charles B. Wright and Margaret J. Maclachlan. The two met at Sermaize, where they both spent varying periods of time in 1916 and 1917.
9. Gertrude knew five of these couples: Ruth Clark and Wray Hoffmann, Eleanor Lindsay ('Martha') and Edward West, Margaret Maclachlan and Charles Wright, Ethel Ubsdell and Alfred Fryer, and Lois Young and Harold Trew. In Poland she knew a sixth couple, Lilian Hockey and William Graham.
10. Day, *Round about Bar-le-Duc*, pages 89, 215.
11. Information based on the files recording the registration of foreigners, ADM, Statistique des étrangers, 1911-1921.
12. Textiles, brewing and metallurgy formed the bases of Bar-le-Duc's industrial economy at that time.
13. Henry van Etten, *Chronique de la vie Quaker française 1745-1945*, page 237.
14. Day, *Round about Bar-le-Duc*, Chapters 9 and 10.
15. I have been struck by the number of German or Germanic-sounding names among these acquaintances, to which may be added Dann-Reuther, Krug and Untermehr. Some of these people may have come from Alsace. Madame Kleinknecht certainly did and told Gertrude about Alsatian customs

NOTES 249

and the divisions between German and French circles in the region.
16. See Emile Bugnon, *La Coopérative Meusienne*, page 37.
17. See Ruth Fry, *A Quaker Adventure*, page xxiv.
18. Leonard and Nancy had been fellow-students at the Quaker study centre at Woodbrooke, where his uncle Dr Rendel Harris, a member of the Society of Friends, was the first director of studies.
19. Quoted by courtesy of the University Librarian and Director, The John Rylands Library, The University of Manchester. See Special Collections, TFT/1/963, item 4.
20. Quoted by courtesy of the University Librarian and Director, The John Rylands Library, The University of Manchester. See Special Collections, TFT/1/963, item 8.

Chapter 7

1. With the ending of hostilities, the Society of Friends expanded the name of its relief organisation to reflect the continuing needs of postwar Europe and from September 1919 became the Friends' Emergency and War Victims' Relief Committee.
2. FEWVRC/8/4/3, Letters from Dr Goodall, 20 July 1919.
3. The hotel, converted at the end of the 18th century from a private residence, stood until 1939, when it was destroyed by German bombing during the invasion of Poland and occupation of Warsaw.
4. He later contributed an article on the Polish typhus epidemic, 'Typhus fever in Poland, 1916-1919', to the *Proceedings of the Royal Society of Medicine*, 13, 1920, pages 261-76. See Gaines M. Foster, *The Demands of Humanity: Army Medical Disaster Relief*, Special Studies Series, Washington DC: Center of Military History United States Army, 1983, footnote 9.
5. *The Friend*, 59/5, 31 January 1919, and 59/17, 25 April 1919.
6. In preparing these paragraphs, use has been made of the following sources: Norman Davies, *God's Playground: A History of Poland*, 2 vols, Oxford: Clarendon Press, 1981, revised 2005; Norman Davies, *A History of Europe*, London; New York: BCA, 1996; Richard Doody, *The World at War: Poland 1918-1952*, http://worldatwar.net/timeline/poland/18-52.html, accessed 5 February 2014; Peter Gatrell, *A Whole Empire Walking: Refugees in Russia during World War I*, Bloomington IN: Indiana University Press, 2005; Jan Karski, *The Great Powers and Poland 1919-1945*, Lanham MD: University Press of America, 1985; Adrian Webb, *The Routledge Companion to Central and Eastern Europe since 1919*, London: Routledge, 2008; Adam Zamoyski, *Warsaw 1920: Lenin's Failed Conquest of Europe*, London: Harper Press, 2008.
7. Foster, *The Demands of Humanity*, page 84.
8. Foster, *The Demands of Humanity*, page 89.
9. Foster, *The Demands of Humanity*, page 84.
10. Foster, *The Demands of Humanity*, pages 85-94. Chapter 5, on 'Disease in the aftermath of war: disaster aid to Poland and Russia after World War I', gives a detailed account of US army medical participation in anti-typhus operations in Poland.
11. FEWVRC/8/4/9, general needs and programmes of work.
12. Fry, *A Quaker Adventure*, page 252.
13. FEWVRC/8/4/2, General Committee minutes, 11 August 1919.
14. Fry, *A Quaker Adventure*, page 253.
15. FEWVRC/8/4/3, Letters from Dr Goodall, 24 September 1919.
16. M.A.L., Special Correspondent, 'Fighting the typhus plague in Poland: the relief work of the Friends', *Manchester Guardian*, 30 December 1919, page 6.
17. Foster, *The Demands of Humanity*, page 86.
18. FEWVRC/8/4/3, Letters from Dr Goodall, 17 August 1919.
19. FEWVRC/8/4/1/1, Executive Committee minutes, 30 August 1919; FEWVRC/8/4/3, Letters from Dr Goodall, 30 August 1919.
20. FEWVRC/8/4/3, Letters from Dr Goodall, 13 August 1919.
21. FEWVRC/8/4/3, Letters from Dr Goodall, 27 August 1919.
22. Between October 1919 and January 1920, the *Manchester Guardian* carried four articles on the FEWVRC's work at Zawiercie: a report by John Hoyland on his visit of inspection to Poland in September 1919 (he and Gertrude had met briefly in Paris on 11 September), which appeared on 17 October 1919; and three articles carried on 30 December 1919 and 1 and 3 January 1920 by the newspaper's special correspondent Miss M. A. Linford (M. A. L.), who was in Zawiercie in mid-December 1919.
23. FEWVRC/8/4/2, General Meeting minutes, 15 September 1919.
24. FEWVRC/9/1/4, Zawiercie relief, 5 November 1919.
25. FEWVRC/8/4/2, General Committee minutes, 6 October 1919; FEWVRC8/4/1/1, Executive

Committee minutes, 21 October 1919.
26. FEWVRC/8/4/5, correspondence from Cuthbert Clayton, 3 December 1919.
27. The Polish spelling of place names, which is the form used by the three travellers, has been retained in this account. Many of the places they visited are now in Ukraine and appear with Ukrainian spelling. It would, however, become cumbersome to give a double spelling in each case.
28. A copy of Wallis's undated notes, entitled 'Report of visit of investigation to East Galicia and West Ukrainia', is held in FEWVRC/8/4/11.
29. This mission arrived in Poland in the spring of 1919 to support the formation of a professional army for the new state. Its aims were to improve the general organisation of the army, to give material assistance and most importantly to offer instruction and officer training. The mission was under the command of General Henrys. Lieutenant-Colonel Faury was in charge of the educational and training programme, in which he was assisted by Captain Charles de Gaulle. De Gaulle's attachment lasted from April 1919 to January 1921. The mission remained in place until 1939.
30. Several French artists by the name of Roux were active in the first decades of the 20th century, but none of them appears to have been known only as Gaston Roux, and two possible candidates would seem to have been either too young or too old for military service. See Bénézit, *Dictionary of Artists*, vol. 12, Paris: Gründ, 2006, pages 40-46.

Chapter 8

1. FEWVRC/9/1/6/1, Typhus, medical, anti-TB, letter from Colonel A. J. Chesler, 10 December 1919; report from Dr Merrick, 1 January 1920.
2. The US government's Centers for Disease Control and Prevention offer an overview of rickettsial and related infections, of which epidemic typhus is one. See Marina E. Eremeeva and Gregory A. Dasch, 'Rickettsia (spotted & typhus fevers) & related infections (anaplasmosis & ehrlichiosis), in chapter 3, 'Infectious diseases related to travel', in *Travelers' Health*, Atlanta GA: CDC, 2013. Online: http://wwwnc.cdc.gov/travel/yellowbook/2014/chapter-3-infectious-diseases-related-to-travel/rickettsial-spotted-and-typhus-fevers-and-related-infections-anaplasmosis-and-ehrlichiosis, accessed 28 February 2014.
3. FEWVRC/8/4/11, Sydney Wallis, 'Report of visit of investigation to East Galicia and West Ukrainia', undated, page 10.
4. The translations and one of the handwritten copies are stamped 31 March 1925. These late dates presumably indicate the moment when the family finally acquired the certificates.
5. FEWVRC/9/1/6/1, Medical work Mar 1919-Jan 1922, letter of 21 December 1919.
6. Letter dated 24 October 1957 from Hetty Budgen, Europe Department, Friends Service Council, to Agnes Powicke.
7. One of these headstones records Amelia Kurlandzka (1898-1976), the other Stanislaw Brzóska (1931-2009). When the author visited again in June 2014, the cemetery manager explained that the lease on Gertrude's grave would have expired after twenty years, leaving it open to being reused. The Kurlandzka-Bróska family took a new lease on the plot, citing a connection with Gertrude. I still have to explore the exact nature of the connection.
8. When the New Union was opened, the plaque was given to Gertrude's old school, Milton Mount College. The college itself has since had several moves and reorganisations, and the present whereabouts of the plaque is unknown.
9. This memorial, funded by women's subscriptions, now contains a totl of 1,153 names from the First World War. At the time of its dedication in June 1925, 1,465 names were listed. (Conversation with Vicky Harrison, Collections Manager, York Minster, 7 October 2014).
10. The text of Miss Burstall's address is recorded in Agnes Powicke's memoir, pages 248-251.
11. Unidentified and undated letter.
12. FEWVRC/9/1/4, Zawiercie relief.
13. FEWVRC 9/1/1, Administration Departments.
14. See Lyndon S. Back, 'The Quaker Mission in Poland: Relief, Reconstruction, and Religion', *The Bulletin of Friends Historical Association*, 101, Fall 2012, No. 2, page 8.
15. *The Friend*, 62/13, 31 March 1922.
16. Fry, *A Quaker Adventure*, page 299.
17. *The Friend*, 99/4, 24 January 1941, carried what was said to be confirmation of her death, but a later report in June 1941 (*The Friend*, 99/25, 20 June 1941) denied this and presented the somewhat different account of what had happened.

Sermaize

1. Jacky Béon, *Eglise de la Nativité de Marie*, n.p., 2012, preface.
2. See Charles Rémy, *Sermaize: Ville d'eaux, 1873*. Facsimile of second edition, published in the series Monographies des villes et villages de France, edited by M.-G. Micberth, Paris: Le Livre d'histoire-Lorisse, 1993.
3. Hilda Cashmore, 'Relief Work in the Marne and the Meuse', page 14.
4. Sanitary work could include the removal of animal remains: FEWVRC/2/5/1-2/5/4, report for June 1915. The disposal of dead horses and other animals, let alone human remains, was a serious problem in the aftermath of the fighting of autumn 1914.
5. Fry, *A Quaker Adventure*, page 16.
6. FEWVRC/2/5/1-2/5/4, statistics for house repairs and construction, November 1914-November 1917.
7. Personal conversation, 3 August 2012, and subsequent email, 6 August 2012.
8. Confirmation from Monsieur Pauphilet in an email of 2 September 2014. For information on the site I am indebted to a letter of 7 May 2012 from Monsieur Raymond Dzieja, the then mayor of Sermaize-les-Bains, and to Monsieur Pauphilet.
9. Fry, *A Quaker Adventure*, page 51.
10. Walter G. Bowerman, 'Quaker relief in wartime France', page 41.
11. Edith M. Pye (ed.), *War and its Aftermath*, page 33.
12. Hilda Cashmore, 'Relief Work in the Marne and the Meuse', pages 13, 16.

Verdun

1. Malcolm Brown, *Verdun 1916*, Stroud, UK: Tempus Publishing Ltd., 2000, page 21.
2. The literature on Verdun, starting immediately after the war, is copious, both in historiography and analysis and in memoirs and fiction. Useful bibliographical information is contained in Ian Ousby's *The Road to Verdun: World War I's Most Momentous Battle and the Folly of Nationalism*, London: Jonathan Cape, 2002; New York: Doubleday, 2002, pages 347-79. To this may be added Malcolm Brown, *Verdun 1916*; Bernard Crochet and Gérard Piouffre, *La 1ere guerre mondiale*, pages 167-82; John Keegan, *The First World War*, pages 300-308; Michelin, *Les champs de bataille*.
3. The first marker takes the form of a monument and now stands at the Bar-le-Duc end of the road to Verdun. The memorial was inaugurated by the former president, Poincaré, on 21 August 1922. The name Voie Sacrée is attributed to Maurice Barrès, a French journalist, novelist and politician, who devised the concept of a 'sacred' road after a visit to Verdun in 1916. It was confirmed by an official decree of 30 December 1923.
4. Much useful information is carried in Louis Gautier, 'La Voie Sacrée et le "Meusien"', *Bulletin des Sociétés d'Histoire et d'Archéologie de la Meuse*, no. 2, 1965, spéciale 14-18, pages 19-33. See also Michelin, *Les champs de bataille*, pages 200-209; Malcolm Brown, *Verdun 1916*, pages 81-90.
5. For a biographical note on Georges Scott (1873-1942), see Bénézit, *Dictionary of Artists*, vol. 12, Paris: Gründ, 2006, page 886. The image in *L'Illustration* was reproduced in the *Illustrated London News* of 18 March 1916.
6. See the museum's website, Chemin de Fer Historique de la Voie Sacreé, http://www.traintouristique-lasuzanne.fr/index.php/fr/, accessed 25 May 2014.

Gertrude and Wilmer in Paris, 1918

1. Ashwell (1869-1957), an actor and theatre manager, formed her own company to take entertainment to the troops in both Britain and France during the First World War.

Luxembourg and Germany, May 1919

1. This is clear from Barclay Baron's memoirs, as edited by Michael Snape, *The Back Parts of War: The YMCA Memoirs and Letters of Barclay Baron, 1915-1919*, Woodbridge, UK: The Boydell Press, 2009. Baron had served extensively in France since 1915 in YMCA posts close to the front line. Following the armistice he was put in charge of the organisation's work with the British army of occupation.

References

1. Unpublished papers
Good, Dorothy. Private correspondence with Powicke family, 7 December 1919-25 November 1920

Powick, Wilmer Chrisman. Private correspondence, 3 November 1918-18 January 1920

Powicke, Agnes Eva. 'Memoir of Gertrude Mary Powicke, Dec 19. 1887 – Dec. 20. 1919', dated 28 October 1957. Typescript

Powicke, Frederick Maurice. Private correspondence, 2 October 1910-4 February 1919

Powicke, Gertrude Mary. Private correspondence, 13 October 1907-31 January 1915
    Private correspondence from France, 6 June 1915-1 August 1919
    Private correspondence from Poland, 5 August 1919-3 December 1919
    Diaries (engagements), 1913, 1914, 1915, 1916, 1918
    Diaries, France, 5 June 1915-17 July 1919
    Diaries, Poland, 18 July 1919-2 December 1919

Powicke, Susan Irvine Martin. Private correspondence, 9 July 1911-3 December 1916

2. Archival sources
Archives départementales de la Meuse (ADM), Bar-le-Duc:
    E dépôt 460/1204 W/3
    E dépôt 460/1431, Statistique des étrangers, 1911-1921

Library of the Society of Friends, London:
    Friends Emergency and War Victims Relief Committee archives: Relief Missions in France and in Poland

Médiathèque Jeukens, Bar-le-Duc, Ms 821/2

University of Manchester, The John Rylands Library, Special Collections, Papers of Thomas Frederick Tout

3. Printed and online sources
Alexander, Rachel F. 'Before the armistice'. Bar-le-Duc relief report for November 1918, *Reconstruction*, 1/10, January 1919, pages 165-66

Back, Lyndon S. 'The Quaker Mission in Poland: Relief, Reconstruction, and Religion'. *The Bulletin of Friends Historical Association*, 101, Fall 2012, No. 2, pages 1-23

Becker, Annette. *Les Cicatrices rouges 14-18: France et Belgique occupées*. Paris; Fayard, 2010

Bedford, Jane. 'Margaret Ashton: Manchester's "First Lady"'. *Manchester Region History Review*, 12, 1998, pp. 3-17

Bénézit, *Dictionary of Artists*, vol. 12, Paris: Gründ, 2006

Béon, Jacky. *Eglise de la Nativité de Marie*, n.p., 2012

Binyon, Laurence, *For Dauntless France: An Account of Britain's Aid to the French Wounded and Victims of War*, London: Hodder and Stoughton, 1918

Birrell, Francis, Harold F. Trew, Maurice S. Hutchinson, Sophia M. Fry, and James A. Babbitt, 'Beginnings at Verdun', *Reconstruction*, 1/10, January 1919, pages 153-57

Bowerman, Walter G. 'Quaker relief in wartime France'. Chapter 4 in Edward Thomas, *Quaker Adventures: Experiences of Twenty-three Adventurers in International Understanding*. New York; Chicago: Fleming H. Revell Company, 1928, pages 38-45

Brown, Malcolm. *Verdun 1916*. Stroud, UK: Tempus Publishing Ltd., 2000

Bugnon, Emile. *La Coopérative Meusienne*. Bar-le-Duc: Imprimerie du Barrois, 1959

Carey, Howard L. 'With the wounded and the peasants'. Chapter 5 in Edward Thomas, *Quaker Adventure: Experiences of Twenty-three Adventurers in International Understanding*, New York; Chicago: Fleming H. Revell Company, 1928, pages 46-53

Cashmore, Hilda, 'Relief work in the Marne and the Meuse', Report to the Friends' War Relief Committee in London, from November, 1914, to April 20th, 1915, inclusive, Society of Friends' War Victims' Relief Committee

Chevalier, Pol. *A Bar-le-Duc pendant la guerre*. Bar-le-Duc: Contant-Laguerre, 1935

Collot, Jean. 'Bar-le-Duc en août 1914'. *Bulletin des Sociétés d'Histoire et d'Archéologie de la Meuse*, 2, 1965, spéciale 14-18, pages 35 - 45

Crochet, Bernard, and Gérard Piouffre. *La 1ere Guerre Mondiale*, Paris: Nov'Édit, 2008

Crofton, Eileen. *The Women of Royaumont: A Scottish Women's Hospital on the Western Front*. East Linton, East Lothian, Scotland: Tuckwell, 1997

Dandelion, Pink. *An Introduction to Quakerism*. Cambridge: Cambridge University Press, 2007

Davies, Norman. *God's Playground: A History of Poland*. 2 vols, Oxford: Clarendon Press, 1981, revised 2005

Davies, Norman. *A History of Europe*. London; New York: BCA, 1996

Day, Susanne Rouvier. *Round about Bar-le-Duc*. London: Skeffington & Son, Ltd., 1918, facsimile reprint by Nabu Public Domain Reprints, 2012

Doody, Richard. *The World at War: Poland 1918-1952*. Online: http://worldatwar.net/timeline/poland/18-52.html, accessed 5 February 2014

Dubé, Paul, and Jacques Marchioro. Du temps des cerises aux feuilles mortes, 2001-2012. Online: http://dutempsdescerisesauxfeuillesmortes.net/paroles/quand_madelon.htm, accessed 22 May 2014

Duménil, Georges. *Bar-le-Duc: ses rues, places, ponts et cours d'eau*. Bar:

Imprimerie du Barrois, 1987
Edwards, Lynda. 'Milton Mount College, Gravesend, to be demolished'. *Kent Archaeological Review*, 26, Autumn 1971. Online: KAR Articles, http://cka.moon-demon.co.uk/KAR026/KAR026_Milton.htm, accessed 19 May 2014
Ennever, Barry. 'The Pelman School of Memory, The Pelman Institute and Pelmanism'. Online: http://www.ennever.com/histories/history386p.php, accessed 20 May 2014
Eremeeva, Marina E., and Gregory A. Dasch. 'Rickettsia (spotted & typhus fevers) & related infections (anaplasmosis & ehrlichiosis)'. In chapter 3, 'Infectious diseases related to travel', in *Travelers' Health*, Atlanta GA: CDC, 2013. Online: http://wwwnc.cdc.gov/travel/yellowbook/2014/chapter-3-infectious-diseases-related-to-travel/rickettsial-spotted-and-typhus-fevers-and-related-infections-anaplasmosis-and-ehrlichiosis, accessed 28 February 2014
van Etten, Henry. *Chronique de la vie Quaker française 1745-1945*. 2nd edition, Paris: Société Religieuse des Amis (Quakers), 1947
Foster, Gaines M. *The Demands of Humanity: Army Medical Disaster Relief*, Special Studies Series, Washington DC: Center of Military History United States Army, 1983
Fry, Anna Ruth. *A Quaker Adventure: The Story of Nine Years' Relief and Reconstruction*. London: Nisbet and Co. Ltd., 1926
Gatrell, Peter. *A Whole Empire Walking: Refugees in Russia during World War I*. Bloomington IN: Indiana University Press, 2005
Gautier, Louis. 'La Voie Sacrée et le "Meusien"', *Bulletin des Sociétés d'Histoire et d'Archéologie de la Meuse*, 2, 1965, spéciale 14-18, pages 19-33
Howarth, Janet. 'Fawcett, Dame Millicent Garrett (1847-1929)'. *Oxford Dictionary of National Biography*, OUP, 2004
Illustrated Michelin Guide to the Battle-fields (1914-1918). The Americans in the Great War, vol. 3, Meuse-Argonne Battle (Montfaucon, Romagne, St. Menehould). Clermont-Ferrand: Michelin & Cie; London: Michelin Tyre Co Ltd; Milltown NJ: Michelin Tire Co., 1919. Facsimile reproduction, Easingwold, York, UK: G. H. Smith & Son, 1994
Karski, Jan. *The Great Powers and Poland 1919-1945*. Lanham MD: University Press of America, 1985
Keegan, John. *The First World War*. London: Hutchinson, 1998
Leneman, Leah. *In the Service of Life: The Story of Elsie Inglis and the Scotttish Women's Hospitals*. Edinburgh: Mercat, 1994
Lengel, Edward G. *To Conquer Hell: The Battle of Meuse-Argonne, 1918*. London: Aurum Press Ltd., 2008
Les Amis du Patrimoine de Mouzon, *The Abbey church Notre-Dame de Mouzon, Ardennes - France*. Sedan: Imprimerie Soupault et Cie., 2008
Les Amis du Patrimoine de Mouzon. *Mouzon il y a 100 ans*. Sedan: Imprimerie Soupault et Cie, 2009
McPhail, Helen. *The Long Silence: Civilian Life under the German Occupation of Northern France, 1914-1918*, London: I. B. Tauris, 1999
Macdonald, Lyn. *The Roses of No Man's Land*. London: Penguin Books, 2013 [first published London: Michael Joseph, 1980]
Michelin. *Les champs de bataille: Verdun, Argonne, Saint-Mihiel*. 92100 Boulogne-Billancourt: Michelin, 2011
Morris, Joseph. *The German Air Raids on Great Britain 1914-1918*. First

published 1925, republished in a modern edition, Stroud, UK: Nonsuch Publishing, 2007

Nivet, Philippe. *Les Réfugiés français de la Grande Guerre (1914-1920): Les 'Boches du Nord'.* Hautes Études Militaires, no. 27. Paris: Economica, 2004

Nivet, Philippe. *La France occupée 1914-1918.* Paris: Armand Colin, 2011

Ousby, Ian. *The Road to Verdun: World War I's Most Momentous Battle and the Folly of Nationalism.* London: Jonathan Cape, 2002; New York: Doubleday, 2002

Powell, Anne. *Women in the War Zone: Hospital Service in the First World War.* Stroud, UK: The History Press, 2009

Powicke, Gertrude M. 'C'est la guerre!' *The Englishwoman*, 38, April-June 1918, no. 114, June 1918, pages 150-154

Punshon, John. *Portrait in Grey: A Short History of the Quakers.* 2nd edition, London: Quaker Books, 2006

Pye, Edith M (ed.). *War and its Aftermath: Letters from Hilda Clark, M. B., B. S. from France, Austria and the Near East 1914-1924.* [London: Friends Book House, 1957]

Rémy, Charles. *Sermaize: Ville d'eaux, 1873.* Facsimile of second edition, published in the series Monographies des villes et villages de France, edited by M.-G. Micberth, Paris: Le Livre d'histoire-Lorisse, 1993

Russell, Parvin M. 'Among refugees in the war zone'. Chapter 6 in Edward Thomas, *Quaker Adventures: Experiences of Twenty-three Adventurers in International Understanding.* New York; Chicago: Fleming H. Revell Company, 1928, pages 54-62

Smith, Henry W. *A Story of the 305th Machine Gun Battalion, 77th Division A.E.F..* New York: Modern Composing Room, 1941

Snape, Michael (ed.). *The Back Parts of War: The YMCA Memoirs and Letters of Barclay Baron, 1915-1919.* Woodbridge, UK: The Boydell Press, 2009

Society of Friends' War Victims' Relief Committee. 'Report on three months' work at Châlons-sur-Marne from Dec.1914 to Feb. 1915', signed by Hilda Clark

Stockport Metropolitan Borough Council. 'Hatherlow conservation area character appraisal', October 2006 (updated 2012). Online: http://www.stockport.gov.uk/2013/2978/8803/9020/12299/hatherlowapp1, accessed 19 May 2014

Sumner, Ian. *French Poilu 1914-18.* Illustrated by Giuseppe Rava. Oxford: Osprey Publishing, 2009

Sumner, Ian. *The First Battle of the Marne*, Oxford: Osprey Publishing, 2010

Sutters, Jack. 'The red and black star'. American Friends Service Committee. Online: https://afsc.org/story/red-and-black-star, accessed 21 May 2014

Tunnicliffe, Alan. *Powicks Past and Present.* Christchurch, New Zealand: Alan Tunnicliffe, 1989

Twigge, Stephen, Edward Hampshire, and Graham Macklin, *British Intelligence: Secrets, Spies and Sources,* London: The National Archives, 2008

Unikoski, Ari. 'The war in the air – bombers: Germany, Zeppelins'. firstworldwar.com: a multimedia history of world war one, 22 August 2009. Online: http://www.firstworldwar.com/airwar/bombers_zeppelins.htm accessed May 2014

War Victims' Relief Committee of the Society of Friends, 'Behind the battle lines in France: the report of a month's work by a group of members of the mission sent by the above', with an introduction dated March 1915 by T. Edmund Harvey MP

Webb, Adrian. *The Routledge Companion to Central and Eastern Europe since 1919.* London: Routledge, 2008

Zamoyski, Adam. *Warsaw 1920: Lenin's Failed Conquest of Europe.* London: Harper Press, 2008

4. Press and periodicals

Echo de l'Est, published at Bar-le-Duc from 1830 to 1939

The Friend: A Religious, Literary, and Miscellaneous Journal, New Series, vols. 54-60, 1914-1920, and vol. 99, 1941.

Index

Illustrations are included in italics

Accounts 87-89, 159, 194
Ashton, Margaret, social campaigner and governor of MHSG, 24, 25
Alexander, Jean, 70, 119, 158, 233
Alexander, Rachel, 83, 100, 107, 116, 119, 120, 136, 138, 233
–awarded medal, 150
–embroidery schemes, 70
–Maison des parents, Revigny, 113, 114
–offers Gertrude Powicke work, 158
–soldiers' canteen 104, 105, 246
American Expeditionary Force, 24
American First Army, 124, 132, 134, 135, 217
–army engineers' dumps, 141, 148
–feeding refugees, 137
–presence in Bar-le-Duc, 109, 124-125, 143-144
American Friends, 125-126, 149
American Friends Service Committee, 43, 126
American Red Cross Society, 43, 49, 54, 126, 131, 138
–clothing for relief work, 184, 187
–representatives in Moulins, 133
–representatives in Poland, 180, 194, 195, 196, 198, 200
American Relief Administration, 180, 206, 237
American Relief Clearing House, 49
American-Polish Relief Expedition, 180, 237
Anglo-American Mission of the Society of Friends, 126
Anti-typhus measures, 178, 180, 192, 207, 228-231
–clothes disinfection, 184, *185, 187*
–delousing, 184-186, *186, 206*, 207
–disinfecting stations in eastern Poland, 229
–house disinfestation, 185
Argonne, 51, 52, 124, 134, 135, 136, 142
Armistice, 51, 122, 135, 136, 147, 157, 215, 226
Auzéville, 52, 135, 136

Babbit, James, Dr, 125, 215
Ball, Richard Reynolds, 175, 194, 195, 196, 197, 199
–burial, 201-202
–illness and death, 200-201
Bar-le-Duc, 65, *66*, *68*, 72, 92, 99, *100, 142*
–awarded Croix de guerre, 122
–bombing raids, 99, 114, *118, 119*, 246
–foreign population during war, 161-162, 244
–hospitals, 93, 102, 110
–railway station, 92, 99, 102, *103*
Bar-le-Duc équipe, 60, 65, 66-67, 76, 79, 90, 142, 144, 151, 165
–addresses in Bar, 65, 143
–assistance at covered market, 73, 98
–assistance at Maison des parents, 111, 113

—assistance at soldiers' canteen, 103, 104
—assistance at soldiers' club, 107
—bomb precautions, 116, 120, 121
—contacts with local society, 163-164
—daily life, 151-154
—relations among colleagues, 89-91, 157-161
Barrie, J. M., 62, 243
Batten, Agatha, 104
Białowieska, Jadwiga, 176, 188, 193, 207, 208
Bidet family, 140
Boller, Charles, 71, 72, 110, 163
Bollot, René, Father, 211, 215
Borszczów, 195, 199, 229
Boughton Leigh, Edith, 175, 194, 200
Boulevard de la Rochelle, 65, 66, 85, 89, 118, *119*, 121, 122, 143, 144, 151, *152*, 219
Bourgeois, Léon, senator for the Marne, 48
British Committee of the French Red Cross, 111, 126
—investigates FWVRC's work, 48-49
—sponsor for FWVRC volunteers, 48-49, 156
British Expeditionary Force (BEF), 45
British military, 41, 49, 226, 227
British Red Cross Society, 49, 181
British Urgency Cases Hospital, 102, 245
Brizeaux, 52, 62, 145, 147, 149
Brockway, Fenner, 27, 233
Bulley, Margaret, 89
Bungener family, 122, 165, 165, 166, 171, 191
—Madame Bungener 102, 108, 140, 164, 165
Bungener, Wanda, 78, 88, 165
Burstall, Sara, headmistress, MHSG, 21, 22, 35, 38, 161, 167, 169, 170
—memorial address for Gertrude Powicke, 205

Carey, G. Cheston, 126-127
Carpenter, Carl, Reverend, 201
Châlons-sur-Marne, 45, 59, 128
—FWVRC maternity hospital at, 49, 52, 59, 61, 129, 234, 239

Chesler, A. J., Colonel, American Red Cross Commissioner to Poland, 194
Chevalier, Pol, senator for the Meuse, 94, 96, 103, 104, 107, 110, 115, 124, 163, 234, 248
—author of *A Bar-le-Duc pendant la guerre*, 115, 245
Clark, Hilda, Dr, 41, 59, 63, 82, 214, 215, 234, 239
Clayton, Cuthbert, 174-175, 188, 189, 190, 200, 201, 202, 206
Clermont-en-Argonne, 52, 114, 131, 141
Cole, Samuel, 206
Connah, Sarah, 202
Conry, Kathleen, 176
Conscientious objectors, 40, 41, 83, 159, 175, 237
Covered market, 73, *97*, 97, 110, 111, 112, 113, 144
Crown Prince Wilhelm, 92, 217, 218

Dalglish, Eliza, 28, 67, 70, 71, 90, 244
Dann-Reuther, Madame, 164, 165, 171
Day, Susanne, suffragist, playwright and author, 67, 70, 80, 88, 90, 106, 154, 158-159, 164, 235
—book *Round about Bar-le-Duc*, 159
—play *Fox and Geese*, 159
Dinely, Emily, 70, 114, 158, 232
Dogs, *84*, 146-147, 152, *165*
Domrémy, 52, 90
Driving experiences, 82-86, 128, 130, 131, 136, 139, 142, 145, 146, 193, 194, 227
—driving instruction, 36, 82
—driving permits, 36, 37, 156
Dunbar, Ethel, 175, *186*, 194, 200
Dyckoff, Anette, 134, 164
Dyckoff, Charlotte, 122, 134, 164

Earp, Rosslyn, Dr, 150
Eastern Galicia, 43, 177, 178, 194-199, 207, 228-232
Edis, Olive, photographer, 144, 248
Evangelical-Reformed cemetery and church, Warsaw, 201, *204*
Evans, Gwladys, and Powicke family, 15

Evans, Richard, 175-176, 202

Fains, 52, 132, 135, 136
Ferry, Elsie, 192
Finances, family, 14, 18, 20, 168
–Gertrude's finances, 18, 20, 168
Fleas, 38, 67, 183, 192
Foyer des alliés, 103, 104-106, 113, 122, 124, 125, 143, 170, 245, 246, 248
Foyer du soldat, 76, 106-108, *108*, 109, 124, 125
Franco-Prussian War, 1870–1871, 42, 216
French acquaintances, 102, 122, 144, 146, 150, 164, *165*, 166, 170, 248
French civil authorities, 49, 51, 56, 57, 61, 95, 129, 132, 133, 135, 150, 153, 156, 157, 162, 163
French military, 42, 58, 92, 94, 102, 104, 106, 129, 130, 137, 215, 218, 247
–close liaison with FWVRC, 46, 48, 131, 132
–presence in Bar-le-Duc, 66, 92, *94*, 99-101, *100*, *101*
–uniform, 58, 64, 66, 100, 245
French military mission to Poland, 199, *199*, 250
French Red Cross Society, 37, 49, 129, 156, 161
Friends' Ambulance Unit, 41, 44, 49, 128, 157
Friends' Emergency and War Victims' Relief Committee, 175, 182, 188, 189, 190
–Emergency Committee on Poland, 190
–First General Meeting, 190
–London Committee, 182, 187, 188, 189, 202
–renamed from FWVRC, September 1919, 45, 249
Friends' Emergency and War Victims' Relief Committee, Polish unit, 173, 181, 186, *186*, 187, 192, 197, 200, 201, 207
–different nature of work, 176
–executive committee, 175, 182, 189, 194
–extending work to eastern Poland, 194, 197, 207
–general committee, 174, 189
–maintenance committee, 175, 176, 189
–Poland project, 149
Friends' Emergency Committee, 41
Friends' League for Women's Suffrage, 28
Friends Service Council, 203
Friends' War Victims' Relief Committee, 9, 10, 28, 37, 41, 46, 52, 125, 126, 130, 141, 180, 181, 212, 247
–agricultural work, 57-59, 213
–British Committee of the French Red Cross inspects work, 49
–earlier committee with same name, 42
–extent of work in Europe and Russia, 44-45, 157-158
–financial accounting, 43, 87, 88
–funding and fundraising, 43
–leading role of Society of Friends, 42
–marriages within French unit, 248
–negotiations with French authorities, 46, 48
–numbers of volunteers, 44
–medical work, 61-63, 214-215
–organisation and style of work, 41, 42, 160-161
–Paris office, 53-54, 88, 140, 161, 147-148
–policies and practices towards refugees, 60, 61, 147
–programme of work in France, 55
–relief work, 59-61, *60*, 66-67, 96, 213-214
–remuneration, 43, 63, 168
–shops, 61, 67, 74, *144*, *147*
–uniform, 43, *71*, 154, 155, *155*, 168, 223
Fry, Margery, 71, 161, 167, 215, 235, 236
–advises Gertrude Powicke on career, 167-168
Fry, Ruth, FWVRC general secretary, 41, 43, 49, 83, 156, 189, 235, 236, 238, 242, 243
– author of *A Quaker Adventure*, 44
– comments on spiritual value of FWVRC work, 43-44, 212

–interviews Gertrude Powicke, 37
–visits Poland, 181, 183, 190, 191
Fry, Sophia, 83, 106, 132, 150, 161, 165, 233, 236

de Gaulle, Charles, Captain, 197, 259
German advances and retreats in France, 1914, 45-46, 47, 50, 92
–planned retreat, 51, 123
–renewed advance, 1918, 51, 127
German anti-war posters, 247
German bombing raids on Bar-le-Duc, 114-122, 246
German Fifth Army, 92, 135, 217
German military behaviour towards French population, 55, 59, 137, 140, 210
German occupations of Poland, 177, 186, 207-208
Germany, 14, 42, 53, 135, 139, 178, 181, 226
–FEWVRC assistance to, 45
–Gertrude Powicke's stay in Germany, 1907-1908, 17-18
–Gertrude Powicke's trip to Germany, 1918, 86, 225-227
Gilpin, Eva, 89
Ginisty, Charles, Monsignor, bishop of Verdun, 117
Glover, George W., 33-35, *34*, 166
Goigoux, General, 107, 110, 124
Good, Dorothy, 173, 176, 182, 200, 201, 202, 206
Goodall, Edward W., Dr, 173, 175, 181, 186, 188, 189, 192
Gotha aircraft, 115, 120
Grange-le-Comte, 52, 141, 144, 161
Griggs, Mrs, 108, 111, 246
Grillon, Jean, sub-prefect and prefect, 132, 133
Gruver, Major, 194, 197, 229
Guiness, Mary, 162

Harris, Leonard, 31, 166, 249
Harvey, T. Edmund, MP, 41, 58, 84, 126, 234, 236, 238
–and conscientious objectors, 159, 237
–intervenes with President Poincaré, 48, 155

Henderson, John, 190, 191, 202
Hockey, Lilian, 193
Hoover, Herbert Clark, US president, 180, 182, 183, 206, 237
Hotel Angielski, 174, 200
Hôtel Britannique, 53, *54*, 222
Hotels for visiting relatives, *see* Maison des parents
Housing construction 50, 51, 55-57, 56, 133, 196, 207, 212-213, *213*, *214*
Hoyland, John, 190, 191
Hupmobile, 83-84, *84*, 85, 86, 87, 136, 140, 225, 227

Imperial War Museum, London, 205
Influenza, 20, 136, 200, 206, 224, 247

Jackson, Clare (Mrs Jackson), 69, 90
Janiczewski, Dr, Polish minister of public health, 181
Jewish population, 183, 188, 201, 231, 239
Joffre, Joseph, Marshal, commander-in-chief, 45, 48, 99, 217, 243
Johnson, Bertha, 105, 248
JUR (Jencow Uchodzcow i Robotnikow), 196

Kamieniec Podolski, 179, 195, 198, 201, 230, 231
King, Frederic Truby, Dr, 175, 238
Kleinknecht family, 164, 171, 248
Kraków, 179, 193, 194
Kurlandzka, Amelia, 203, 250

La Besace, 52, 136, 137-139, 155, 157
Lamb, Gilbert, 160
Lansdell, Connie, 19, 21, 24, 25, 171
Lee, Henry Austin, Sir, 28, 238, 243
Lemberg, *see* Lwów
Lendrum, Miss, 162, 164
Lindsay, Eleanor ('Martha'), 160, 190, 248
Linford, M. A. (M. A. L.), *Manchester Guardian* correspondent, 249
London Yearly Meeting, 242
–position on women's suffrage, 28
–supervises FWVRC, 41
Lucas, E. V. and family, 62, 238

Lunn, Florence (Dolly), fellow student and teacher at MHSG, 22, 32, 35, 36, 190
– writes appreciation of Gertrude Powicke, 205
Luxembourg, 15, 47, 86, 94, 146, 225, 227
Lwów, 179, 194, 195, 196, 198

McHardy, Elizabeth, 200
'Madelon', 100, 245
Maginot, André, National Assembly deputy for the Meuse, 117, 118
Maison des parents, in Bar-le-Duc, 107, 110-113, *112*, *113*
– in Revigny, 113-114, 158
Manchester Guardian, 32
– articles on FEWVRC relief work in Zawiercie, 249
– Gertrude Powicke working on article on Zawiercie, 190
– obituary of Gertrude Powicke, 205
Manchester High School for Girls, 9, 24, 35, 36, 38, 43, 73, 75, 167, 168
– Gertrude Powicke teacher at school, 20, 21-23, *21*
– history of school, 20-21
– Nancy Powicke student and teacher, 16
Manchester University, 9, 19, 25, 27, 36, 204
– George Glover a student, 33, 166
– journal, 204
– motto, 203
– Harry Pickles a student, 29, 32
Manchester University and Powicke family, 21, 241
– Agnes Powicke a student, 15
– Gertrude Powicke a student, 19-20
– Maurice Powicke, student, assistant in history department, professor of history, 14-15, 166
– Nancy Powicke a student, 16
Marne, department of, 48, 50, 51, 55, 56, 57, 59, 65, 104, 210
– First Battle of the Marne, 46, 92
– Second Battle of the Marne, 130
Martyl, Nelly, 109
Médaille de la reconnaissance française, 150, *150*, 163, 248
Merrick, Margaret, Dr, 200, 201, 206

Meuse, department of, 49, 50, 51, 52, 57, 59, 65, 94, 102, 117, 129, 141, 234
Meyer, Philip, 88
Mikosz, Paul, 193, 194
Mikosz, Stanley, 193, 194
Military Service Act, January 1916, 40, 159, 237
Miller, Jane, 175
Milton Mount College, 17, *17*, 18, 25, 205, 241, 250
Montford, Ernest, 64, 67, 149, 160, 175, 200, 202, 206, 211
Motor vehicles, 43, 80, 81, 83, 212, 244
– petrol, 76, 85, 86, 131, 154, 192, 194
Moulins, 132, 133, 134
Mouzon, 52, 147-149, 248

Nadworna, 179, *206*, 207
National Union of Women's Suffrage Societies, 23, 24, 27, *27*, 28, 87, 242
– effect of war on organisation, 28, 37
– North of England Women's Suffrage Society, 23, 24
– Romiley branch, 24, 24, 25, 26, 27, 87
Nivelle, Robert, General, commander-in-chief, French army, 48, 123, 217

Oise, department of, 127, 128
Ouvroir, Bar-le-Duc, 69, 70, 72, 73, 74, 75, 79-80, 83, 87, 105
– children and teenagers, 68, 77-79, 171, 172
– Gertrude Powicke's management, 70, 158, 161, 163
– women attending, 73, 74, 75, 76

Paderewski, Ignacy x 2 (7)
Paris, 45, 47, 53-54, 64, 80, 118, 127, 140, 141, 145, 173, 218, 222-225, 238
Paris Peace Conference, 145, 149, 177, 181
Passport, 16, 38, 156, 202, 248
Permits, 48, 155, 162
– bicycling permit, 81, 82, 156
– *carnet d'étranger*, 48, 51, 156-157
– driving permit, 84, 156

–group transit visa, 173, *174*
–residence permit, 156, 157
–safe-conduct pass, 156, 157
Pershing, John, General, 124, 125, 134, 135, 149, 180, 247
Pétain, Philippe, General, 123, 217, 218
'Peter', *84*, 146, 147, 150, *165*, 171, 202, 205
Pickles, Harry Thornton, 29-33, 160, 241
–death, 32-33, 166, 172
–enlists, 29, *30*
–marriage, 31-32, 166
Piette, Maurice, prefect of the Meuse, 49, 129, 132, 150, 247
Piłsudski, Jósef, Marshal, 176
Place de la Fontaine, *142*, 143
Podwoloczyska, 196, 207, 231
Poë, W. Hutcheson, Lieutenant-Colonel Sir, 49
Poincaré, Henriette (Madame Poincaré), 107, 117
Poincaré, Raymond, President, 48, 251
Poissons, temporary équipe, 52, 86, 129, 130-131, 132, 162
Polish language lessons, 173, 175, 176, 193
Polish Ministry of Public Health, 149, 180, 181, 192. 201
Pontefract, Jane, 131, 136, 154, 158
Powązowski cemetery, 201
Powick, Wilmer, 80, 140, 154, 170, 205, 221, 222-225, 239
Powicke, Agnes Eva, 13, 15, 17, 20, 21, 22, 32, 36, 87, 226, 244
–earlier memoirs of Gertrude Powicke, 10, 11
–manages Gertrude's finances, 168-169
–reunions with Gertrude Powicke, 1919, 145-146, 224-227
–works with YMCA, 15, 145, 146, 225, 226
Powicke, Annie Collyer (Nancy), 13, 16, 20, 21, 29, 31, 32, 145, 166, 175, 201, 203, 249
Powicke, Elizabeth Viccars (Betty), 13, 20, 25, 26, 30, 31, 32, 36

–family manager, 16
Powicke, Frederick James, Reverend, 13, 14, 15, 16, 24, 25, 36, 38, 168, 190
Powicke, Frederick Maurice, 13, 14, *19*, 38, 146, 166, 203, 241
–academic career, 14-15
–attends Paris Peace Conference, 1919, 145
–financial support to Gertrude Powicke, 18, 19-20, 168
–influence on Gertrude Powicke, 19, 172
–reunion with Gertrude Powicke in Paris, 1919, 145, 169, 170
–war work, 15, 145
Powicke, Gertrude Mary, 9, 13, 71, 81, 144, 155
–article in *The Englishwoman*, 75, 134, 244
–awarded medal, 150, 150, 163, 233
–burial, 201, 202
–childhood, 16-17
–death, 201, 202
–depression, 172
–diaries and letters, 10, 11
–experiences of bombing raids, 114-122
–family's views on her welfare, 39, 145, 224
–grave, 11, 202-203, *204*, 250
–health, 16-17, 86, 145, 149, 169, 170, 193, 200-201, 214, 241
–memorials, 204-205, 250
–nicknames, 16, 106
–nursing work in Bar-le-Duc, 69
–ouvroir, 70-80
–Polish unit, 149, 174, 175, 176, 188, 189, 190, 191, 192, 193, 206
–preparation for war work, 35-36
–relationship with Harry Pickles, 29-33
–relief work in Bar-le-Duc, 67-69
–religious beliefs and attendance, 19, 22, 26, 171-172, 190
–schooling in Britain and Germany, 17-18, *17*, *19*
–student at Manchester University, 19-20
–suffrage activities, 23-29, *24*, 241
–teacher at MHSG, 20-23, *21*

–views on career, 158, 161, 166-168
–views on Society of Friends, 143, 176
–views on war, 39, 124
–visit to Eastern Galicia, 194-199, 228-232
–work with French organisations, 98-112, *see* also entries under 'Bar-le-Duc équipe'
Powicke, Martha (born Collyer), 13, 14, 16, 83, 203
Powicke, William Alfred (Will), 13, 16, 20, 38
–army chaplain in Egypt, 15
–plans earlier memoir of Gertrude Powicke, 11
Prisoners-of-war in France, 118
–British prisoners-of-war, 139
–French prisoners-of-war 60, 73
–German prisoners-of-war, 62, 114, 148, 198
–Prisoners-of-war in Poland, 45, 178, 196, 207
–Russian prisoners-of-war 200
–Ukrainian prisoners-of-war, 201, 228
Proctor, Helen, 90
Protestant community in Bar, 107, 162, 164, 171, 172
Pye, Edith Mary, 37, 58, 63, 239
–awarded Légion d'honneur, 61-62

Quaker star, 42, 154, *155*, 242

Rajchman, L., Dr, 181, 192, 194, 200, 248
Refugees, Belgian, 35, 36, 43, 44, 161
Refugees in Bar-le-Duc, 66, 93-94, 141-142, 143, 144
–influx from Verdun, 96-99, 112
–numbers, 95, 97, 121
–provenance, 94, *95*, 146
–shelter and accommodation, 67-68, 72, 95-96, 107-108
Refugees in France, conditions of life, 53
–government allowances, 60, 75, 95, 96
–new waves of refugees, 1918, *127*, 129, 130-132
–official categories, 53, 55, 243
–official strategies, 49, 59, 97
–refugee responses, 59, 99
–responsibility for care, 49, 59, 95, 163
Refugees in the Meuse and neighbouring departments, 132, 135-136, 137-139
Refugees in Poland, 45, 177, 178, 180, 196, 207, 228
Refugees in Russia, 44-45
Register, Edward C., Colonel, 196
Reichel, Lieutenant, 137, 138, 139
Restrictions on correspondence, 157
Revigny, 52, 82, 92, 102, 113, 114, 116, 158, 234, 245
Rheims, 45, 52, 62, 123, 127, 128, 145, 247
'Robin', nickname, 16
Robson, A. W. Mayo, Major, 49
Roux, Gaston, 199, 250
Russia, 127, 178, 179, 180, 196, 200, 229, 230, 231, 236
–FWVRC assistance, 44-45, 175, 190, 247
Ryder, Dr, 182, 192

Sampson, Lila, 105
Save the Children Fund, 190
Scattergood, Henry, American Friends' Commissioner with the ARC, 126, 141
Scattergood, Margery, 126
Scott, Georges, artist, 109, 219, 251
Scottish Women's Hospitals, 37, 88, 175, 242
Sedan, 47, 52, 86, 135, 137, 138, 139, 140, 147, 247
Serbia, 43, 44, 149, 158, 175, 192
Serbian Relief Fund, FWVRC co-operation with, 44, 149
Sermaize-les-Bains, 47, 52, 64, 82, 116, 156, 164, 210-216, *211*
–garage, 81, 83
–'garden city', 57, 212-213, *213*, *214*
–hospitals, 62, 63, 125, 169, 214-215
–regional headquarters for FWVRC, 50, 57, 141, 159, 171, 212-215
Sheavyn, Phoebe, Women's Tutor at Manchester University, 25
Shewell, Wilfrid, FWVRC secretary

for France, 54, 136, 146
Skoraczewski, Ladislas, 176, 193, 195
Society of Friends, 9, 11, 40-41, 42, 45, 54, 74, 105, 113, 166, 168, 238, 242, 243, 246
–awarded medal, 248
–delegation to Poland, 181
–interest in co-operative movement, 165
–offer of help to France, 46, 61
–offer of help to Poland, 149, 181, 189, 248
–representatives of Society of Friends in Poland after 1924, 203, 207
–response to war, 40-41
Soldiers' canteen, see Foyer des alliés
Soldiers' club, see Foyer du soldat
Soviet Union, FWVRC assistance, 45
–Bolshevik government, 177, 178, 207, 247
Spring Rice, Bernard, 158, 233
St Mihiel, 47, 52, 66, 92, 114, 132, 134
Staveley, Mary, 90
Streatfeild, Granville, architect, 55, 239

Tarnopol (Tarnapol), 179, 195, 196, 197, 198, 207, 228, 229, 230, 231
Tatlock, Robert, 63
Taube aircraft, 115, 116, 117, 136
Tilley, Captain, 130, 131
Tout, Thomas Frederick, Professor, historian, chair of governors of MHSG, 21, 166, 167
–writes obituary of Gertrude Powicke, 205
Townend, Gertrude, 28, 67, 70, *71*, 90
Treaty of Versailles, 177
Trenkner, Dr, 207
Tuberculosis, 49, 53, 54, 69, 234, 238
Typhus, 9, 173, 175, 178, 181, 184, 200, 201, 203, 207
–epidemic typhus, 180, 200, 201, 250
–in Poland, 45, 176, 178, 180, 181, 196, 207, 228, 229, 230, 231, 237, 249, see also entries under 'Antityphus measures'

Ukraine, 43, 178, 194, 195, 196, 228, 229, 231, 250

Upper Silesia, 177, 181, 194, 198
US First Army, see American First Army

Varennes, 52, 62, 86, 135, 136, *147*
Vassincourt, 52, 92, *93*
Vauquois, 135, 136, 142
Verdun, 45, 47, 52, 66, 92, 93, 96, 99, 100, 106, 109, 115, 117, 129, 132, 215, 216-221, *219*, *220*, *221*, 224, 251
Vichy, 134
Vienna, 173, 174, 190, 206
Vitry-le-François, 50, 52, 55
Voies sacrées, 52, 218, *219*, 220, 251

Wallis, Sydney, 193, 194, 195, 196, 197, 202, 231
Warsaw, 9, 173, 177, 178, 179, 180, 188, 190, 194, *195*, 200, 201, 203, *204*, 207
Watts, Renshaw, 175, 193
Webster, Edward Lownes, 126
Werbkowice, 179, 207
West, Edward, 59, 160, 190
Wharton, Edith, 51
Wild boar, 57
Wilno, 179, 194
Wilson, John H., Dr, 175, 188
Wilson, Thomas Woodrow, President, 149, 177, 180, 237
Witherington, Florence, 207
Woodbrooke, 16, 64, 241, 249

York Minster, Five Sisters window, 204
Young Men's Christian Society, 50, 54
–American YMCA, 77, 124, 130
–British YMCA, 15, 104, 145, 225, 226, 251

Zawiercie, 179, 181, 183, 186, *187*, 188, 190, 191, 198, 205, 207, 249
Zbrucz river, 178, 230
Zeppelin attacks, 64, 115, 116, 122, 246
Zivy, Commandant, 102
Zone of French armies, 45, 46, 48, 82, 92